# THE
# REAL L.A.
# CONFIDENTIAL

# PETE NOYES

# TO

Grace, Love of My Life

Granddaughters, Lauren and Michelle


The Memory of Jack Tobin
Friend, Colleague, Mentor

# CONTENTS

# SPECIAL THANKS TO:

Editing Consultants;
Bob & Barbara Tarlau
Robert Blair Kaiser
Elizabeth Beerman Rothbart

Technical Advisors:

Leroy Orozco (LAPD Retired)

Jack Noyes

# PREFACE

There is one simple axiom for investigative reporting that was laid down many years ago by the legendary head of *CBS Television News*, Fred Friendly. "You must be bold and you must be accurate." It's an admonition I've taken quite seriously during more than half century in both print and broadcast news. I've disagreed strongly at times with those in news management who pay lip service to the idea of hard hitting reporting, but then cower at material that uncovers corruption and other forms of wrongdoing because they fear either lawsuits or political repercussions.

One of California's greatest investigative reporters, Jack Tobin of the Los Angeles *Times*, mentored me over the years in the need to authenticate every bit of information obtained from a public facility. It was Tobin's dogma that any court document dealing with a lawsuit or criminal matter must be certified by a court clerk. He insisted it was easy to fool people with information copied on a duplicating machine. A good example was CBS anchorman Dan Rather's ill fated report on President George Bush's National Guard service. An internal investigation found that four duplicated documents used in the report had not been properly vetted and cast doubt on the veracity of the entire story.

"*The Real L.A. Confidential*" is my memoir, a summary of many of the stories I've covered in L.A since my first job on the police beat for Los Angeles City News Service in 1957. Some of the stories in this book took place years before I came of age as a reporter. But new information I uncovered in later years about such infamous crimes as the Black Dahlia and Bugsy Siegel murders led me to include them as part of my memoir.

It's been a rough and tumble career that landed me in the newsrooms of all four major TV networks. Over the years I received a number of death threats over my investigations. A contract was even put on my head by a notorious con man I helped send to prison. Luckily for me the hit man backed out of the deal. Perhaps the scariest investigation of all was the horrific Manson murder case for which I was honored with one of the first Edward R. Murrow awards for investigative reporting.

Success in TV news does not always equal longevity. One of the nation's biggest banks set out to ruin my career after its officers learned I was producing a documentary about Howard Hughes, the so-called "bashful billionaire." Hughes had many millions of dollars on deposit in the Bank of America, which sponsored my show, and he made it clear to the bean counters he didn't want a story about his life on CBS. I paid a small fortune for very rare film of Hughes and his exploits only to have it stolen from the station library the day it arrived. And the bank went so far as to "bug" my conversations at a public event and send a transcript of what I said to my bosses at CBS. The Hughes show was a big success in the ratings and was syndicated nationwide. But a short time later I was out of job. Fortunately there was an opening a few blocks away at ABC.

I was often threatened with libel suits if I pursued certain stories. Stands I took on behalf of what I considered "integrity issues" probably cost me one or two jobs over the years. But I can truthfully look back and say there was never a dull moment, and I loved every minute of it.

# 1

# L.A.'S THE PLACE

As far as I'm concerned there's no other city in the world that measures up to Los Angeles when it comes to headline news. Some may think it's because of the celluloid glamour created by Hollywood, but there's much more to L.A.'s dark soul than the drivel coming out of the tinseltown's publicity machines. Los Angeles is the city where five different murder cases have each been referred to at times as "The Crime of the Century." First, there was the deadly bombing of the Los Angeles *Times* by union anarchists in 1910 which left 21 news people dead, and scores of others badly injured. The secretary of the Iron Workers Union and his brother pled guilty to the murders and escaped the death penalty. But the reputation of their defense attorney, the legendary Clarence Darrow, was left in shambles after he was tried and acquitted of bribing two jurors despite overwhelming evidence of his guilt.

The unsolved 1947 mutilation murder of the so-called "Black Dahlia," a beautiful 22-year-old aspiring actress named Elizabeth Short, attracted worldwide attention and resulted in a score of books and movies. Hundreds confessed to the crime but the real killer was never found. Five months later in nearby Beverly Hills the mobster credited with inventing Las Vegas, Benjamin (Bugsy) Siegel was shot to death at the home of his girlfriend. Some thought that, too, qualified as a crime of the century.

The 1968 assassination of Senator Robert Kennedy at L.A.'s Ambassador Hotel by the young Palestinian militant Sirhan Bishara Sirhan just hours after RFK was declared the winner of the Democratic Presidential primary election in California also qualified as another "Crime of the Century." Sirhan had murdered the man who very likely might have become the next president of the United States. Sirhan escaped the death penalty when the California Supreme Court declared it unconstitutional.

The following year the "Manson Family" murders terrified the people of Los Angeles like nothing else in the history of the city, another "Crime of the Century." The lives of Charles Manson and his followers were likewise spared by the same court ruling.

Twenty five years later football star turned actor O.J. Simpson was brought before the bar of justice for murdering his estranged wife, Nicole, and her friend, Ron Goldman, in what was described as the most publicized criminal trial in recorded history, attracting an audience like none ever seen before on live television. Needless to say, Simpson was acquitted of still another "Crime of the Century" despite a preponderance of scientific evidence that seemed to have established his guilt.

There were many other L.A. cases that achieved notoriety for a variety of reasons. Three reigning beauty queens died young in Los Angeles, Thelma Todd, Jean Harlow and Marilyn Monroe, and to this day conspiracy theories abound about their deaths.

There were troubling days in Hollywood long before the "talkies." The famous silent film comedian Roscoe Conkling (Fatty Arbuckle) was accused of killing a young starlet in his room during a wild party at the St. Francis Hotel in San Francisco in 1921. He was tried three times for manslaughter, but never convicted. Fatty never made another movie. One of the greatest directors of the silent screen era, Thomas Ince, was shot to death aboard a yacht owned by William Randolph Hearst, and there are many who believed the legendary newspaper czar pulled the trigger, intending to kill comedian Charles Chaplin for romancing Hearst's mistress, actress Marion Davies. William Desmond Taylor, another famous silent film director, was murdered in his home, a bullet to the back of his head. The case was never solved.

Television's first *"Superman,"* the ruggedly handsome George Reeves who made his movie debut in *"Gone with the Wind,"* also died from a bullet to the brain in his home. The cops called it a suicide. But relatives and friends were convinced he was murdered on the orders of a film studio mogul who suspected *"Superman"* had bedded down his wife.

Apart from stories about crime and punishment, L.A. seems to have had one disaster after another. The 1933 earthquake left 125 dead and millions of dollars in property damage. As a small boy I remember sleeping in the park next to the L.A. Memorial Coliseum after our home was nearly destroyed by the 6.4 magnitude quake.

In 1938 "a storm of the century" practically washed away Los Angeles. Several thousand homes from the San Fernando Valley were tossed out to sea as the Los Angeles River overflowed its banks. Nearly every bridge was torn away in surrounding communities within 100 miles of L.A. The beachfront community of Malibu, home to some of

Hollywood's biggest stars, experienced one disastrous fire after another in its surrounding hills since 1919 when officials first began keeping records.

A nuclear power plant in the San Fernando Valley had a major meltdown in 1959, much worse than the one at Three Mile Island. But the feds kept the accident secret for 20 years and housing developments sprang up all around the radioactive facility resulting in an unusual number of cancer cases and deaths.

In politics we gave the country two presidents, Herbert Hoover, who got most of the blame for the "Great Depression," and Richard Nixon, who resigned from the nation's highest office in disgrace over the Watergate scandal. Then, too, there was the Governor of California, Earl Warren, who was appointed Chief Justice of the United States and presided over the historic Supreme Court decision that banned racial segregation in public schools. All three were the subjects of prolonged and bitter controversy, which seems to go with the political territory in California.

Twice in the 20th Century "burn baby burn" became the battle cry as black rioters rose up against the established order in the "City of the Angels." The first riot in August of 1965 seemed to have been fueled by an intemperate remark by the chief of police about African Americans. The National Guard had to be called out to restore order on the streets. Forty-five persons were killed, most of them rioters, and 800 were wounded.

The second riot in 1992 came about after a jury acquitted four white LAPD officers of brutality charges stemming from a beating they gave a black man they captured after a high speed car chase. The rioting started after video of the incident filmed by a homeowner was played on TV news broadcasts. There were 34 deaths, 800 wounded, 3,000 arrests and widespread property damage. (Two of the officers who took part in the beating were later found guilty of different civil rights crimes at a federal court trial.)

L.A. has been a refuge for the questionable activities of billionaires such as Howard Hughes and Armand Hammer, both of whom liked to think they kept politicians in their hip pockets. L.A. Oilman William Doheny was one of the major industrialists implicated in the Teapot Dome oil leasing scandal in the 1920s that brought down the crooked ways of President Harding's Interior Secretary, Andrew Fell. In return for an estimated $400,000 in bribe money, Fell swapped government oil leases to Doheny and Mammoth Oil Company president Harry Sinclair. Fell was fined $100,000 and given a one year prison sentence, the first presidential cabinet secretary to end up behind bars. Sinclair received three months for jury tampering, but Doheny got off scot-free. It was said at the time that Doheny tried to soothe his guilty conscience by donating a huge library to the University of Southern California and by building a Catholic Cathedral near Downtown L.A., something my Irish grandmother disdainfully called "the church of the holy oils."

Growing up in California where my parents were natives, the very mention of "oil" was almost a dirty word in our family. Much of the anti-oil company sentiment resulted from the Teapot Dome scandal. But there were other factors including the decimation of one of the best rapid transit systems in the United States, the fabled Red Car lines which had been around since before the turn of the 20th Century. At its peak the Pacific Electric Company operated high speed trains on 600 miles of track, much to the dismay of "Big Oil" and the Detroit car makers, which lobbied long and hard for a freeway system. They got what they wanted and the Red Cars could soon be found in local junk yards after the entire system was dismantled.

In its early years Los Angeles seemed to have a culture of political corruption. As a boy my father, a pharmacist, told me about the crooks in government who had to be bribed if you wanted a building permit or a license to sell liquor. At one time during the 1930s an estimated 1,000 houses of prostitution in Los Angeles County operated freely with the consent of the powers that be. The city's leading madams were on a first name basis with members of the police vice squad and their guest lists included lots of cops. Gambling ships operated by the mob were parked a few miles from the coastline and small boats ferried bettors to them night and day.

My first real brush with journalism came when I attended Loyola University in Los Angeles (now known as Loyola Marymount), a school run by the Jesuit priests with an enrollment of less than a thousand young men. I worked on the campus newspaper, first as a reporter, then sports editor and finally editor in chief which provided me with a partial scholarship. Real news suddenly became very much a part of my life in 1950. Despite its small enrollment, Loyola had a first class football team and was undefeated when the time came to play Texas Western University in El Paso, Texas.  A few days before the scheduled game, the school notified Loyola that our black athletes were not welcome to participate. The Loyola players voted to go ahead and play the game because they didn't consider Texas Western much of a challenge. But Father Charles Casassa, the university president, said he could not abide racial segregation in athletics and called off the game.  Casassa said Loyola would reimburse Texas Western the $50,000 fee called for under its contractual obligations.

Apart from being a major news story, it was a bonanza for Loyola, both in good will and financial help. Nationally syndicated columnist Drew Pearson was so impressed with Loyola's stand against sports segregation he raised over $300,000 for the university. Ironically, 16 years later the same Texas school became the first team with an all black starting lineup to win the NCAA basketball championship by defeating the University of Kentucky.

My plans to become a working journalist on one of L.A's five newspapers were put on hold by the start of the Korean War in 1950. I was draft eligible the moment I was graduated and decided to take my chances with the United States Navy.

One of my Loyola classmates, Lonnie Castle, was killed in the first wave during the invasion of Inchon, South Korea. I had almost joined the Army's 40th Division Reserve unit with Castle, but changed my mind at the last moment, considering it an unwise move despite promises by recruiting officers that signing up was a sure way to avoid combat.

So two months after getting out of Navy boot camp in 1952, where did I end up? In South Korea of course, assigned there by the office of Commander Naval Force Far East to cover the war effort. Specifically, I was to report on the evacuation of a Marine unit close to enemy territory at the 38th Parallel. It was a hair-raising experience. We embarked up a river in a Navy LCU (Landing Craft Utility) piloted by a veteran Chief Petty Officer who appeared to be imbibing a little too much.

Our worst fears were realized when the boat crashed into some big river rocks and the port engine blew out. The chief's bloodshot eyes had failed to follow his river road map. We limped to the evacuation area on just one engine in the dead of night. At five the next morning, just before dawn, about 25 battle weary Marines climbed aboard the landing craft. We were warned that we must depart immediately because the Chinese Communists would start shooting at us the minute they saw the light of day.

One big problem, though. With so much weight on the landing craft and one engine dead, the boat wouldn't budge. So all available hands got off the boat and we pushed and pushed in the muddy water until the engine turned over just like my old Model "A." As we sailed off daylight arrived and, as predicted, the Chinese started shooting at us. But luckily we escaped without a single casualty. This was too much of an ordeal for my photographer who had a nervous breakdown and was sent back to the United States.

A few months later I was assigned to *Pacific Stars and Stripes*, the Far East version of the military newspaper that came to prominence during World War Two with such legendary figures as literary great Alexander Wolcott, Bill Mauldin, the Pulitzer Prize winning editorial cartoonist, and Andy Rooney, the gruff, outspoken commentator on the CBS program "Sixty Minutes."

I learned the opening on *Stars and Stripes* came about because reporter Murray Fromson was kicked off the paper for making an unauthorized trip to the top secret island of Koje-do where Communist prisoners were held, sort of an earlier version of the prison for terrorists at Guantanamo Bay, Cuba. Fromson was quickly discharged from the Army and went to work for *United Press* in Tokyo. Later we both worked together at CBS Television. He was a gutsy guy and those were big shoes for me to fill.

At 22 years old I was just where I wanted to be, working on a daily newspaper, albeit a military one tightly censored by General Douglas MacArthur's staff in Tokyo. *Stars and Stripes* was published seven days a week with eight different editions stretching from Korea to Indochina (now Vietnam). The paper had no advertisements.

Our city editor, Army Master Sergeant Herb Scott, came to us via the Chicago *Tribune*. He was a good editor but as nasty a man as I ever met. Once in a rage, he called our movie critic Al Ricketts a "pus belly" because of something Scott considered to have sexual overtones. Ricketts fled to the basement print shop where he threw up. Scott was one of those old timers who never learned how to use a typewriter. If he rewrote a story he did it with a pencil, and then handed it back to the reporter to retype.

I mentioned there was censorship which we fought endlessly. There was a squawk box next to the city desk and the voice on the other end was usually a major at the Army's high command in Pershing Heights who frequently questioned us about stories we planned to run. At one point Army Intelligence launched a major investigation into the background of all editorial personnel. Why? Because *Stars and Stripes* ran an *Associated Press* story that said the Russians had completed a cross country railroad to Siberia. Cold War paranoia was at a fever pitch in those days.

One day while manning the city desk, I got a call from Air Force Captain Lee Campbell who invited me to dinner at a Tokyo restaurant. Lee was a college classmate who said he was somewhat troubled and needed to chat with a friend. I wondered what was on his mind and he told me after a couple of drinks. His job was to fly the bodies of our men killed in Korea back to Tokyo every week. He did it because he was under orders but he didn't like it one bit. He said he wished he could change places with me. Soon after the war ended Lee resigned from the Air Force.

A year later he died from a heart attack. Lee Campbell never fired a weapon. But he was truly an unsung hero in America's forgotten war.

From time to time I like to remind my co-workers that 43,000 American men and women were killed in Korea in less than three years, and thousands more severely wounded, a horrible toll. We cheered in the city room when President Eisenhower declared the fighting over on July 27, 1953 even though there was no real Armistice, just a cease fire. It seemed there would be no end to the "cold war" with the Communist world for the foreseeable future.

On Sept. 6, 1954 a full blown international incident was in the making when a U.S. Navy patrol plane was shot down by two Soviet MIG fighter jets over the Sea of Japan roughly 45 miles off the coast of Siberia. Nine of the 10 Navy men aboard the downed plane were rescued and flown to the U.S. Naval Base at Atsugi, Japan, a distance of about 60 miles from our offices in the Roppongi District of Tokyo. The Navy called a press conference to lay out the official version of what happened and city editor Scott assigned me to the story, telling me and my Japanese driver to "bust our butts" to get to Atsugi in time for the presser. The driver took Scott at his word and was doing 80 miles an hour when we were stopped for speeding a few miles from our destination by two Navy shore patrolmen. My Stars and Stripes press card made it clear that I was not to brook any interference while covering a story. It stated that I was to be given "the privileges and courtesies normally accorded civilian correspondents."

But the Navy cops busted my driver and took him to the stockade, and I had to continue the drive to the base. Once there I ran into a Navy public information officer and demanded that my driver be freed at once.

He told me he'd look into it and suggested I get to the press conference. It was a crowded affair and I was lucky to find a seat in the last row. An Admiral was describing how the two Soviets MIG fighter jets opened fire on the Navy plane without warning. Suddenly I got a nudge from a young petty officer who saw the Stars and Stripes patch on my shoulder and said, "This is all B.S. Come with me to the enlisted men's barracks and you'll get the real story from a guy who was on the plane."

So I rushed out of the press conference and went to the enlisted men's quarters where I was introduced to the Navy gunner's mate who was aboard the downed air-craft. "So what happened?" I asked the young sailor from Oklahoma. "I'll tell you what happened," he declared without a moment's hesitation. "Those Commies were coming right at us and they were in my sights so I started shooting and they started shooting back." I asked why he fired the first shot and he said "I knew they were about to fire at us so I let them have it. I hope I got one of them." Another sailor who was aboard the plane verified the story.

Now this was the 1950s and the conventional wisdom was that in situations such as this the Communists shot first because they were the bad guys. I called *Stars and Stripes* managing editor Gene Miller, a civilian from Buffalo, New York, and dictated a story describing how the gunners mate appeared to have provoked the shooting. "Pete," Gene said, "if you're wrong about this I'll lose my job. You've got to know how those people at Pershing Heights are going to react." I finished dictating the story and then Gene told me to come back to the office. I departed after I got my driver released from the stockade where he told me he was forced to stand with his hands raised above his head the entire time I was gone. My byline appeared on the front page of *Stars and Stripes* the next day but there was no mention of what I had learned from the Navy gunners mate. The Commies were to blame and that was that! Another reporter got tired of my bellyaching over the censorship of my story and told me, "You'd better get used to it kid."

My two-year tour of duty was coming to a close and to my surprise I was rewarded with a plush assignment back in the states, where I would wind up in Washington D.C. working as a correspondent out of the Pentagon for *Armed Forces Press Service* and *Stars Stripes*. My colleagues included Max Frankel who would eventually succeed the legendary Abe Rosenthal as executive editor of the New York *Times* and Myron (Mike) Kandel who, after working for the New York *Herald Tribune*, became a respected financial analyst for *Cable News Network* (CNN).

Going to work in the Pentagon was a real eye opener for this young reporter.

Charles Wilson, the chairman of General Motors, (not to be confused with the Texas Congressman who was the subject of the movie "Charlie Wilson's War") was picked by President Eisenhower to run the Defense Department and he made for great copy. Wilson became known as "Engine Charlie" after he was immortalized in Pentagon lore for his famous line, "What's good for General Motors is good for the country." He was a jovial character who really seemed to like reporters. I was in some pretty fast company this time around. The New York *Times* desk was manned by Anthony Leviero who won a Pulitzer Prize while covering the White House. The *Associated Press* was led by Yates McDaniel, *United Press* by Charles Cordray and the Chicago *Tribune* by Lloyd Norman. Norman would eventually collaborate with me in an investigation that led a wrongly condemned (in my opinion) Los Angeles soldier win a last minute reprieve when the commanding general at Leavenworth refused to carry out his execution.

There wasn't space for me and my co-worker in the small Pentagon press room so our desk was located directly across the hall in the office of Press Secretary Herschel Schooley. I sat a few feet away from Air Force Major Bob White, known throughout the Pentagon as the "Secretary for Flying Saucers." Bob had countless stories to tell about the UFO true believers who tried to convince him aliens had indeed invaded our planet.

One day Bob said to me, "Pete, let's go to the Pentagon entrance. It's a sight you've got to see." There on the steps of the Pentagon was a former Marine major, Donald Kehoe, one of those true UFO believers. Kehoe had authored several books on the subject including "The Flying Saucer Conspiracy." And there he was in all his glory on the Pentagon steps, this ramrod straight ex-Marine, dressed in bathrobe, pajamas and slippers.

Major Kehoe insisted he had come across some incredibly new information about alien sightings, and was so excited he forgot to change clothes before he left home. White told the major he could not go inside the Pentagon in his current garb or he might get locked up as a security risk.

For a good 20 minutes while a curious crowd of onlookers watched and listened. Kehoe talked about the newest sighting and said he would soon have photographic evidence to prove it. White finally told Kehoe to go home and have breakfast after promising he would investigate the merits of the latest sighting. It was like that day after day for Major Bob White as UFO mania seemed to be sweeping the country. But Bob had a genial personality and temperament that helped him survive his mind boggling ordeal.

Perhaps my biggest thrill in Washington was getting a printed invitation from Presidential Press Secretary Jim Haggerty to attend a White House news conference for President Eisenhower, thanks to my friend at *the Copley Press* Bureau, Frank Macomber. It was a sit down affair in the East Room of the White House with eight reporters in attendance. The engraved invitation warned that Mr. Eisenhower's voice could not be recorded. And if he said something "off the record" it was not to be repeated. The President was a genial host. The president seemed at ease seated on a sofa, taking time to answer questions in a careful, measured tone. But there were snickers at times from some of the reporters when Ike garbled his syntax, a problem he frequently experienced in ad lib situations. I filed my story, well aware my military career as a Washington correspondent was coming to a close at the end of my four-year stint in the Navy and I would soon have to begin looking for a real job in the civilian marketplace.

One day I got a call from New Hampshire asking if I would be interested in going to work for the radical right wing newspaper, *The Manchester Union Leader*. I said thanks but no thanks. Max Frankel said he thought he could get me an entry level position at the New York *Times* where he was on staff. Thought about that one quite a bit, but my heart was in Los Angeles. Little did I realize my next job as a reporter would be in what some called the "salt mines of journalism." But I would never regret the move back West because L.A.'s was truly the place for news.

# 2

# THE SALT MINES OF JOURNALISM

My return home in 1956 following a four year tour of duty in the Navy was met with lots of rejection. All five metropolitan newspapers in L.A. rejected me for employment as well as the three national wire services and a half dozen community newspapers. No one cared that I had risen to the rank of editor on *Stars and Stripes*, interviewed Ike at the White House and helped get a condemned G.I. off death row. So I applied and was accepted into the UCLA Graduate School of Journalism where I was introduced to some very fine minds including Fred Warner Neal, a former State Department big wig who served as an assistant ambassador to Yugoslavia, and Kirby Ramsdell, the chief editorial writer for the Los Angeles *Times*. Kirby liked to say that California Governor Goodwin J. Knight was "so conservative before he was elected that he believed in shooting poor people." Joe Brandt was the former head of the Journalism School at the University of Oklahoma. It was an incredible faculty. They introduced me to the likes of Lincoln Steffens, Richard Harding Davis, Walter Lippman and a host of other journalism greats. We took courses in writing style, ethics, newspaper history, socialist revolutions.

We interviewed authors, historians, men of the cloth. They even threw in the notorious bigot Gerald L.K. Smith to test our objectivity.

About three months into our studies, Charley Katzman, a job hunting specialist for the Journalism School, asked me I'd be interested in going to work at Los Angeles City News Service (CNS), which was modeled after the legendary City News Service of Chicago. I said I was uncertain if I could work and still get my degree. Katzman said no problem "Take the job while you can get it; there may not be another one for a year or two." So I went to the old Cotton Exchange Building in the heart of Skid Row in downtown L.A. and told city editor Chuck Riley I needed a job. He liked my experience and hired me in a matter of minutes to start work right away. Several friends suggested I was going to work "in the salt mines of journalism" but I never gave it a second thought. The salary was minimal, about $35 a week after taxes. Plus I paid $1 a day for parking. I would have to live with my parents and four younger brothers and sisters because I couldn't afford to rent an apartment.

Each week day I attended grad school in the morning, then drove downtown to police headquarters where CNS had a desk in the press room. When I started working the police beat in 1956 I was about as green as they get. I soon discovered that local reporters and their editors had a racist perception of the world they covered. Black crimes against black people were never reported in the four metropolitan papers. "Pass on it, it's black" were the bywords in the press room.

Black crime against whites was always reported, because in the minds of the editors that was real news. That's the way it was, a microcosm of the greater society at the time.

But the editors at City News Service covered black on black crimes, mainly because the local wire service had several "Negro" newspapers as customers. So at first I sat in lonely isolation in the police press room, ignored by the "real" newspaper reporters who labeled themselves "the syndicate," and regarded me as an outsider because of my affiliation with City News Service and because, in their view, we reported non-newsworthy stories. It was a battle day after day.

The "syndicate" was a tradition that went back almost to the start of American newspapering. The legendary muckraker, Lincoln Steffens, wrote in his autobiography that in 1893 while working on the *Evening Post* in New York City police reporters had a "combine" for covering the news. It was almost identical to the syndicate in the LAPD press room. The syndicate demanded that the information submitted to their editors be identical. There could be no deviation, no reporter grandstanding by hyping a story with information that would set it apart from what his peers in the press room wrote. And at first the syndicate would have nothing to do with me.

One day I was quite curious when a police spokesperson called the press room and said interviews were available with an officer who had killed a narcotics suspect, a "Negro." The officer bragged that he killed the guy, choking him hard "… trying to get back the dope he swallowed when he saw me coming." The syndicate passed on the story, and advised me to do likewise. I didn't heed the syndicate's advice and the story appeared on the CNS news wire. Another reporter thought my story gave the LAPD a "black eye."

The prevailing attitude of editors at the time manifested itself in the summer of 1965 when the predominantly black community of Watts exploded in a firestorm of violence.

The Los Angeles Times did not have a single black reporter on its editorial staff so the city editor turned to the advertising department where he recruited a black salesman to cover the story.

There was the day in the late 1950s that the Santa Monica Police Department called the police press room to advise us that a young actor named Rock Hudson had been arrested for having sex with a young boy on the Santa Monica Pier. The syndicate reporters passed on the story but CNS ran it, much to the chagrin of the studio flacks who were charged with protecting the rising young star's image. The PR types passed the incident off as a case of mistaken identity by the Santa Monica police. The studio bosses even arranged a phony marriage for Hudson to protect his image. Hudson was never prosecuted and it was about 30 years later his homosexuality became public knowledge when we learned he was dying of AIDS.

In the view of the newspaper brass, if a story wasn't in print in one of their papers, it wasn't news. It wasn't news when an L.A. *Times* reporter – discovered by his editors to be a homosexual – leaped to his death from an upper floor in the newspaper building.

As for "pass, it, it's black," that policy gradually disappeared after a story I wrote for City News Service described the slaying of an African-American father of eight who was stabbed to death "by a man who heard voices." Columnist Paul Coates of the Los Angeles *Mirror-News* picked up the story and found it hard to comprehend why the murder of a solid citizen under unusual circumstances was given nary a mention in the L.A. newspapers until he wrote about it.

I got my job on the police beat because City News Service owner Joe Quinn decided he would break with tradition and assign a woman to the CNS desk in the police press room. The syndicate decided she had to go. There had never before been a woman on the police beat and the syndicate wasn't about to break with precedent. So they set her up, each reporter pretending to call his respective desk with a story that L.A.'s headline grabbing mobster, Mickey Cohen, had been shot to death in Griffith Park. The CNS reporter overheard the Cohen report and gave the details to her desk editor. The subsequent bulletin from CNS was read on half a dozen L.A. radio stations and several television stations. The young woman was fired immediately when the story was unveiled as a hoax. None of the reporters who took part in the deception was disciplined. Just a case of boys being boys, I guess. So from the very start I was leery about doing business with the syndicate.

Reporter Jake Jacoby of the *Herald-Express*, who was not involved in the hoax, took a liking to me and decided to help school me in the art of police reporting. Jake was a warm, friendly person who considered it his responsibility to help young journalists and ignored the rants of the "syndicate" for fraternizing with me. (Twenty years later Jake broke in my son on the police beat at my old City News Service desk. After his death the police press room was named in his honor).

The press room was a sight to behold. Half the reporters had booze stashed in their desks and sober moments were few and far between. The talk of the town was the case of a reporter who stopped at the police press room to have some libation one Friday night.

After a time the guy disappeared into a small back room with a sofa and most of the reporters thought he was simply trying to sleep it off. Three days later there was the stench of death in the press room. A reporter opened the door and the guy's lifeless body lay on the couch. There was no room for sentiment. Just call the coroner.

Legendary Police Chief Bill Parker was a tyrant when it came to reporters. He loved to dress us down and tell us how stupid we were. Everyone was pretty much aware that Parker had a drinking problem and reporter Sid Smith of the *Examiner* decided to seek revenge on the chief for all the brickbats he hurled at us. *Examiner* city editor Jim Richardson, commonly referred to by news types as "the last of the wild men," decided Smith and a cameraman would tail Parker as he went from bar to bar. The plan was to catch Parker coming out of a bar and getting into his car. Then Smith would radio police headquarters with a "502" call meaning a drunk driver – a so-called "deuce" was on the road and police assistance was needed.

Once a police car was at the scene, the newspaper cameraman would photograph the tipsy Parker and the confrontation with his underlings. Smith and his camera-man tailed Parker for several weeks but were never able to catch him emerging from a bar. The suspicion was that the chief got wind of the plot from a press room snitch and decided to quit drinking, at least in public.

A sometime visitor to the police press room was mob boss Mickey Cohen who almost salivated every time he met a reporter. On one occasion Mickey handed out $100 bills to reporters (I wasn't one of them), than launched a tirade against his chief tormentor, Chief Parker. The midget mobster loved news guys because the man who made him famous was city editor Jim Richardson of the *Examiner*. The Cohen legend started after he and seven of his thugs beat up a loan shark who had evicted an eld-erly woman from her home because she was late on a payment for a cheap radio she had purchased on a time account. As far as Richardson was concerned, the former bantamweight boxer and his tribe were the citizens of the month. An editorial cartoon in the newspaper depicted Mickey as Snow White and his hoodlum followers as the seven dwarfs. Cohen's popularity became so immense that he opened up a very profitable men's clothing store on L.A.'s trendy Westside, and shed his wife, La Vonne, first for stripper Liz Renay followed by another exotic dancer named "Candy Barr." The Mick's bookmaking income rose to $25,000 a month and he loved playing the role of a big money guy, living the life of a night clubbing celebrity on L.A.'s glittering Sunset Strip.

One of the people who helped me get started was Florabel Muir, a nationally syndicated Hollywood columnist who often lectured me on the history of newsgathering in L.A. She once owned City News Service and had news sources just about everywhere. Florabel was on the Mickey Cohen beat the night of July 20, 1950, when the midget mobster was holding court at a popular night club on L.A.'s Sunset Strip. Outside a group of rival mob gunmen hiding behind cars on the street were planning to assassinate the Mick. Cohen partied until late in the evening. When it was time to leave Florabel and the Mick began walking out together when suddenly Cohen stepped into the restroom to wash his hands, a move that saved his life. Florabel turned to summon Mickey when suddenly gunfire erupted from several directions. The columnist was shot in the derriere and Mickey was winged in the shoulder, but the wounds to both were not serious. One of Mickey's closest buddies, Edward (Neddie) Herbert was killed.

One of those who didn't like the Mick one bit was Jack (the Enforcer) Whalen, one of the toughest bookmakers on the L.A. scene. On Dec. 2, 1959 Cohen and his associates were dining at one of their favorite pasta hangouts, Rondelli's Restaurant in North Hollywood, when who should burst through a kitchen door and come charging at Cohen's table, but a growling Jack the Enforcer. Apparently the big guy was there to collect money from two of Cohen's sidekicks who had welshed on some bets. Suddenly there was a burst of gunfire and Whalen slumped over dead from a bullet to the brain. Police said they couldn't find any witnesses to the killing in the crowded restaurant. Cohen was charged with the murder but escaped prosecution for lack of evidence. One of his sidekicks, Sam Frank Locigno, was eventually convicted of the crime. Years later a deputy LAPD police chief wanted to know all about the Whalen killing but no one in the department could find the murder book. So the homicide dicks called me and I sent them my entire file on the case.

In a footnote to the murder, Jack Whalen left behind a 16-year-old daughter, Karen, who was the president of the teen-age fan club of Baxter Ward, one of L.A.'s most popular TV anchormen. I got to know Ward quite well because he frequently used my investigative stories on his top rated TV news broadcast on *KCOP* (Channel 13). Ward was so smitten with Karen Whalen that he dumped his first wife and married the teenager. Ward eventually left TV for politics and was elected an L.A. County Supervisor despite his refusal to accept campaign contributions. He served just one six year term, and was defeated in his bid for re-election. In 2002 I got a call from Ward's son, Torrey, who told me his 81-year-old father had died of lung cancer, just two weeks after it was diagnosed, at a hospital in the state of Washington. Torrey said he knew his father would have wanted to be remembered to me. Then Torrey added that his father died a lonely death because he could not reach his bedside in time. I asked Torrey where his mother was. "In prison for fraud," was the reply. Somewhat surprised, I mumbled a "sorry about that" and wished Torrey a good life. Just another L.A. story.

As for Mickey Cohen, he beat one rap after another over the years, serving just one brief jail sentence, until the tax man caught up with him. Doing the catching was Donald (Bulldog) Bowler of the Internal Revenue Service's Intelligence Division, one of my college classmates. Mickey was accused of not paying taxes on nearly $400,000 in income, most of it from bookmaking. Convicted, he was sentenced to five years in prison. Once behind bars he was nearly killed by another inmate who clubbed him on the head with a board. When he returned to L.A. a few years later Cohen was a shadow of himself, a broken man, his organization in shambles.

During my learning years on the police beat I worked on occasion with columnist Florabel Muir, who when not covering Mickey Cohen, was always looking for a good story. Pretty soon she was assigning me to sub for her on the Hollywood beat. Most of my assignments were for her main customer, the New York *Daily News*, and most were Hollywood "fluff." But the money wasn't bad and helped supplement my meager salary at a time when I was thinking of getting married. Eventually Florabel turned the job at the Daily News over to me and retired.

I became acquainted with a long list of famous Hollywood  headline makers such as Fatty Arbuckle, Thelma Todd, Jean Harlow, George Reeves  and a host of silent film stars who partied themselves to death. Australian-born actor Errol Flynn generated tabloid copy everywhere he went. Flynn's death in 1959 while bedded down with his teenage lover, Beverly Elaine Aadland, was fantastic grist for the tabloid mills. Four years earlier Beverly was proclaimed the "Explorer Scout of the Year" by Sheriff Eugene Biscailuz. But then she put her good deeds behind her, turning into a teen-age call girl whose services commanded a pricey $100 a night.

Beverly's activities had the full support of her mother, Florence Aadland, who was derisively referred to as "Mother of the Year" by cops and reporters alike. At just 16 Beverly settled down with Flynn on a permanent basis and a few months later his heart gave out while they were touring Vancouver, British Columbia. Reporters were at a loss to describe Beverly. It wouldn't be fair to call a teenager a prostitute or a hooker. So CNS city editor Chuck Riley and I hit on the idea of calling the teenager Errol Flynn's "protégé," and the moniker stuck. The philandering Charlie Chaplin fled the country after attorney Joseph Scott, who was at least 20 years older than the comic, referred to him as a "dirty old man" at his trial for impregnating youthful actress Joan Berry. The jury verdict favored Chaplin but the trial almost destroyed his reputation and he took off for Europe, where he was eventually knighted as Sir Charles Spencer Chaplin in his native Great Britain. It was many years before he would leave England and return to the United States to be honored by the Motion Picture Academy in 1972.

Then came the really big story of the 1950s – the fatal stabbing in Beverly Hills of mob glamour boy Johnny Stompanato in the bedroom of his lover, actress Lana Turner. She, of course, was the one time "sweater girl" who according to Hollywood legend was discovered at a soda fountain at Schwab's drug store on the Sunset Strip and became one of tinsel town's most celebrated beauty queens.

Stompanato came to L.A. from Chicago with mobster Benjamin (Bugsy) Siegel. After Bugsy was assassinated in 1947 a few blocks from Turner's home, he became a bodyguard for crime boss Mickey Cohen who inherited much of Bugsy's L.A. turf. Years later while doing a TV special about the case I was chided by my colleagues for writing that "Stompanato had a record that stretched from L.A.

to Chicago" and that he was stabbed to death in Lana Turner's "pink bedroom." Dare say it was a little tabloid, but I thought it clearly summed up the story.

City Editor Riley had decided I was to take charge of the Stompanato story and find out the truth of what happened in Lana's pink bedroom. It's no exaggeration to write that most news guys believed that Turner, not her 15-year-old daughter Cheryl Crane, had committed the killing because the "Stomp" beat her regularly. I took off for Beverly Hills in my rusty 1949 Ford and asked questions everywhere I went in the upscale community where virtually every car seemed to be a Cadillac or Rolls Royce, and where blacks and poor white trash couldn't get past the city line at night without being stopped by the cops.

I asked people on the street, "Did you see Lana Turner and Stompanato together?" "Did you know Johnny Stomp was tied to the underworld? That he worked for Mickey Cohen and Bugsy Siegel?" and on and on. Finally I dropped into a hardware store in the heart of Beverly Hills and asked the manager if Lana Turner ever shopped there. "Hell yes," he replied "Just a week or so ago she came in and bought the knife used to kill that gangster." He went behind the counter and showed me what he was talking about, a shiny nearly foot-long butcher knife. God knows, I had a scoop. More questions, and then I walked out of the store and into the waiting arms of two Beverly Hills cops. I demanded to know what they wanted and they said they were taking me to police headquarters at City Hall. I wanted to know what heinous crime I had committed "Did I spit on the sidewalk? "Was I being fined for not driving a Caddie?" The very stoic cops didn't think I was one bit funny. Once at the station I was introduced to Lt. Jack Egger. I knew who he was immediately. Before he became a cop he worked security at the Florentine Gardens, a night spot in Hollywood, that was one of several hangouts of Elizabeth Short, the murdered

"Black Dahlia. "What are you doing in our town?" Lt. Egger asked. I told him I was covering the Stompanato story. "Not any more," said Egger, "you don't have a Beverly Hills press pass." As far as I knew Beverly Hills didn't issue press passes. I had an LAPD pass but that didn't matter. Egger told me to get out of town and if I came back they'd lock me up and throw away the key. So I got out of town quickly and went back to City News where I promptly reported the incident at the hardware store. The possibility that Miss Turner purchased the knife shortly before Stompanato was killed was never introduced as evidence and she was never questioned about it as far as I could determine. That only fueled my suspicions of a possible cover-up.

Next up was the coroner's inquest in the old L.A. Hall of records which tilted like the Leaning Tower of Pisa. The inquest jury absolved Lana Turner of any involvement in the crime after she sobbed quietly on the witness stand, and pinned the blame on the teen-age daughter Cheryl. Miss Turner was never asked if she had purchased the knife shortly before Stompanato was killed. It's been falsely reported in some books that it was a trial. It was not. An inquest by the coroner usually meant that the police and district attorney were unsure of their evidence, and a finding by the jury would determine if the killing in question was justified or not. The District Attorney's ducking of the case seemed to me a major concession to Lana Turner's lawyer, Jerry Giesler, a guy known for getting things done in Hollywood. The inquest was a slipshod legal proceeding. People wandering the hallways of the old Hall of Records were picked at random by deputy sheriffs to sit on the six person jury. Most of them appeared to be in their 60s and 70s. The elderly jury foreman never took his eyes of the immaculately primed actress as she testified and cleared her tears away with a lace hankie. About10 minutes after testimony ended the jurors returned with a verdict of justifiable homicide.

***Actress Lana Turner holds back the tears as she testifies at the 1958 inquest into the death of her lover, mobster Johnny Stompanato.***

It was the perfect ending to a Hollywood tragedy, much to the joy of Miss Turner and lawyer Giesler, who had contacts with every important law enforcement official in L.A. beginning with the district attorney's office. There was no doubt in my mind that Lana Turner killed Johnny Stompanato. The common reportorial view seemed to be that the killing of the Stomp was good riddance, a public service, so to speak.

Hollywood stories seemed quite intriguing to this young reporter. One that I never chronicled came to me from a newspaper editor who told me I was the one reporter in town who could help him with a terrible family crisis. He said his well-known actress- niece, a movie beauty queen, was in the habit of having sex with a gentleman caller in the presence of her very young daughter. I suggested he contact a friend of mine in the LAPD's intelligence division who was quite skilled at dealing with Hollywood problems. Not long after that the cop told me the problem had been resolved. Today the story would be fodder for the tabloids, but not then. There were some stories that were simply considered to be "in bad taste" and not printable. I was surprised one day when I answered the press room telephone and Beverly Hills Police Chief Clinton Anderson was on the other end of the line. Anderson said, "Noyes, I've got a story for you." I asked "Why the story chief? You never tell us anything." Then I reminded him of the threat to jail me while I was covering the Stompanato killing. Ignoring my remark he said, "Noyes, here's the story. Last night we arrested Bing Crosby's brother, Bob for being drunk and disorderly and fighting with his wife in front of the children." "Why tell us?" I asked in a snide voice, feigning disinterest? Chief Anderson responded, "The guy got drunk and beat up his wife in front of their kids last night. I want the son of a bitch out of Beverly Hills and I want him out now." The syndicate didn't shy away from the story and it ran in the newspapers. Two weeks later Bob Crosby, a bandleader by profession, had moved his family to a new home in Orange County. I guess the moral of the story for me was, "Don't mess with the Beverly Hills cops." Despite Chief Anderson's bullying tactics there was some sadness in the police press room when his only son was killed in the Vietnam War. Colleagues on the department said Anderson was never the same after that.

It's easy to become cynical when covering the police beat. Deadly violence becomes a way of life night after night. After awhile it's hard to develop compassion for the victims and their families. But every so often there is a story that really tugs at your heart despite the daily turmoil. I had become friends with a homicide cop named Jose Castellanos who took a liking to me and became extremely helpful in providing background on murder cases. Not too far away in another room at the station was one of the most famous police sketch artists in the country, Ector Garcia. When provided with a description of a criminal suspect, Ector would, in a matter of minutes, turn out a sketch that nine times out of ten would prove to be a dead ringer for the suspect once he or she was apprehended. But Ector got bored with his desk job and asked for, and got an assignment in LAPD's vaunted Robbery-Homicide detail.

Ector was paired up with my friend, Detective Castellanos. On Ector's first night on the job, February 5, 1959, he and Jose got a call to a disturbance in a Hollywood bar where a drunken truck driver had shot and killed one man and wounded two others. I was on the city desk at City news Service when the call came over the police radio. There was a violent shootout at the scene. Jose Castellanos was killed and Ector was blinded in both eyes. The shooter, George J. Arevalo, had fired on them from ambush. Although Ector couldn't see, he returned a volley of shots and killed Arevalo.

After undergoing three operations Ector regained the vision in his right eye, and exactly 11 months after the shooting he went back to work in his old job, police sketch artist, which he held until he retired many years later. A picture of Jose Castellanos was placed in the court of honor at police headquarters. Ector Garcia, it turned out, had been a newspaper editorial cartoonist before joining the force. He was a cop who loved to hang out with reporters, and almost nightly could be found at the bar of the Los Angeles Press Club keeping the news guys up to date on all the intrigue at the cop shop. I wrote a story about his career and return to duty which appeared in the old Hollywood *Citizen News*. Ector loved my profile of him and wanted to buy me a drink every time he ran into me at a local watering hole. Seeing him back at work at Parker Center was certainly one of my most fulfilling moments as a young police reporter.

# 3

# A NEWSMAN'S LEARNING CURVE

Sometimes luck has a lot to do with earning a reputation as a good reporter. When I first met George Miller, a suave kind of guy who came to work in a suit and tie, highly improbable clothing for the police beat, I was at a loss to understand why he was working for City News Service, the lowest paying news organization in L.A. Miller, who was at least 15 years my senior, looked like someone from the cover of a men's magazine, and could articulate on just about any subject brought to his attention. He claimed to be on a first name basis with just about every politician in town. So why was he working the cop shop one particular night and why was I on the city desk, editing everyone's else's copy? I soon found out, all part of mastering the learning curve.

It became pretty obvious after Miller broke one of the biggest stories in California. And it was another learning experience, basically don't wait for the press releases. L. Ewing Scott was a handsome silver-haired con man who for many years made a living ripping off wealthy but vulnerable widows. He was in his 50s when his latest conquest turned out to be one of the richest women in

L.A., Evelyn Throsby, a socialite from the upscale community of Bel Air on L.A.'s Westside. He charmed Evelyn into marriage during a vacation in Mexico in 1949 and quickly began looting her bank accounts. Then one day in 1955 Evelyn disappeared and it became the talk of the town. After filing a missing persons report, Scott told reporters Evelyn would be coming home any day soon. He said he thought she was undergoing treatment in a sanitarium. He didn't know exactly where. "Evelyn, I love you," he would blurt out while the TV cameras were rolling. "Please come back to me." From the start there were those who suspected he might have buried Evelyn in the path of the San Diego (405) Freeway which was under construction a few blocks from the Scott home. One wag even suggested it be renamed the "Evelyn Throsby Scott Memorial Freeway" after Evelyn's dentures, eyeglasses and cosmetics were found buried in shallow ground in the backyard of her home.

Scott had been leading the good life, a flashy new car every year, a Brooks Brothers wardrobe, a Rolex watch and other accouterments befitting a man of his social standing. He rubbed elbows with some of the city's biggest movers and shakers at the exclusive Jonathan Club. Investigators determined Scott had a history of fleecing widows, and when the Grand Jury found out he had stolen a lot of Evelyn's money, perhaps as much as $250,000, through forgery and other illegal acts, he was indicted on larceny charges and he became a man on the run, fleeing to Canada.

Several months later while I was on the city desk George Miller ran into the newsroom and shouted, "Noyes, get away from the teletype. I'm going to punch out the hottest story in the nation." I demanded to know what the story was but George said, "Stand over my shoulder and learn kid."

It was a big story all right. L. Ewing Scott had been arrested by the FBI when his vanity got the better of him. As was Scott's custom, he had to have a new car every year.

So true to his life style, he risked crossing the Canadian border at Windsor to buy a car in Detroit. He paid cash for a new Ford Fairlane and was attempting to head back into Canada when border patrolmen recognized him from a wanted poster and held him for the FBI. I asked Miller about his sources and how was it that he was the only reporter who knew about Scott's arrest. "Pete," he said. "I was standing at the urinal in the men's room at Parker Center between two cops who were talking about Scott's capture and the circumstances leading up to it. They thought I was a cop, too, and told me everything I needed." It was the big story of course and Miller played it for everything he could. A month later he was working at the New York *Times*. Scott, meantime, was returned to L.A. by armed guards and indicted for killing his wife. On the flight back to L.A he sat next to the city's premier TV newscaster, George Putnam, and told him, "I just can't wait to get Evelyn in court." Despite his bluster Scott was fair game for J. Miller Leavy, the D.A.'s top prosecutor. Leavy put together a chain of evidence that left no doubt that Evelyn was murdered by Scott although the cops never found her body.

In an historic decision, a jury found L. Ewing Scott guilty of first degree murder in November of 1957 and he was given life in prison. At the time it was described as the first, first degree murder conviction in the history of American law in which a body was not recovered. The shaken Scott was taken in shackles to San Quentin Prison. Twenty one years later at the age of 81 a feeble and not so debonair Scott was given his freedom and returned to L.A., still protesting his innocence at every turn. A few years later he consented to cooperate with writer Diane Wagner for a book about his murder case called "*Corpus Delicti*."

During a taped interview with Wagner, Scott finally admitted killing Evelyn because, in his words, "she was a terrible person." Scott said he pounded her over the head with a hard rubber mallet, put her body in his car trunk and drove to Nevada where he buried her body in the desert sand. Not many people were surprised by his admission although some believed he was not telling the truth about where he dumped the body, that Evelyn's remains were under the 405 Freeway near his old neighborhood. Scott died at 91 from the complications of old age. No tears were shed. By any standard L. Ewing Scott wasn't a very nice guy.

*L. Ewing Scott (right) with a deputy outside the courtroom where he was found guilty of murdering his wife. Her body was never found.*

Many of the stories I worked on the police beat were forgettable, but some were quite horrific and all part of a young reporter's learning curve. A reporter never forgets covering a plane crash for the first time. On a Saturday evening, January 26, 1958 I was having a drink with a friend in a beachfront bar when the music suddenly stopped on radio station KMPC and the announcer said there was a "Sig Alert" caused by a plane crash in the city of Norwalk ("Sig Alert" was named after Lloyd Sigmon, a legendary broadcaster who pioneered radio traffic reporting). I jumped in my car and 20 minutes later I was the first reporter to reach the scene of a terrible aerial collision over the Norwalk Sheriff's Station. A Navy patrol bomber with eight reservists had collided with an Air Force C-118 transport plane that carried 35 passengers and a crew of six.

The tail of the transport plane was torn off and landed squarely on top of a gas station. The bulk of the plane slammed down across the street on a gasoline storage area directly behind the sheriff's station, wiping out 15 cars including eight patrol vehicles.

As I got out of my car I came across body parts every where and I gagged at the smell of burning flesh. I had never experienced such human devastation, not even in Korea. I found a pay phone and called the City News Service desk. In a matter of minutes they had me voicing phone reports with half a dozen radio stations who were clients of the wire service.

Then a deputy sheriff asked me to join him in searching for the Navy patrol bomber. We found it in nearby Santa Fe Springs and to our astonishment two of the men aboard were alive and in fairly good shape. To this day I find it hard to understand how anyone could have survived that head-on crash.

The final toll was 48 dead from both planes. One civilian was killed, a woman hit by falling metal as she went outside her home to summon her children. The crash was witnessed by a goodly number of persons scanning the skies for a glimpse of Explorer I, America's first satellite.

It may have been my imagination but the smell of burning flesh that permeated the crash scene that night lingered with me for many months before I finally got it out of my system. Other reporters who had covered plane crashes and deadly fires told me they had pretty much the same experience. A fireman told me, "You never get used to the smell of burning flesh."

Following the mid-air collision, the Navy ordered a halt to all low-flying flights in the area, and unveiled a series of plans to prevent a repetition of such mid-air crashes. Unfortunately 29 years later history repeated itself when an Aero Mexico DC9 passenger plane collided with a small privately owned Piper Apache over the neighboring community of Cerritos. The big plane slammed to earth destroying every home within its reach. Eighty two people were killed, 64 passengers and crews on the two planes, and 15 persons on the ground. The scene was much uglier than the first crash in 1957. But at any time reporters must be prepared to cover such terrible stories. But they're very hard to forget.

# 4

# LIFTING THE SECRECY VEIL

One of things I didn't learn in college was the art of checking public records, which was never mentioned in any of the classes I took at the UCLA Graduate School of Journalism. One day Deputy Police Chief Thad Brown, a legendary detective for the LAPD, came into the press room and invited all of us to come to his office and learn the fundamentals of finding public records. He said from reading our stories he could tell we had a lot to learn. Only two of us showed up for the class but it was a God send. Public records could be found everywhere, the Los Angeles County Hall of Records the most prominent place. Every public agency keeps its records on file and with few exceptions all you had to do was ask to see them. It was an excellent learning experience. Brown told us exactly where we had to go to look.

My first big public records quest began at City News Service in 1959 when a real estate agent named Claire Arney called me to say a group of developers were secretly planning to seize roughly eight miles of beachfront land along the Southern California coast so they could build high rise condominiums and marquee hotels. She said local councilmen were "on the take" to build the massive project which was never discussed at public meetings.

Mrs. Arney said the developers planned to seize the land through eminent domain proceedings with the quiet cooperation of public officials in three beach cities and thousands of homeowners stood to lose their homes at give away prices. This was in the days before the California legislature passed a law requiring elected officials to hold nearly all their meetings in public. Using what I learned from Thad Brown, we went to the local planning departments in three beach cities and asked to see the various building requests on file. I guessed correctly. Plans for the huge beachfront development were on file, under wraps so to speak, in the offices of the three city clerks. Then Mrs. Arney and a group of local homeowners began monitoring city council meetings in the cities of Manhattan Beach, Hermosa Beach and Redondo Beach and bombarded their elected representatives with questions about their deal making. "Were they taking bribes from the developers?" the homeowners wanted to know. "Where was the money coming from to finance this huge project?" Local television news stations picked up the story and before too long there were demands for an investigation by the District Attorney's office. No legal action was taken but the developers quickly backed off and plans for the beachfront condemnations were dropped.

It's a story that's been told over and over again in land rich Southern California. Several developers told me it was impossible in those days to build anywhere in the Los Angeles area without paying off a councilman, a county supervisor or planning department official. In 1951 L.A. City Councilman, Eddie Davenport, dropped dead while boozing it up at a bar. Ambulance attendants found he was carrying $50,000 in cash, a lot of money at the time.

Davenport was long regarded at City Hall as a man on the take.

When L.A. County Supervisor Frank Bonelli died, authorities found $1 million in cash in his safe deposit box at a local bank. You can be sure Bonelli didn't get the money playing the stock market. In Bonelli's memory his fellow supervisors named a park after him in the San Gabriel Valley. After all he didn't do anything the rest of them wouldn't do.

In 1959, Ed Roybal, the first Mexican-American elected to the L.A. City Council, was engaged in a tough race for the L.A. County Board of Supervisors against fellow councilman Ernest Debs. Roybal got scant recognition from the downtown "Anglo" newspapers so his campaign chairman, Joe Fox, decided to concentrate his hopes for coverage on City News Service and its list of clients that included many small newspapers as well as most radio and TV stations in the L.A. area. The strategy seemed to pay off. Roybal was out in front on election night after the votes were first counted. But overnight there were several recounts and the next morning Debs was declared the winner by a slim margin. The Roybal camp cried foul and Fox alleged the election was "fixed." But the grand jury took no action. The fact of the matter was that Ernest Debs had long been the chairman of the L.A. City Council's Planning Committee which was notorious for letting developers know if they wanted to build they would have to pay off  Planning Committee members.. One developer told me, "It was just the cost of doing business in those days." So Ernest Debs would be a perfect fit for the Board of Supervisors who controlled building projects in all unincorporated areas of L.A. County. And the powers that be were not about to allow an unknown such as Ed Roybal to intrude on their territory. Mexican-American groups cried racism. But it wasn't all about race. It was about money, although race obviously played into it.

In recent years, as far as I can determine, developers don't make cash payoffs to politicians. They don't have to. They make campaign contributions. Years ago at the start of the 20th Century, an Eastern politician told the muckraking Lincoln Steffens, "The only thing worse than a bribe is a campaign contribution." So the more things change the more they remain the same. But there's one positive effect of all this, namely that politicians can wind up in jail if they fail disclose their campaign contributions which are available in the public record for anyone taking the time to inspect.

# 5

## THE CURSE OF BARBARA GRAHAM

There were plenty of ups and downs for me in my side job as a Hollywood stringer for the New York *Daily News*. You could work all week on a story and not get paid if what you wrote didn't end up in print. One summer day in 1961, I got fairly excited when *Daily News* editor Ruth Reynolds called and said she had a "hot one" for me.

The story was this: In 1955 Barbara Graham, a strikingly beautiful Los Angeles woman, and two male confederates, Jack Santo and Emmet Perkins, a pair of career criminals, were executed on the same day at San Quentin Prison for the murder of an elderly widow in suburban Burbank. They were convicted of the fatal bludgeoning of Mrs. Mabel Monahan, 70, whose nephew worked the gaming tables in Las Vegas. The conspirators believed Mrs. Monahan was hoarding gambling money stolen by her nephew and decided to rob her in plot hatched in the parking lot of the fashionable Smokehouse Restaurant in Toluca Lake near the home of comedian Bob Hope. They used a ruse to get into the old woman's home. Graham knocked on Monahan's front door, said her car had broken down, and she needed help. When Mrs. Monahan opened the door Barbara and her two armed male accomplices stormed inside. When Mrs. Monahan failed to lead them to the money they beat her so viciously blood began pouring from her head and she lapsed into unconsciousness. Then they departed empty handed.

Baxter Shorter, standing lookout outside the Monahan home, overheard Graham and her confederates talking about the beating. Later he called the Los Angeles Police Department, telling a desk officer what had happened. "Not our territory," said the cop who then hung up. If he had been doing his job, the LAPD cop should have referred the call to the Burbank Police Department and it might have saved a life. Three days later Mrs. Monahan finally bled to death, and now it was a case of murder. The lookout- turned-snitch was subsequently killed by the Graham gang. Finally Graham and her two accomplices were brought to justice, convicted by a jury and sentenced to die.

Barbara Graham personally pleaded with California's most famous TV news anchorman, George Putnam, to intercede with Governor Goodwin Knight on her behalf. But because of the gravity of the crime Putnam declined. "It broke my heart," Putnam told me. "She was such a beautiful young woman."

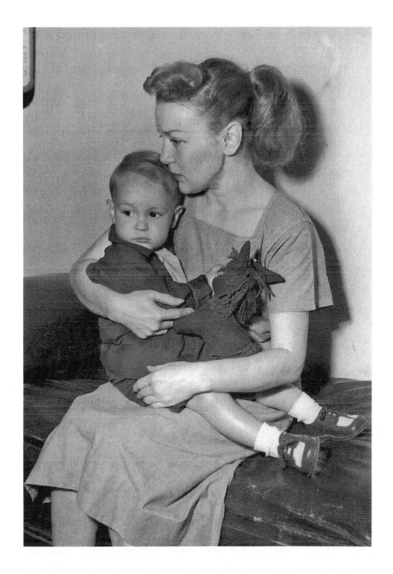

***Barbara Graham hugs her 2-year-old son before being taken to San Quentin Prison where she was put to death in the gas chamber in1955.***

Graham and her two male accomplices were executed in quick succession in the San Quentin gas chamber on June 3, 1955. Now lots of myths were floating around about Barbara Graham, the principal one being that the cops caught the wrong woman. Actress Susan Hayward won best actress honors for her sympathetic portrayal of Graham in the Academy Award winning movie "*I Want to Live*" in 1958. It was duly noted by some critics that Graham was just as beautiful as Hayward.

I called Clinton Duffy, the warden who changed San Quentin Prison from a hell hole into a somewhat livable place and asked him about "The Curse of Barbara Graham." In no uncertain words Duffy told me the story was a fabrication. "Barbara confessed her sins to a Roman Catholic chaplain," Duffy said, and then she was taken to the gas chamber "quivering and shaking, not uttering a word as she went to her death." Duffy gave me the names of several witnesses to the execution and each confirmed the warden's version.

I called Editor Reynolds at the *Daily News*, told her what Warden Duffy said and about my personal misgivings about the entire story. She said she thought a story about Graham's "curse" had appeared in the L.A. *Herald-Express* and suggested I visit the paper's morgue where old stories were filed. I must confess I had missed it in the newspaper. Herb Krauch was the managing editor of the *Herald-Express*, and I had gone to the UCLA Graduate School of Journalism with his son, Bob, who also worked on the paper. Bob Krauch arranged for me to meet with his father, a real gentleman who was very gracious to this young reporter. Krauch looked over the story and without hesitation told me the reporter who wrote it could be found downstairs in the "11 11" bar next to the newspaper. So I went to the bar and found the reporter, the only person there, face down in a drunken stupor. I said "please help me out on this one. My editor at the New York *Daily News* wants me to do a follow-up to your story, 'The Curse of Barbara Graham.' " Without even looking up he told me, "I made the whole God damn thing up. Now get out of here." I called Reynolds at the New York *Daily*

*News* and told her what had transpired. She responded, "Noyes, you've got a negative attitude. You're fired." A week later I got a termination check for $25 for labor that had consumed at least three weeks of my time.

At this point in my young life I found several of my most cherished beliefs about the integrity of journalists little more than an illusion. Time after time since then I've seen it happen; Clifford Irving with his phony autobiography of Howard Hughes, and reporters at some of the nation's best newspapers who were good at fiction, but not real news. Even a great paper like the New York *Times* was fooled into printing stories that were purely the imagination of a young reporter. And there were those tabloid newspapers and TV shows which didn't hesitate to pay for information and interviews, thereby tainting their stories from the onset.

A few years later I got a call from a different editor at the New York *Daily News*. "Pete" he said "we want you to do a story for us on the Jack Kirschke murder case." Kirschke, a high ranking member of L.A. District Attorney's staff and a close personal friend of D.A. Joe Busch, was suspected of murdering his wife and her lover in their home in the fashionable Belmont Shores area of Long Beach. He claimed he was in Nevada when the murders took place. I reminded the *Daily News* editor what had happened to me when I engaged in truthful reporting and how I was still incensed over that $25 fee. But I did the story, obtaining an exclusive half-hour television interview with Kirschke. The *Daily News* ran my story on three consecutive days and paid me the lofty sum of $3,000. Sometimes good things happen when you least expect them. Incidentally, Kirschke was convicted of killing his wife and her lover and served seven years in prison. I was told that D.A Joe Busch was crestfallen at the crimes committed by his close friend and top aide. Busch died a few years later. He was only 47.

# 6

## THE DARK SIDE OF OLD L.A.

Corruption in Los Angeles was widespread during the first half of the 20th Century. It's hard to believe, but at one time there were an estimated 1,000 house of prostitution in the city. One madam after another maintained a cozy relationship with the LAPD. The fairest queen bee of the madams was fashion-conscious Brenda Allen who kept key members of the Vice Squad on her payroll. On one occasion Brenda drove downtown from her pad on the west side, and parked her car near the L.A. *Times* building. A well-dressed man with a fedora entered her car from the sidewalk and they began chatting. Suddenly a somewhat raggedy thug stuck a gun in the car window announcing a holdup. The well dressed man, without hesitation, pulled out a revolver and shot the robber dead. The shooter was the head of the LAPD Vice Squad. He was there to accept his monthly "protection" stipend from the madam, hat in hand. The Chicago Mafia had a strong presence in L.A. at the time. Al Capone's man, Willie Bioff, ran the motion picture craft unions with an iron hand. Johnny Roselli, known as the mob's ambassador to Hollywood, did Capone's bidding with the studio bosses and even had a hand in producing several movies.

Clifford Clinton was a courtly, well educated gentleman who ran a downtown restaurant, Clifton's Cafeteria. People down on their luck during the depression could always get a free meal at his place. Clinton was fed up with the corruption, the prostitution, the organized crime figures who forced merchants to install slot machines in their stores; the politicians who took big bribes from developers, and the cops who paid their superiors as much as $1,000 for a promotion,. Clinton may have run a cafeteria but he was a fearless crusader who knew his life would be at risk if he took on the corrupt regime running L.A.

Somehow Clinton persuaded a judge to appoint him to the grand jury where he proceeded to launch his own investigation into corruption L.A. style. He knew it wasn't going to be easy. The majority of the grand jurors opposed the investigation, but Clinton decided to do it under the guise of a minority report. Clinton hired a burly ex-cop, Harry Raymond, to be his chief investigator. Raymond was the former police chief of the nearby beach community of Venice which had been recently annexed to big brother L.A. He found corruption everywhere he went, in the LAPD, the DA's office and especially at City Hall where Mayor Frank Shaw and his "bag" men were usually up to no good. This was the real L.A. Confidential. One day a bomb blew up Raymond's car while he was parked on the street. But this one tough cop survived and testified before the grand jury with nearly 200 bomb fragments still in his body. Later a police intelligence officer was sentenced to 10 years in prison for planting the car bomb. Clinton's home was also torched one night but he and his wife and children were not home. (Many years later, on Aug. 6, 2006, Clinton's surviving 83-year-old daughter, Jean Roeschlaub, was stabbed to death in her gated Glendale penthouse complete with security cameras. There was no signed of forced entry. The crime was never solved).

It was the beginning of the end for the administration of Mayor Frank Shaw and his cronies. Shaw was booted out of office in a recall election in 1938 and replaced by a reform minded judge, Fletcher Bowron. But L.A. was still a tough place to clean up.

The LAPD was saddled with so much corruption that Bowron hired William A. Worton, a retired U.S. Marine Corps General, to restore order in the department.

Gradually the hookers, the madams, the slot machines and the offshore gambling boats pretty much vanished from obvious view in the city of the angels. After several years General Worton was replaced by Bill Parker, a tough Irish cop who came up through the ranks, and his iron discipline turned the LAPD into an organization that was praised by some as setting an example for other police departments across the nation. But there were others who disdainfully called the LAPD under Parker "a paramilitary organization."

In the state capital in Sacramento, another political cleanup was in the works led by newly elected Republican Governor Earl Warren, who later was named Chief Justice of the United States by President Eisenhower. California Attorney General Fred Howser was accused of running a cesspool of corruption, so bad that Gov. Warren appointed one of the state's most prominent attorneys, Warren Olney III, to investigate Howser as well as the head of the State Board of Equalization, William "Big Bill" Bonelli and other scoundrels involved in the business of government. It was pretty much common knowledge that if you wanted to obtain a license to sell liquor in California you had to grease Big Bill's palm with thousands of dollars. It was also no secret that Howser, the state's top cop, had offered protection for a price to L.A. gang lord Mickey Cohen, thus enabling the mob to set up countless criminal activities throughout the area. Years later Mafia snitch Jimmy Fratianno told the feds that Howser personally assigned a state policeman, Harry Cooper, as Cohen's bodyguard.

Before he was elected attorney general, Howser served as L.A. District Attorney and was notorious for doing nothing about the rampant prostitution and gambling in the city. Olney's probe, which led to a scathing assault on Howser by the California Crime Commission, rattled the attorney general's political cage so loudly that he was defeated in his bid for reelection in 1950. Many years later I incurred Howser's wrath when I mentioned his checkered past and reported he had just been named city attorney of the small Indian town of Cabazon near Palm Springs. Howser screamed a number of profanities at me over the phone and demanded a retraction. I asked why the retraction and he replied in his best Nixonian verbiage, "I am not a crook." I told him to call our lawyers but he never did. His record spoke for itself. He once filed a defamation suit against nationally syndicated columnist Drew Pearson who alleged Howser presided over massive corruption in Los Angeles. Howser lost that one.

Bonelli, who accumulated massive wealth selling liquor licenses during his tenure in office, fled to Mexico in the face of a grand jury indictment. Year after year Bonelli told reporters he planned to return to California to face his accusers and clear his name. But he never did, and eventually he died in Mexico. Warren Olney III became a United States Attorney and was considered one of the best by his peers. President Lyndon Johnson thought so much of Olney he named him chief legal counsel for the Warren Commission. But FBI Director J. Edgar Hoover, perhaps envious of Olney's crime fighting record and viewing him as a threat, objected so strongly that LBJ withdrew Olney's name. It was just one of things that caused so much doubt about the conclusion of the Warren Commission that Lee Harvey Oswald acted alone in killing President Kennedy. Olney was replaced on the Warren Commission by prominent L.A. Attorney Joseph Ball whose legal footprints were all over what I call "The Case of the Watch Stem Rapist."

# 7

# THE CASE OF "THE WATCH STEM RAPIST"

One of the most intriguing cases I first came across on the police beat spoke loudly to the political corruption of the 1950s that stretched from the back rooms of L.A. to the governor's office in Sacramento. Edward Simon Wein, a product of one of L.A.'s wealthiest neighborhoods, became known as the notorious "Watch Stem Rapist." Just 5 feet 5 inches tall and weighing 130 pounds, Wein seemed like anything but a sadistic predator. He was well educated and lived in the upscale Rancho Park area on the city's Westside with his parents and two sisters who doted on Eddie. His father was a prosperous painting contractor with an exclusive contract to paint L.A.'s public schools. But little Eddie was a twisted psychotic sex maniac who years later told a prison psychiatrist he had a deep seated hatred of women, and raped and tortured them without remorse.

Before Eddie was eventually caught, police estimated that this pint-sized predator had raped at least 50 women whose names he usually found in the "for sale" sections of newspaper classified ads or those placed on market bulletin boards. His method of operation went something like this: Eddie would call the person who placed the ad and if a woman answered he would make an appointment to view the merchandise. Once inside the house Eddie would inspect the product, then bend over and pretend he was looking for the stem to his watch. Typically the woman would join Eddie in searching for the watch stem at which point Eddie would jump on her, pin her to the floor and rape her. It was not unusual for cheap watches to become easily disassembled in those days, and to see someone looking for a lost stem or crystal.

**Eddie Wein, described as the worst rapist in the history of California.**

The plot was carried out time after time with few variations. One of Eddie's victims was a young concert pianist who was attempting to sell her fur coat and a dining room set so she could make ends meet. She said after Eddie pulled the watch stem ploy she tried to fight him off but he choked her so viciously the blood vessels ruptured in both her eyes. The woman fled California after she was raped, so traumatized she never again played the piano.

Another woman was raped after Eddie locked her 5-year-old son in a closet where the child cowered while his mother screamed for help. Not a nice guy this Mr. Eddie Wein. Then there was the case of the woman who didn't fall for the "Watch Stem" ruse. The next day Eddie returned with a friend. They broke into the woman's home by smashing a window. The second man held the woman down while Eddie raped and orally copulated her.

Police took a task force approach to capturing the "Watch Stem" rapist, assigning a score of officers to track him down but Eddie kept eluding them. Authorities as far away as Arizona reported several rapes using the same "Watch Stem" line.

Eddie hit numerous communities from the Hollywood Hills to the Port of Long Beach. Finally the cops got the break they were looking for in what might be best described as a one in a million fluke. The critical link was a good looking Hollywood woman who had been raped in her home in October of 1956 by a man answering a furniture ad she had posted in a local market. Trying to escape the nightmare of her horrifying ordeal, the woman headed south to the oceanfront to listen to some good music at a popular Long Beach supper club. It was Saturday night and the club was jammed with customers. The woman had made a reservation, and she slowly nudged her way through the crowd to her table when suddenly she stepped on someone's foot, a man's foot to be sure. The foot belonged to Eddie Wein, who was seated at a table with another man.

The woman let out a blood curdling scream and security guards rushed to her side. "This is the man who raped me," she cried out. Police were summoned and arrested Wein despite the protestations of his drinking buddy, an off duty L.A. County Deputy Sheriff, Delbert Crawford. The deputy insisted it was a case of mistaken identity; that Eddie Wein was a law abiding citizen, a member of a respected west side family. Crawford, it turned out was Wein's roommate. The Long Beach Police didn't buy the deputy's story and hauled Eddie off to jail, suspecting he matched the description of a suspect in a local rape case.

The cops' instincts proved correct. Wein appeared in a lineup and was identified by a score of women as their attacker. The District Attorney charged him with 22 felonies including eight counts of rape, six counts of sex perversion, two counts of kidnapping, and five counts of kidnapping for the purpose of robbery, the last charge a death penalty offense under California's "Little Lindbergh Law." Wein initially pleaded not guilty and not guilty by reason of insanity, but later withdrew the insanity defense.

One of his defense attorneys was Russell Parsons, a mob lawyer who years later helped represent Sirhan Sirhan at his trial for murdering Senator Robert Kennedy at L.A.'s Ambassador Hotel years later. (In 1975 when Parsons was past 80, he was forced to surrender his license to practice law by the State Bar Association for stealing $1 million from a dead woman's estate he held in probate for 30 years He was never prosecuted and died soon afterwards.)

Parsons had a well deserved reputation as a "fixer," and his reasons for taking the Wein case will become clear shortly. Apart from the parade of victims who testified at the trial, there were expert witnesses who said the sawed-off rapist had a psychopathic personality as witness the brutal-ity and cunning in his assaults. One witness said he would not be surprised that Wein would kill someone if he should go free, a very prophetic statement. A psychiatrist told the court Wein's wave of sexual assaults was prompted by his hatred of his mother, Esther, who died in 1954 at the age of 62. He began assaulting women almost immediately after his mother's death. Wein insisted the cops got the wrong man, but apart from the testimony of the women he raped, there was physical evidence, a fingerprint he left on a drinking glass at the home of one of his victims.

In April of 1957 Wein was convicted by a jury on all 27 counts and given five death sentences. The judge concurred with the verdict and sentenced Wein, whom he described as the worst rapist in California's history, to die in the gas chamber at San Quentin Prison.

At the time Eddie Wein was sent to death row another occupant taking up space there was Caryl Chessman, the so-called "red light bandit" who was condemned to die under the same Little Lindbergh law. Chessman had been convicted of kidnapping and raping a teen-age Catholic high school girl who subsequently suffered a mental breakdown. Chessman represented himself at his trial, and Judge Charles Fricke, commended him for offering a brilliant defense. But the verdict was guilty and Fricke ordered Chessman put to death. Chessman wrote a book about his ordeal which became an international best seller and stirred heated controversy. Governor Edmund G. (Pat) Brown postponed the execution once, but then decided not to grant Chessman clemency and ordered him put to death at San Quentin. The execution took place in the gas chamber on May 2, 1960 even as the governor's son, Jerry Brown, a future governor himself, joined the picket line outside San Quentin in protest.

Chessman came from a dismal family background. Eddie Wein, conversely, was the product of affluence, a spoiled child whose parents gave him anything he wanted. Wein's execution date in the gas chamber was scheduled for December 5, 1958. Various religious and civic groups in Los Angeles campaigned to have Governor Brown overturn the death sentence. And Eddie's father, David Wein, was said to have confided to associates he would spare no expense to save Eddie's life.

In appealing the death sentence defense attorney Parsons charged the prosecution with misconduct by comparing Wein to Chessman, The court transcript quoted the prosecutor as telling the jury that Chessman was "...a rank amateur compared to Edward Wein."

But Parsons' claim went for naught as the California Supreme Court upheld Wein's death sentence. So what happened? Why did Caryl Chessman die in the gas chamber for the rape of just one woman, while Eddie Wein, the condemned multiple rapist, eventually become a free man?

Investigations conducted by the California Attorney General, the Los Angeles County District Attorney, and the Los Angeles Police Department were hushed up for years. But I learned from the best of sources in these agencies that Russell Parsons, the fixer, did his job well. There was a high level payoff that enabled Eddie Wein to escape the gas chamber and to eventually walk out of prison.

Investigators told me that Wein's father, desperate to save his son, persuaded his business associates at a major paint company to advance him $10,000, a considerable amount of money in those days. Anxious to maintain a good relationship with the school district's chief painter, the company forked over $10,000 to the senior Wein. He handed the money over to Russell Parsons who knew what to do next. The money was turned over to one of L.A.'s most prominent lawyers, Joseph Ball, a power in Democratic politics later appointed to the Warren Commission by President Lyndon Johnson. Ball carried the cash to Sacramento where it was delivered to a person in "close contact" with Governor Brown. This is not to suggest that Governor Brown personally took the bribe money. But his actions were quite suspicious to say the least. On June 4, 1959, the governor commuted Eddie Wein's death sentence to life imprisonment without the possibility of parole. Such a commutation was not considered unusual since during eight years in office Brown spared the lives of 22 condemned men.

But what happened on Dec. 22, 1966 was considered most unusual in the view of law enforcement which considered Wein a danger to society. On that date, shortly before yielding office to Ronald Reagan, Brown removed the "no parole" provision he had originally placed on Eddie Wein. He said technically Wein did not kidnap any of his victims in "...the true sense of the word" so he should qualify for eventual parole.

When I interviewed Brown with reporter Furnell Chatman in 1982, the former governor defended granting clemency to 22 condemned men on California's death row. He said in his opinion most were leading productive lives. As examples, he said one man had become a scientist, another, a millionaire in the business world. But his face turned ashen when we asked him, "what about Eddie Wein?" He said it was his "only mistake." It turned out to be a very big and deadly mistake, as we shall see.

While in prison Wein insisted to anyone within earshot that he wanted to be free so he could care for his sisters and his elderly father who did not have long to live. But parole officials considered him a chronic criminal, a perverse sexual predator, and repeatedly denied him freedom. But in a great irony The U.S. Supreme Court opened the prison gates for Eddie when it ruled California's "Little Lindbergh Law" was unconstitutional. It wasn't any help to Caryl Chessman who never killed anyone and was rotting in his grave. But the ruling gave little Eddie Wein the opportunity to walk back into society's mainstream in 1974 after being locked up for 17 years. Now he was free to resume his evil ways, this time with murder on his mind.

Once back on the streets of L.A. Wein walked straight into a job with the very paint company that bankrolled his escape from death row. He moved back into the family home in Rancho Park with his ailing father and two sisters. They wondered if Eddie was going to carry on the family name and marry again. In his early twenties Eddie was married for several months but it ended in a bitter divorce in which his wife told the court he beat her violently and engaged in "sexual deviation."

Shortly after Eddie came home his father died at age 82, and almost immediately the ugly pattern of sexual violence emerged just as it did after his mother's passing two decades before. But there was a new generation of cops on the job and putting two and two together in the latest version of the "Watch Stem Rapist" proved difficult at first.

Take the case of Mrs. Dorothy George who decided she had one recliner too many in the crowded walk-up apartment she shared with her husband in suburban Westchester near Los Angeles International Airport. So the 52-year-old woman posted an ad for a lounge chair on a bulletin board at the neighborhood self-service laundry. A few days later, on August 8, 1974, a man called and said he wanted to inspect the chair. We know the man was Eddie Wein but we don't know if used the "watch stem" ruse because Mrs. George did not survive his visit.

When her husband returned home that evening, there was water flowing down the stairs leading to his apartment. He found his wife's body in the bathtub, the water still running. Mrs. George had been sexually assaulted, gagged and strangled. An eyewitness, a neighbor, told the cops he saw a slightly built man walking hurriedly to his car from the direction of Mrs. George's apartment. He was able to provide a good physical description of the killer and a partial license number of his car.

Just 27 days later, Wein struck again at apartment house in Palms, a few miles from his home. The victim, a very attractive woman, had posted an ad for a bed on a market bulletin board. The slightly built man who answered the ad pulled the "watch stem" ruse shortly after arrival. Then he bound the woman's hands and feet and forced her to copulate him. She was convinced he was going to kill her after the man turned on the water in her bathtub, apparently planning to drown her too. Suddenly a door slammed loudly in the next apartment and scared the intruder who fled. During the same time frame another woman who advertised household goods for sale on a market bulletin board was raped and murdered 70 miles away in San Bernardino.

The various cases linked by so many threads still stumped LAPD investigators. The murder of Mrs. George and the Palms rape case came up for discussion at a luncheon meeting of homicide investigators, some of whom had retired. The mention of the "watch stem" ruse tugged at the cobwebs in the mind of Robert Wright, a retired LAPD homicide officer. Wright recalled a case in the 1950s involving the so-called "Watch Stem Rapist" who usually found his victims names and phone numbers in ads on market bulletin boards. Wright couldn't remember the rapist's name but thought the guy had been executed at San Quentin.

A new team of investigators led by LAPD Homicide Detective Larry Kallistad began checking out the old cop's information, and literally hit the jackpot. After poring through old files they found the "crime book" on Edward Simon Wein, the notorious "Watch Stem" rapist. No, Wright was wrong, Wein had not been executed. And yes, he was back on the streets of L.A. According to the eyewitness who saw the killer leaving Mrs. George's apartment, an old mug shot of Eddie Wein was a perfect match. And the partial license plate description also matched the one on Wein's car. Meantime, the second rape victim, whose name was never made public, promptly identified Wein as her assailant.

The legal process was swift. Wein was arrested at his home and carted off to the Los Angeles County Jail. Interviewed in his cell by my colleague, Dick Carlson, Wein tearfully proclaimed his innocence, calling it a case of "mistaken identity" just as he had done some 20 years before. He said his family disowned him because of his latest legal problems. But a few minutes later a Beverly Hills lawyer showed up at the jail and ordered reporter Carlson to leave immediately. Eddie's sisters had hired the lawyer, just as their father had done long ago.

At a dramatic jury trial, prosecutor Bob Altman confronted Wein with the testimony of four of the women he had raped in the fifties using the "watch stem" ruse. One of those called to testify was the former concert pianist whose career was shattered by his violent sexual assault. She was still so traumatized she could not appear in person and her testimony had to be read into the court record. On May 24, 1976 a jury of nine men and three women convicted Edward Simon Wein of the rape-murder of Mrs. George and the near fatal assault on the second woman 27 days later.

There was no death penalty in California at the time because of a ruling by the California Supreme Court. So in pronouncing a life sentence on Eddie Wein trial Judge Charles Woodmansee of the Santa Monica Superior Court implored the California Department of Corrections never again to allow his release from prison. The jurist described Wein as a "violent and compulsive killer." The judge added: "The nature of his brutal and sadistic crimes indicate he will always continue to be an extremely dangerous man."

Year after year parole boards took the judge's counsel to heart and denied Eddie Wein parole. In 1985 I showed up for one of his parole hearings at the California Men's Colony in San Luis Obispo. When Eddie saw me standing there with a cameraman, he refused to enter the room. But the hearing went on, and as usual, parole was denied. Prosecutor J. Miller Leavy told me the Wein case "one of the darkest moments in California's legal history.

A few years later, Wein's left leg was amputated as the result of severe diabetes. On June 8, 2002, he died in a prison hospital. No one sang a requiem for Eddie Wein, the "Watch Stem Rapist."

# 8

# THE BIRTH OF "THE BIG NEWS"

By the time I had spent five years in the salt mines of journalism at City News, working my way up to city editor and a salary of $100 a week, I married my wife, Grace, in 1959, and a year later, we had a healthy son, Jack. I even managed with the help of a G.I. loan to buy a home for $15,000 in the San Fernando Valley. And I found time to cover a lot of interesting people and events. In 1960 the Democratic Party held a powwow at the Biltmore Hotel in downtown L.A. and an attorney friend of mine, Ed Foley, suggested I meet him there after work and see what was going on. Our first stop was the main bar at the Biltmore. There was only one person seated at the bar, Senator Jack Kennedy of Massachusetts. His wife, Jacqueline, was seated in a large chair as far away from the bar she could get and seemed to be staring daggers at him.

So Foley and I joined Kennedy for a drink at the bar where he was downing Scotch and water. When I told him I was a reporter and speculated he might win the Democratic nomination for the presidency, he really opened up, talking about the need for civil rights legislation, among other things, and promising to end farm price supports. He asked who ran City News Service and I told him Joe Quinn. I said his wife, Grace, was a loyal Democrat but Joe was a right-wing Republican. "Doesn't matter," Kennedy said. "I'll get him on board. He's Irish isn't he?" Three days later Joe Quinn was a member of Kennedy's California campaign committee. Quinn came to like politics so much he eventually served as deputy mayor of Los Angeles. After Joe died, his widow, Grace Quinn, a lawyer, started a law firm and was much honored for her legal work on behalf of the elderly.

I had several job offers in my last years at City News. One was that of assistant city editor at the Los Angeles *Herald-Express* where the legendary Aggie Underwood was city editor. But the paper was rife with labor problems and I decided not to chance it. Then, out of the blue I got a call from Sam Zelman, the news director at the local CBS station, who told me he was looking for a city editor and would like to chat with me. Sam said he was told I knew my way around L.A. He seemed impressed that I had a master's degree in journalism from UCLA and that I had written my thesis on the start of the L.A. freeway system which I found to be obsolete from day one when the first patch of asphalt was put down.

In a meeting that lasted about 15 minutes Zelman said he was going to change the face of television news. At the time local news broadcasts usually ran just 15 minutes, five minutes for news, five minutes for weather and five or sports. The national CBS broadcast anchored by Douglas Edwards also ran 15 minutes. The network and local broadcasts ran back to back on most stations, with lots of headlines but hardly much news of substance.

Sam said he was going to start out with a 45-minute broadcast called "*The Big News*," and eventually hoped to expand it to an hour, something that had never been done before on American TV. Then he said, "Pete, I want you to come on board." When he said he would triple my salary I accepted without hesitation because we had been pretty much living day to day on my City News Service wages and stringer fees from the New York Daily News. It was a life altering change for me. I knew nothing about TV writing or production. Sam said "...not to worry. It's going to be easy for you to pick up." A few weeks after I arrived I was ready to quit when the show editor tore a piece of my copy to shreds shouting "It wasn't worth a crap." A couple of days later Sam posted one of my stories on the bulletin board with a note saying, "This is type of copy I want." I started feeling more at home.

I had hardly walked in the door when major news stories seemed to be crashing down all around me. On Nov. 6, 1961 scorching Santa Ana winds that bedevil Southern California in the fall triggered a torrid fire ball that wiped out 400 homes in the exclusive enclave known as Bel Air. After working 12 hour days I fought the fire at night and managed to help save the home of my wife's family on the outskirts of the fire, the flames shooting up to the back fence before retreating.

The Big News debuted in late 1961 as a 45-minute broadcast, airing weeknights at 6 p.m. before the 15-minute CBS National News with Walter Cronkite, who replaced Douglas Edwards. Our anchorman was Jerry Dunphy, a TV dynamo from Chicago who was to become a broadcasting legend, known for his on-screen presence and his opening catch phrase, "From the desert to the sea to all of Southern California, a good evening."

As the new kid on the block I was under constant scrutiny to produce stories that had not first appeared in the newspaper. It was a real challenge. Local TV news broadcasts usually picked up stories from the morning newspapers, and regurgitated them. My first big break came on April 10, 1962 when, after years of controversy amid charges of a land giveaway by the city, Dodger Stadium opened for its first major league baseball game in Chavez Ravine. A huge public housing project had once been planned on the land but was abandoned in the early 1950s after the Director of the City Housing Authority, Frank Wilkinson, appeared before Congress and admitted he was a member of the Communist Party.

After the game had ended I got a phone call from an old colleague of mine at City News Service, Ridgley Cummings, who said he had been at the game and when he got thirsty could find only one drinking fountain in the entire stadium. I did some checking and the story rang true. Team owner Walter O'Malley, long considered a skinflint when the team played in Brooklyn, apparently decided too many drinking fountains would hurt beer sales.

I wrote the story the next day, but the producer didn't think it was important and held off placing it in the Big News lineup until the last segment, Jerry Dunphy's "Reporter's Notebook," usually a potpourri of interesting but minor news items. The phones started ringing almost immediately from outraged viewers. Equally outraged were those members of the city council who had bitterly opposed O'Malley's presence in Chavez Ravine. But not Sid Ziff, a sports columnist for the L.A. *Times*. Ziff told his readers the Big News story had to be fiction and he would personally conduct his own inspection to prove it at the ballgame that night. Alas, the apologetic Mr. Ziff wrote the next day that he could not even find the one drinking fountain mentioned in the Big News story. Then the predictable battle erupted at City hall. Opponents of the Dodger deal on the City Council demanded O'Malley's scalp or a reasonable facsimile in the form of an apology in addition to installing a satisfactory number of drinking fountains. O'Malley complied at once, placing the blame on a construction oversight. The bad press didn't hurt the Dodgers one bit with the team and its new stadium becoming one of the most successful franchises in major league history, annually luring more than three million fans to its games with beer sales greater than the late Walter O'Malley could have ever imagined.

A few months later, on August 4, 1962 the lessons I learned on the police beat were quickly tested when America's reigning beauty queen, actress Marilyn Monroe, was found dead in her Brentwood home. She was just 36 years old. Our coverage dwarfed the opposition which didn't quite seem to grasp the significance of the story. We went full bore for each and every detail, telling how the blonde actress seemed to lose her bearings after being kicked off the movie set of "Something's Got to Give" produced by 20th Century Fox. Our extensive coverage ended with a closing video shot of Monroe's small dog following two ambulance attendants as they carried her body out of the house on a stretcher. The eastern establishment didn't quite understand the importance of the story either. Monroe's death was the last item reported on The CBS Evening News and ran just 45 seconds. Hardly time to catch the viewers' breath.

Sometimes when I reflect on those days I'm shocked at what transpired. The coroner's office allowed a number of voyeuristic reporters to view Monroe's naked body on a slab at the morgue. And the teenage son of one of the autopsy surgeons checked out slides of Monroe's body and showed them to his high school buddies.

It appeared that Monroe had accidentally overdosed on prescription medication although autopsy surgeon Thomas Noguchi, a headline grabber who was soon to become known as the "Coroner to the Stars," held out the possibility that her death might be a suicide resulting from "acute barbiturate poisoning." But there was no suicide note. The findings in Monroe's death were not seriously challenged until ten years later when author Robert Slatzer's book, *"The Life and Curious Death of Marilyn Monroe,"* advanced the theory that she was murdered on orders from President Kennedy or his brother, Robert, the U.S. Attorney General. Slatzer claimed she had been romanced by both brothers. He even quoted her as saying "Bobby Kennedy promised to marry me." I knew Slatzer fairly well. He claimed he was married to Monroe in 1952 in the Mexican border town of Tijuana, two years before she wed baseball legend Joe Dimaggio. Slatzer said although their marriage lasted only a few weeks, he and the actress remained the best of friends over the years and she confided in him about her romances with the Kennedy brothers.

I have no quarrel with those who claim Marilyn Monroe was acquainted with John Kennedy. After all she did belt out a very sexy rendition of "Happy Birthday Mr. President" at JFK's 45th birthday party in Washington D.C. on May 19, 1962 which was shown on network television across the country. But doesn't it seem a little far fetched to accuse the Kennedy brothers of plotting to murder her so soon after the birthday party. And to me it seemed even more far fetched to unveil the allegations years later after both Kennedy brothers had died at the hands of assassins and were unable to defend themselves. There was even an allegation that Senator Robert Kennedy was seen in Monroe's neighborhood at the approximate time she died. My investigation determined that the U.S. Attorney General was in nearby Santa Monica that evening, attending mass at a Catholic Church.

Among the other perpetrators of the Monroe conspiracy theory were several retired police officers who were active in ultra right-wing circles and had been previously involved in branding California Republican senator Thomas Kuchel a "homosexual." The married Kuchel persuaded the District Attorney's office to charge the Senator's critics with "criminal libel." They were convicted but never served time.

Did we in the media know that Jack Kennedy was a philandering type? Most certainly! In contrast, Robert Kennedy, the father of eight, had an almost puritanical reputation. One of our Big News cameramen shot film at the Santa Monica Airport of JFK boarding a small plane with actress Angie Dickinson. But we never broadcast the film. Our news director said if they were indeed having an affair it was their business and not for public consumption. Years later Miss Dickinson did go public about her involvement as the President's mistress in an interview with Larry King on CNN. But does that prove that Mr. Kennedy wanted Marilyn Monroe dead? Did she know state secrets that might endanger the nation if made public? Was she engaged in pillow talk with JFK that made her a national security threat? I didn't think so then and I don't think so now.

We had great talent on the Big News besides the good looking anchorman Jerry Dunphy. Maury Green, a former Los Angeles *Times* reporter, was our lead investigative reporter. One of Green's first big scoops was the shutting down of two L.A. newspapers, the *Examiner* and the *Mirror-News*, before their own staffs even knew about it. Gil Stratton, a baseball umpire with 17 screen credits, including a featured role with William Holden in the movie, "*Stalag 17*"was the sports editor. His signature opening, "Time to call 'em as we see 'em," became a classic part of the Big News lore. The weatherman was Bill Keene, a meteorologist by profession, who turned out to be one of the wittiest men on TV. The golden-voiced Ralph Story, host of TV's "*$64,000 Challenge*," presented a segment called "The Human Predicament." Story's piece on little John Jr. saluting the flag-draped casket of his assassinated father, President John Kennedy, resulted in thousands of viewer requests for scripts written by Nate Kaplan, a legendary news figure himself.

A few hours after President Kennedy was shot, Big News reporter John Hart was on the scene in Dallas with a camera crew securing a brief but exclusive interview with accused assassin Lee Harvey Oswald. We didn't hesitate to go anywhere a major news story was taking place in the nation.

Hart worked with me on my first investigative piece on the Big News. It concerned a board member of the Southern California Rapid Transit District who was also a director of the New York consulting firm of Coverdale & Colpitts. Scouring scores of public records we learned that the transit district had doled out thousand of dollars in consulting contracts to Coverdale & Colpitts and that our conflicted transit director had voted yea on every one of them. No doubt, this was an obvious conflict of interest. But apart from a few phone calls there was hardly a ripple of protest. The *Times*, in its usual display of journalistic arrogance, never mentioned the story. But a *Times* reporter, who once worked with me downtown, called and offered congratulations on the "beat." Another reporter from City News Service advised me that she had talked to a county supervisor about the story and he told her there was nothing to it. He predicted the story would just "fade away" and it did. I knew L.A. to be as corrupt as any major city in the country. No one seemed to be policing the public store, not the cops, not the press. Not yet, anyway, but we hoped to change all that. George Reasons, a Pulitzer Prize winning reporter for the L.A. *Times* with whom I played an occasional game of tennis, once told me, "It isn't news until it's in the Times." He was referring to a story I broke about the local FBI chief, Wesley Grapp, shaking down a Beverly Hills banker for a huge interest-free loan after the banker's kidnapped son was rescued by FBI agents. The *Times* ran the story several days later, better late than never. Grapp lost his job.

My next investigation concerned a team of scoundrels who had obtained a Teamsters Pension Fund loan of $12 million, ostensibly to build a luxury home and golf course community known as "Beverly Ridge Estates" on land adjoining Beverly Hills. But I found this was just a typical ruse by teamsters President Jimmy Hoffa to dole out big bucks to his buddies. The $12 million quickly disappeared and all that was left were a couple of signs directing traffic to the vacant development. The project ended up in bankruptcy court. I asked the federal judge presiding over the case to let me review the file. He was more than happy to oblige and it was eye popping. One of the shakers and movers behind the project was Nate Stein, one of Hoffa's closest friends. Leonard Burston, a former U.S. Attorney, was considered the project's prime mover. Just a few years before Burston was convicted of federal income tax evasion. The newspapers were quick to pick up my story. Anything linked to Jimmy Hoffa was considered big news. The Hollywood *Citizen News* ran a page one story on the scandal under my byline and included the entire transcript of the presentation on the Big News.

The top of our story read:

"It isn't easy to misplace $12 million- even in these days of high financing. But it apparently has happened here in Los Angeles. The $12 million belonged to the Teamster Union pension fund of the southeast and southwest. It came into the Los Angeles area in the form of a loan to develop a luxury community and golf course in the hills *between Los Angeles and Beverly Hills, a community to be known as Beverly Ridge Estates. But today, five years after the project began, the 350 acres earmarked for development are virtually barren and on May 9 of this year Beverly Ridge Estates went into bankruptcy."*

The story preceded a federal grand jury indictment of four persons on a variety of theft and fraud charges. Three got off for various reasons. One defendant was let go after he proved he had worked for the C.I.A. Leonard Burston was the only one who did jail time, less than 30 days. A veteran courthouse reporter told me, "If you rob a bank of $10,000 you'll get 20 years. If you're a white collar thief and steal a million, you'll probably walk out of prison in five years, or maybe even get probation."

A story exemplifying the coverage problems we faced in the early days of the Big News took place on Dec. 14, 1963 when the JFK assassination was still fresh on everyone's mind. Frank Sinatra Jr., son of the legendary crooner, had been kidnapped and the FBI scheduled a news conference for 10 a.m. The bureau planned to announce that young Sinatra had been rescued in good health, his four young male kidnapers caught and the ransom money recovered. But no one knew that going into the news conference. Reporter Saul Halpert was assigned to cover the story at FBI headquarters in West Los Angeles. I was working the assignment desk when a very nervous woman called and told me she lived close to the Baldwin Hills Dam in the center of the city and water from the dam was leaking down nearby La Brea Boulevard. I checked with the communications center at police headquarters and was told an alert had just gone out warning that the dam could collapse at any minute.

I paged reporter Halpert at the news conference and when he phoned in I told him to get his camera crew out of there and head for the Baldwin Hills Dam. "You must be crazy," Halpert screamed at me, "this is the biggest story in the country." "Not anymore," I shouted. "Get your butts out of there. This is a direct order."

It was a timely move. Halpert, cameraman Doug Dare and soundman Pierre Adidge were standing on the top left ridge of the dam when its center gave way. In an instant a huge wall of water, 250 million gallons, swept down on the homes beneath the dam and our camera was trained right on the entire episode. Five persons were killed but hundreds of other lives were spared because police had warned residents well in advance to evacuate.

There was just one problem about the Big News coverage. We were at the right place at the right time, but our three-man crew was trapped atop the gutted dam. We did not have the capacity to broadcast live pictures in those early TV days so all we could do at the station was run a bulletin with no film to support it, But then I noticed that KTLA (Channel 5), the only station in town with the ability to go live, was on the air with its helicopter feeding back coverage of the disaster. I called KTLA news director Stan Chambers, a former college classmate, and he gave me permission to take the helicopter feed off his air. Thank God for small favors. A police helicopter finally lifted our three- man crew from the top of the dam with their precious film and we were able to get it on the air later in the evening. It was spectacular footage like nothing I had seen before. The dam, weakened by years of drilling in surrounding oil fields, broke loose with a tremendous roar and the wall of water literally drowned the 300 homes on the slopes beneath it. Oh yes, the Sinatra kidnapping was the last story on the news that night.

I got my first real taste of big time politics in 1964 when I produced CBS local coverage of the California primary election in which Senator Barry Goldwater defeated Nelson Rockefeller. CBS pulled out all the stops on this one, setting up shop at the Biltmore Hotel with a lavish set and production facility. Walter Cronkite was to anchor the first half hour for the network and then, with one minute to spare, we were to take over the set for an hour of local coverage. Fred Friendly, the legendary head of CBS News, took me aside, and gave me some cautionary advice. "Pete, you've got a real problem to deal with." What, I wondered, could he be talking about. Friendly said, "At the end of our broadcast, as you know, Eric Sevareid does an analysis to which he's given a great deal of thought. After he concludes his presentation he goes into a trance and doesn't move for five to 10 minutes. In all probability he'll end up sitting right next to Jerry Dunphy when your broadcast begins."

I was seized with a state of near panic. The CBS program ended, and a one minute commercial break came up. I ran up to Sevareid on the set and he seemed frozen in time. I yelled at the top of my lungs, "Mr. Sevareid, get out of here or you'll be seen on local news." Sevareid came to, jumped out of his seat and bolted from the set as Friendly and Cronkite roared with laughter. "Nice job kid,' Friendly said. After giving it some thought, I decided it was fairly funny.

I had lots of help learning the fundamentals of TV News from Pat O'Reilly, a former wire service reporter and Jim Vinson, an ex-Texas newspaperman. They came down hard at me at times but I deserved it. O'Reilly was the assistant news director and Vinson was the first producer of the 45 minute Big News. O'Reilly used to tell me he never trusted a newsman who didn't drink. His interviewing of potential employees was usually done at Brewer's musty bar across the street from the station. That's how he hired Dave Browning, who went on to become a top

"*60 Minutes*" producer at the CBS network and Bob Long, who eventually became an NBC vice president for news.

Pat was as polished a news writer as I had ever met, and greatly influenced me. His biggest problem seemed to be he could not make up his mind if he were a Catholic or an atheist. One time I had to laugh when he asked me why I wasn't running a story about the Catholic Cardinal of Los Angeles, James Francis McIntyre. I told him it wasn't newsworthy and he jumped all over me. "I'm not going to hell because of you," he shouted. His views on religion seemed to change from day to day.

When the Big News expanded to a full hour in 1963 my job changed from city editor to producer. I didn't particularly want the job because of all the stress involved but O'Reilly and Vinson didn't want it either. Vinson was the first choice, but called in sick on the day the hour-long show was to debut. O'Reilly stepped into the production slot, shuffled through some news copy, then turned to me and said, "Noyes, you've got the job." O'Reilly put on his hat and headed across the street to Brewers for a libation. The person I picked as my associate producer was Bob Flick, who once worked with me at City News Service, and had outstanding news credentials. Years later Bob was on assignment for NBC when mad man Jim Jones caused the slaughter of more then 900 persons at Jonestown. Bob was one of the few to escape alive.

My first venture into documentary reporting began in 1965 after President Lyndon Johnson, who had defeated Senator Barry Goldwater in the 1964 election, launched his "War on Poverty." The Neumeyer Foundation was hired to oversee the start of the program in the Los Angeles area, and the first projects were designated to take place in Venice Beach, Ocean Park and Santa Monica, all on the Westside of town. Santa Monica was a fairly well-to-do community, but Venice and Ocean Park had more than their share of slums, gang violence and poverty.

In the early 1900s Venice was developed as a resort city with picturesque canals and artful bungalows. But its municipal government collapsed and Venice was left almost in ruins before it was annexed by the City of Los Angeles. The canals were filled with yellow water that smelled of sewage, and mounds of debris and slum housing could be found everywhere. I was quite impressed with the Head Start program designed to improve the educational and social levels of children, especially minorities. But quelling the terrible gang violence in Venice had to be a major undertaking by law enforcement and the poverty we came across was sickening. We found homes with human and animal defecation scattered throughout the interiors, others with no utilities. There were single mothers trying to raise as many as six or seven children in rat trap housing. The anti-poverty people had their work cut out for them. We called our documentary "*Appalachia by the Sea.*" The one-hour program broadcast in prime time in August of 1965 produced tremendous ratings. A critic for the Los Angeles Times wrote that had the program been broadcast before the deadly Watts riots, it might have prevented the violence that occurred earlier in the summer. But the local newspaper, the Santa Monica *Outlook*, was not exactly pleased. The paper's bold black headline on August 27, 1965 read: "**VENICE LEADERS AGHAST AT TV'S POVERTY SHOW.**"

The newspaper, often referred to as the "Santa Monica Outrage" because of its volatile attacks on those who disagreed with its editorial stance, described our story as a "public relations job" for the Neumeyer Foundation and the Johnson Administration's "War on Poverty." It quoted one woman who said the people of Venice were much better off than those in the movie colony of Malibu because they had sewers, a public library and parks, and Malibu had none of those. If the truth can be told, the wealthy denizens of Malibu simply didn't want such facilities. It can be said President Lyndon Johnson's war on poverty had a profound effect on Venice. The community eventually rebounded and now has fairly good schools. The canals are a beautiful sight to behold and upscale housing can be found throughout the area.

The dual job of producing documentaries and a nightly news broadcast began to wear on me. One day I got a call from Dean Borba, the program manager at the CBS station in Sacramento, the state capitol and the 20th biggest news market in the country. When Borba offered me the job of news director, I jumped at the opportunity. It was a challenging experience. There were only 14 employees in the news room and I had to produce the nightly news as well as run the administrative side of the business. But we had some success and in 1966 were honored by the *Associated Press* for producing one of the top news programs in California.

The real estate market was fairly bad at the time and it took nearly a year before we sold our home in Los Angeles and my wife and son joined me in Sacramento. Almost every weekend I drove a total of` 800 miles to and from my home in L.A. to spend some time with my family. We purchased a home in a brand new development five minutes from work. My wife was still decorating the place when I got a phone call from CBS Vice President Bob Wood. He told me he was flying to Sacramento the next day and insisted I join him for lunch. I was somewhat surprised that Wood wanted to meet with me since he never said goodbye when I left. All sorts of things crossed my mind. There was a dustup I had with Jerry Dunphy in the studio a few years back. I was producing the 11 o'clock news one night when Dunphy started attacking my writing and production skills during a pre-show rehearsal.

Reporter John Hart kept egging me, asking how long I was going to take Dunphy's abuse. I brushed him off. But then Dunphy really launched an Irish tirade about the "dumb shit in the director's booth" and I couldn't take it any longer. I rushed out to his podium where he was standing next to a buxom young woman, not his wife. I took a wild swing at him, knocked over his podium and water glass, tore up his news script, walked out of the studio and went home. Thanks to co-producer Mike Daniels, the news somehow got on the air, although it was a few minutes late, a no-no at a network station. I went home and went to bed, not telling my wife anything. The next morning I received a call from a secretary at the station saying Mr. Wood wanted to see me promptly at 9 a.m. I told my wife a somewhat sanitized version of what happened at the station, and said I'd better start job hunting. I showed up as ordered at 9 a.m. and Wood looked at me with a straight face intended to engender fear in my person and said, "Noyes, the next time you take a swing at that son of a bitch and miss, you're fired. Now get out of here." So I guess I had impressed Wood somewhere along the line. That night I went back to the studio to produce the news. I apologized to Dunphy – his wife Mary was standing next to him this time. He accepted it, and the show went on. Eventually Jerry and I became good friends after a rough start.

I had no idea what was on Wood's mind when we sat down with for lunch in Sacramento. He told me the ratings were slipping at the Big News and he wanted me to return immediately. "You were our catalyst," Wood said, "and you can't say no to me. We all need you." I asked if he wanted me to be news director, but the answer was no. He said he wanted me to be the managing editor and produce the nightly Big News just as I had done before.

Referring to Captain Queeg in the "*Caine Mutiny*," Wood said, "if I don't watch out some of the people in that newsroom are going to find the strawberries, and then I'll be in real trouble." He was referring to an incident in which one of the newsroom bosses let the air out of the tires of a man who had parked in the wrong space in the company lot. It turned out the car belonged to a top CBS executive from New York, and Wood said the man was very angry.

I really loved the job in Sacramento and especially the short commute to work. But Wood insisted my career would benefit if I returned to L.A., and that Bill Paley, the president of CBS, wanted me back. In all the years I had worked at the L.A. station, I never met Mr. Paley. But I always knew when he was making his annual visit to "Gower Gulch" (our station was at Sunset and Gower and was the site of Hollywood's first movie studio) because workmen always painted the parking lot prior to his arrival. Mr. Paley, I was told, detested ugly parking lots. And memos would go up on the newsroom bulletin board reminding male employees that they must wear a shirt and tie to work, all this to please the big boss. We were soldiers in Bill Paley's army.

So when Bob Wood offered me a $5,000-a-year raise plus an expense account, agreed to pay my moving expenses and restored my CBS pension, I accepted. It came as a shock to my wife, but she began packing right away. I gave my resignation to Bob Wilson, general manager of KXTV and one of the best bosses I ever had, and recommended he replace me with Tom Capra, son of legendary filmmaker Frank Capra. Tom parlayed the job into a great career in TV news in which he wound up as my boss at the NBC station in L.A, and eventually became producer of NBC's Today show in New York.

We returned to L.A, my wife, son, two dogs and two cats, none the worse for wear, and I quietly slipped back into my old job with the added title of managing editor. Grant Holcomb, a savvy street reporter, was promoted to news director, replacing Roy Heatley, who originally recommended me to Big News creator Sam Zelman. Zelman collected his CBS pension several years previously, and after a failed attempt at creating a rival news broadcast down the street at Gene Autry's independent station, KTLA, moved to Atlanta where he helped Ted Turner start up CNN, the *Cable News Network*.

Our success at the Big News was told in the ratings. Most years our audiences were larger than those of all the other L.A. stations combined. Over its life span of 15 years the Big News was said to be the biggest money maker in the history of CBS.

In 1968 our newsroom, located in a somewhat dingy one-story building abandoned by the Bank of America, became a test tube for the creation of one of the most successful shows in the history of television. Actress Mary Tyler Moore, who starred in the *"Dick Van Dyke Show,"* was thinking of branching out on her own. Miss Moore's aunt, Alberta (Berte) Hackett, was the treasurer of the CBS station and frequently regaled her actress-niece with stories of those strange people who populated the newsroom. Yes, there were bottles of booze in the desks of several writers and producers. The smell of burning trash cans resulted from discarded cigarettes that were still lit. And our news anchors were often treated as if they were mere copy boys by the hard bitten news staff. One day when Jerry Dunphy started giving orders in the newsroom demanding that we cover stories he heard on the radio, the news director told him to beat it and added, "Jerry, tomorrow I'm going to bring my dog in for you to kick around."

I warned the powers that be that Miss Moore could be a major distraction for all the red blooded young men in the newsroom, but they said she had promised to make herself inconspicuous. It was Bob Wood who had the real eye for talent and made the decision allowing Miss Moore, her producer and camera crew to spend several weeks in the newsroom filming our activities. Miss Moore was absolutely radiant as she sat at a desk about 10 feet from my command post. Every time I glanced her way she was taking notes. I was told she paid no heed to my frequent screaming outbursts.

At the end of the observation period the producer of Miss Moore's show approached me and said "Mr. Noyes, you'd be perfect for the role of the managing editor." I laughed and said thanks but no thanks. I told him I had had done several plays in college including George S. Kaufman's "*The Big Butter and Egg Man*" but that my acting skills were limited. I said I was honored to be considered but I doubted that a show about a TV newsroom would have much mass appeal. I was dead wrong on that one. "*The Mary Tyler Moore Show*" would soon become one of the biggest hits in television history.

Miss Moore invited me, my wife and young son to the taping of the first show before a live audience and introduced me as the model for Lou Grant, the hard nosed managing editor role played with great success by actor Ed Asner. Miss Moore was a wonderful lady and I was pleased with her success. But I did have one complaint. The show frequently pictured Lou Grant removing a bottle from his desk in times of stress. My mother demanded to know if I kept a bottle in my desk. I told her the truth. I didn't keep one. I asked the producers of the show to get rid of the bottle because it reflected poorly on news people. They complied so Lou Grant lost his bottle of booze.

Bob Wood moved on to CBS Headquarters in New York City where as president of the network division he launched

"The Mary Tyler Moore Show," "All in the Family" and "the Bob Newhart Show," all on Saturday Nights. It was considered some of the smartest blockbuster programming in the history of American television. A few years later Wood was bounced from "The Big Eye," following one of the network's greatest success stories. The possibility of being fired at any moment was sort of a tradition at CBS started by Bill Paley when he dumped the legendary newsman Edward R. Murrow.

My love of investigative reporting made me quite content with my job although I had some trepidation because of Wood's departure since he was my sponsor at that stage of my life.

I didn't make the LAPD happy when I broke the story of a major corruption scandal at the Hollywood Division which included major drug dealing and a cop sponsored burglary ring. The investigation was somewhat hampered when a critical witness was gunned down. I was told investigators believed the killer was another cop, but couldn't prove it.

There were lighter stories too, like the case of LAPD Chief Bill Parker's mother who was a regular customer at my father's drug store. Mrs. Parker told my dad to tell me she was about to lose her job as a school crossing guard because the chief didn't want her engaged in such dangerous activity and I should get in touch with her. "I've been a crossing guard for years," Mrs. Parker told me, "and Bill's not going to get away with this." I asked what she meant. "Well," she said, "Bill's going to ask the city council to do away with civilian crossing guards and turn the job over to uniformed officers." And that's exactly what Chief Parker did. But it all blew up in his face when the Big News reported the chief wanted a cop to replace his mom as a school crossing guard. After the story came out the city council killed the chief's proposal. The moral, I guess, is you should never cross an Irish mom.

All of us genuinely loved covering politics on the Big News. We had bureaus in Washington D.C. and Sacramento, California's capitol, which reported on politically significant events. New York Senator Robert Kennedy's fight for the Democratic Presidential nomination against Senator Eugene McCarthy of Minnesota really caught the imagination of California voters and it was a closely followed fight to the finish in which Kennedy emerged the victor on June 4, 1968.

But what followed, Kennedy's assassination in the pantry of L.A.'s Ambassador Hotel at the hands of a young Palestinian, Sirhan Bishara Sirhan, was as numbing a tragedy as I have ever encountered. CBS cameraman, Jim Wilson, who was covering Senator Kennedy that night, was so emotionally damaged by what he saw that he had a nervous breakdown and died several months later. Immediately there was talk of conspiracies by the right wing to kill the late President's brother. But the truth gradually emerged when the cops found the 26-year-old Sirhan's diary at his Pasadena home. His hatred for Kennedy was spelled out when he wrote over and over "RFK must die."

Sirhan's father said his son became embittered by Kennedy's support of Israel during the "Six Day War" with Egypt. Over the years I checked out at least a dozen conspiracy theories, none of which I could validate. One theory held that Sirhan was simply the tool of Arab terrorists. Another claimed the CIA was behind the assassination. I spent countless hours checking out the assorted theories. But finally I had to agree with the Los Angeles Police Department's investigators who concluded Sirhan acted alone. He was sentenced to death but his life and the lives of several hundred condemned men and women on death row were spared when the California Supreme Court declared the death penalty unconstitutional.

One story that didn't make the Big News broadcasts was a sex scandal involving several members of Governor Ronald Reagan's staff in Sacramento. I can now identify the source of the story because he's dead. It was Lyn Nofziger, the burly former newspaperman turned political consultant who was perhaps Mr. Reagan's closet advisor. Nofziger served as Mr. Reagan's press secretary during his first 22 months as governor. Later, when Mr. Reagan was elected President, Nofziger took charge of the White House Office of Politics and it was he who announced to the world that the President had been shot and nearly killed by a would be assassin in 1981.

In 1969 Nofziger met in Los Angeles with a select group of political reporters including Bill Eames, the Big News Political Editor who soon would edge me out for the job of news director. Nofziger disclosed that a pedophile ring on the governor's staff had molested at least four children at a mountain cabin where they had been taken on camping trips Two of victims were the sons of a state senator. Two others were the sons of a woman who had a key job in the Reagan Administration.

I'm not going to reveal the names of those involved in the scandal because they were never prosecuted. Three Reagan aides resigned at the same time including former pro football star Jack Kemp who in 1996 ran for vice president on the Republican ticket with Bob Dole, who lost to Bill Clinton. Noftziger insisted Kemp was not involved in any way, and he named those who were.

Apparently in concert with CBS management, Eames decided to kill the story. The Los Angeles Times, which was represented at the Nofziger meeting by political reporter

Carl Greenberg, also dropped the story. It simply didn't make sense to me that a story of this magnitude was suppressed. But somehow the story got out, mainly through word of mouth. My parish priest, a former newspaper editor, named those involved in the pedophile ring and wanted to know why I failed to run the story. So did columnist Drew Pearson who called me to say he knew of my reputation and how disappointed he was in me. "Are you all cowards out there?" Pearson asked. About 10 years later a friend invited me to dinner with Nofziger and he still couldn't understand why his leak of such a major story never got out. He said Mr. Reagan wanted the story told and had no desire for a "cover-up."

For those of us who worked in news during the 1960s, it was a very ugly time in American history. Our systems recoiled from shock over and over again with the slayings of President John Kennedy, his brother, Senator Robert Kennedy, Dr. Martin Luther King, the venerable civil rights leader, and Malcolm X, the controversial black activist. But for sheer horrific madness, there was nothing uglier than the so-called Manson murders. It was the most unforgettable story I've ever covered and I'm proud to say, I beat the competition and the LAPD on the story. Once again public records proved decisive in getting the job done, thanks to that lesson I learned on the police beat many years before from an old time cop.

# 9

# BREAKING THE MANSON STORY

In a half century of covering news in Los Angeles, there seems to have been one shocking wave of killings after another. Part of the routine for news people has been tagging the killers with identifiable names that make for catchy headlines. There's been "The Hillside Stranglers," "The Zodiac," "The Night Stalker," "The Freeway Killer," and "The Grim Sleeper" to name a few. Some have been caught, some haven't. But the name that has the greatest recognition of all is simply "Manson." Charles Manson, the personification of evil, according to one prosecutor, "the devil incarnate."

On August 9, 1969, a Saturday, I was producing the Big News Broadcast at the CBS station in Los Angeles when we received word of "police activity" at the home of director Roman Polanski on Cielo Drive in Benedict Canyon. The home was a mass murder scene. Polanski was in London, directing a movie. His wife, the beautiful actress Sharon Tate, was savagely murdered along with their unborn son and four others, coffee heiress Abigail Folger, her boyfriend, Voytek Frykowski, internationally famous hair stylist Jay Sebring, and Steven Parent, a young man who was a friend of the estate caretaker William Garretson, the lone survivor of the bloody rampage. The killers had splattered the walls with the word "Pigs" in bloody lettering, the blood taken from Sharon Tate's mortally wounded body. The presumption for many was the killings had been carried out by the notorious Black Panthers whose verbal calling card always seemed to be "Death to the Pigs." It was eventually determined this was Manson's idea of starting a race war between blacks and whites, "Helter Skelter" he called it after a noncontroversial song recorded by the Beatles. Manson apparently was convinced he would seize power after the race war ended and that he would rule the nation.

Lead detective Danny Galindo and the other cops who emerged from the murder scene that night appeared to be in a state of shock. Small wonder! Sharon Tate was nine months pregnant and her belly had been slashed open, killing her unborn son, the sixth victim, who was to have been named Paul Richard Polanski. Manson follower Susan Atkins later confided that the actress begged her and Charles (Tex) Watson not to kill her baby. But Atkins said she and Watson slashed away at the actress, then bound a noose around her neck, and hanged her from a rafter. Atkins said they acted at Manson's direction although he wasn't present. (A few years later, as a prisoner of the state of California, Watson was given almost unlimited conjugal visiting privileges with a groupie who fell in love with him from afar and was allowed to marry him. I'll have more to say about that shortly.

Joining Atkins and Watson in the bloodletting were Patricia Krenwinkel and Leslie Van Houten, two drug crazed followers of the prophet Manson. All of the victims had been stabbed multiple times. Sebring, Frykowski and Parent were also shot repeatedly with a 22 caliber pistol.

Manson had been to the Polanski home months before when it was leased to music producer Terry Melcher and actress Candice Bergen. At the time he tried to pitch one of his music compositions to Melcher but got a rejection.

The night after the brutality on Cielo Drive the Manson gang descended on another home in the fashionable Los Feliz Hills where they slaughtered a middle aged couple, Rosemary and Leno La Bianca. The killers were driven to the scene by Manson, who then departed for the gang's hideout at the old Spahn Movie Ranch in the San Fernando Valley. The killers put a cord around Leno La Bianca's neck and shoved a fork in his stomach. The word "war" was carved on his chest and "Death to the Pigs" was written in blood on the walls of the home. Rosemary La Bianca was stabbed numerous times. The words "Helter Skelter" were also scrawled on the wall. The killers hid in the bushes until daylight, then hitchhiked back to their hideout at the Spahn Ranch.

The populace of Los Angeles was traumatized by the slaughter like no other murders in the history of the city. While at the Spahn Ranch, the clan executed ranch hand Shorty Shea who apparently annoyed them. Manson follower Steve Grogan was convicted of that murder. While in prison he led detectives to Shea's burial site. As of this writing Grogan was the only Manson follower paroled from prison,

By the end of September LAPD homicide investigators appeared to be clueless about the killers' identity although they still clung to the suspicion that black militants carried out the slayings. Over the years I had become friendly with Sgt. Jerry Stern, an intelligence officer in the Los Angeles County Sheriff's Department. We decided to take a look at the sheriff's homicide files to see if there were any comparable murder cases in their jurisdiction outside the city of Los Angeles.

We went to the old Hall of Justice in downtown Los Angeles where the homicide dicks, known as the "bull-dogs" for their fierce tenacity in solving cases, threw open their murder books to us for inspection. It didn't take long before we came across a report on the July 31, 1969 stabbing death of Gary Hinman, a musician and political science student at UCLA. Mind you, this was just 10 days before the Tate-La Bianca murders.

You didn't have to be a rocket scientist to figure that Hinman's torture killing was somehow linked to the Tate-LaBianca murders. On the wall of Hinman's living room the words "Political Piggy" were splashed with the victim's blood in stark similarity to the Tate and La Bianca murders. A suspect in the case, Bobby Beausoleil, had already been charged with the Hinman murder after he was arrested while driving the slain man's car. Hinman lived in Topanga Canyon, then known as a hippie haven, and had let Beausoleil and other members of Charles Manson's gang live rent-free in his home. He apparently was targeted for death after the Manson family became disruptive and he asked them to leave.

Although Hinman was murdered 10 days before the Tate killings, the sheriff's bulldogs were ready to go to trial in a matter of a few weeks in Santa Monica Superior Court where Charles Manson's name would soon become a matter of public record.

Once testimony started I began monitoring the trial and it soon became apparent that Charles Manson and one of his female sidekicks, Susan Atkins, were deeply involved in the Hinman slaying. A witness testified that Manson ordered Hinman tortured before Beausoleil and

Atkins stabbed him to death. "Charlie told a follower to cut off Gary's right ear," the witness said. "So he did. Then Charlie told the guy to sew it back on. So we sewed it back on."

I learned much more about the leader of this notorious cult and his followers so I decided to discuss my findings with the LAPD. But the commander of the robbery-homicide unit, Lt. Bob Helder, became extremely agitated when I told him what I had uncovered. He swore at me and then hung up the phone after warning me not to bother him again. So I told Sgt. Stern about the reaction I got and he decided to call Helder. Stern told me he was met with the same angry reaction. Apparently the LAPD cops still believed black militants were behind the murders, totally unaware that Manson hoped to provoke a race war.

At least a month went by before the LAPD decided to check out our story with the sheriff's bulldogs, and then the focus quickly shifted to the Manson family. In the meantime we had tracked the Manson clan from the Malibu Sheriff's Station where they had been arrested for loitering, then released, to their first hideout at the Spahn Movie Ranch, and finally to the isolated Death Valley community of Ballarat in Inyo County where they would at last be arrested in a ramshackle desert hideout.

Before their capture I sensed something was in the works and contacted Frank Fowles, the district attorney for California's sparsely populated Inyo County. He told me arrests were imminent. I said we intended to send a reporter and a two-man camera crew to the area and Fowles asked that they come disguised as duck hunters. So I bought hunting outfits for reporter Carl George, cameraman Jack Taylor and soundman Phil Ronney. Next I chartered a small plane and our news team took off for Independence, the county seat. It was Thanksgiving weekend, 1969 and there were no bean counters around to monitor how much money I was spending.

The story unfolded quickly. Our crew got to the trash strewn encampment just moments after the Manson family was arrested without a struggle. A highway patrol officer who had taken part in the arrests confirmed that the Tate-La Bianca murders had been solved.

After shooting a score of interviews our team flew back to Los Angeles. I wrote and produced a 22 minute report which ran the next day. We had beaten everyone on the story. We offered our exclusive report to *The CBS Evening News* with Walter Cronkite, but their producers decided not to run the story after their West Coast correspondent, Bill Stout, said he doubted its veracity.

Our coverage was honored with one of the first Edward R. Murrow awards for investigative reporting. *Broadcasting Magazine*, the "bible" of the TV industry, suggested we may have solved the murder case. I think it was the sheriff's "bulldogs" who deserved most of the credit.

# Broadcasting
## THE BUSINESSWEEKLY OF TELEVISION AND RADIO

December 8, 1969

## Did station first solve murder case?

### TV outlet
### may have had Tate death clues before police

It appears likely that details of the first major break in the bizarre murders in the Los Angeles area of actress Sharon Tate and at least six other persons were forced into the open last week by the private investigations of various news media, among which a television station and a radio station led the way. The television station, KNXT Los Angeles, apparently knew many details of the alleged participation in the murders by a nomadic band of hippies as early as the Thanksgiving weekend and even filmed the most recent encampment of the suspects several days before the Los Angeles police department on Dec. 1 relased details of the case at a general news conference.

KNXT, a CBS-owned station, had been conducting its own investigation since the Tate murder case broke as a news happening last August. On Nov. 28, after piecing together many details of the apparent solution to the crime, managing editor Pete Noyes dispatched a three-man crew to Independence. Aware of the violent nature of the hippie band, the KNXT crew—reporter Carl George, cameraman Jack Taylor and soundman Phil Ronnie—rented a station wagon and traveled disguised as pheasant hunters. Once at the location of the encampment, the crew also rented a helicopter which was kept in the air for 10 hours scouting sites and for shooting film.

Over the weekend, according to his version, Mr. Noyes contacted a high LAPD official and revealed his conviction that there would be a major break in the case and it would involve Independence, Calif. The official supposedly did not refute this information but asked that the story be withheld at the risk of jeopardizing the case. KNXT was prepared to go on the air with a full report of the story with film on the evening of the day the police held a widely attended news conference. The television station did air the story in greater detail than the story revealed by the police.

---

A German magazine offered me $25,000 for my story, as much money as I made in a year at the CBS station. But I was forced to turn it down after a CBS executive warned I could be fired because the network had exclusive rights to the story.

Though they were found guilty of first degree murder in the Tate-La Bianca killings, Manson and his followers escaped the death penalty because of that 1972 California Supreme Court declaring it unconstitutional. Manson and Susan Atkins were also found guilty at a second trial of first degree murder in the death of Gary Hinman.

After five years members of the Manson family became eligible for parole hearings. But time after time they were denied freedom, and time after time Deputy District Attorney Steve Kay was present along with members of Sharon Tate's family to remind parole boards about the horrific nature of the killings.

When I walked out the door of the CBS station in 1972, I dare say it was not on the best of terms. So I was somewhat surprised 22 years later when a new management team at the station offered me a substantial sum of money to return there as an investigative consultant along with my close friend, Leroy Orozco, a retired LAPD homicide officer who was credited with helping solve the so called "Night Stalker" murders in which Richard Ramirez was convicted of killing 14 men and women. A few years earlier Orozco had teamed up with me at NBC when I was writing and producing a weekly program about unsolved murders.

Orozco and I were assigned to do a story with Prosecutor Steve Kay on a matter unrelated to the Manson case when Kay asked me if I'd heard the latest reports on Charles Denton (Tex) Watson, the Manson follower who joined Susan Atkins in thrusting a knife repeatedly into the body of the pregnant Sharon Tate. He said there were reports that Watson had been given special visiting privileges with his wife at the state prison in San Luis Obispo and had fathered a number of children who were on welfare.

I contacted a spokesperson for the Department of Corrections who insisted Watson never received any special visiting privileges at the state prison in San Luis Obispo;

that at most under Corrections policy, he would get no more than four conjugal visits a year. We had learned that Watson now had four children and that fathering that many under such limitations seemed highly unlikely. With that in mind I took off for San Luis Obispo with reporter Drew Griffin, Leroy Orozco and cameraman Ray Armendariz in search of the story.

Once there we found that Watson had been recently transferred from the prison at San Luis Obispo near the coast to an inland facility in Ione, the Mule Creek Prison, which was our next stop. To me Ione seemed a throwback to what California looked like in the 1920s and 30s. The local diner displayed a poster of baseball great Babe Ruth endorsing Camel cigarettes. A bottle of good California wine cost $5 at an old fashioned pub. But the prison, one of the newer ones in California, was very up to date.

We were not allowed to interview Watson. But we were allowed to inspect the quarters where prisoners had conjugal visits. They weren't lavish but very livable. The average apartment included a living room, dining room, kitchen, master bedroom and a smaller bedroom for children. Throw in a big TV set and it made for a very nice weekend. Prisoners and their families had to pay for their groceries, but plenty of everything was available for bargain prices at a nearby compound.

We were really flying blind on the story until I picked up a local weekly newspaper. On the front page was a story about a fire at the home of Mrs. Charles Watson in the Sierra foothills. It wasn't much of a story, the fire didn't do serious damage, but it was our best lead of the day. I called the newspaper and the editor was happy to oblige me with the address of the Watson home. It took more than an hour to find it in the sprawling Sierra, but once we did it was a real revelation. Parked outside the good looking two-story home was a pleasure boat and relatively new SUV. The garage seemed to have been converted into a chapel for followers of Watson's "Abounding Love Ministries" which he founded in prison. There was a cross on the garage door as well as a number of biblical quotations.

Mrs. Watson, the former Kristin Joan Svelte, did not take kindly to our visit. She began screaming at us to leave at once or warned she would call the sheriff. So we left with more unanswered questions. Where did the money come from to support the Watson family life style? Did Watson's followers outside of prison hold services in the garage? Was he still allowed conjugal visits at the new prison with his wife close by?

When LAPD detectives arrived in McKinney, Texas in 1969 with a warrant to arrest "Tex" Watson for his role in the Tate-La Bianca murders, they found out he was a local hero, a star football player in high school and a state record holder in the high hurdles in track. The local sheriff didn't want to turn him over to the LAPD. He said Tex was a "good boy" who may have gotten accidentally mixed up with a bad crowd in Hollywood. This was the same Tex Watson, who according to Susan Atkins, told Sharon Tate, "I'm the devil and I'm here to do the devil's business." Watson had been an honor student at Farmersville High School, and projected the image of the All American youth. He shed the beard and the wild eyed Charles Manson look when he returned to McKinney, but it didn't help. He was whisked back to L.A. where in a separate trial he was found guilty and sentenced to die in the gas chamber. But the court's abolishment of the death penalty set Watson off in a new direction. He found God.

At the San Luis Obispo prison he became an assistant to the chaplain, and founded his "Abounding Love

Ministries." According to other inmates, Watson did a booming business selling religious tapes and tracts all over the country. Kristin Joan Svelte, his bride-to be, was the kind of groupie who falls head over heels in love with serial killers. Watson was so popular with the warden and chaplain that he was permitted to have a full dress wedding in the prison chapel. Tex wore a splendid white tux to the affair and Kristin was attired in a beautiful wedding gown that must have set someone back a few hundred dollars. There was a reception after the wedding and the bride was described as "glowing."

Then the children began arriving one after another until there were four. Several years after the birth of the first two children, county officials briefly arrested Mrs. Watson, accusing her of being a welfare cheat. No one seems to know what actually happened, but the charges were dropped.

In my mind there was one major unresolved issue in this story. Were correction officials being honest with us when they said Watson was treated just like any other prisoner and granted conjugal visits on a quarterly basis? Since the people in the Corrections Department insisted they were following that policy at the San Luis Obispo Prison, I decided to file a public records request for the visitors' logs at the conjugal housing facility. Meantime, I detected an air of skepticism about the story in the newsroom. One person told me that the managing editor, Pat Casey, suspected our trip up north to cover the Watson story was a boondoggle and he assigned a young woman in the newsroom to do a "fact check" on the story.

Under California Public Records Act the Department of Corrections had no choice but to release the visitor logs at the prison. And they showed quite clearly that mass murderer Tex Watson was allowed to have conjugal visits at San Luis Obispo Prison every two to three weeks over an extended period of time. So the fact that the Watsons had four children while Tex was doing hard time shouldn't have come as much of a surprise to anyone. We put the story together and Drew Griffin did a masterful presentation. Then the news director, Larry Perret, called me and Orozco to a meeting with Managing Editor Casey to discuss the story. Casey just didn't like it and wanted the story killed. I became furious, and finally said, "If this guy (Casey) gets his way I'm quitting." No one backed me up so Orozco and I walked out the door and parted company with CBS. At first News Director Perret, didn't support us. But after we left he decided to go with the story which ran in two parts and was awarded an Emmy for investigative reporting. A few months later Perret called me and said "Pete, come back to work, I fired Casey." So I did, but then Perret got fired a few months later and I decided to retire, at least temporarily. When I quit it resulted in a front page story in USA Today.

Drew Griffin went on to become one of the top investigative reporters at CNN, winning a Peabody and a national Emmy for his work. Leroy Orozco went back into law enforcement, working as a welfare fraud investigator for the Orange County District Attorney. What I did is a story for another day, but I just couldn't quit TV news for good. There's no doubt our story about Tex Watson had a major impact. There was so much outrage against the Department of Corrections it was forced to make changes in its conjugal visits policy and mass killers like the Reverend Charles "Tex" Watson would never again be permitted to have them. A postscript to the story, Charles Watson and the former Kristin Joan Svelte were divorced in 2003.

# 10

## THE ANONYMOUS HOWARD HUGHES

Howard Hughes, the reluctant, bashful billionaire, may have been one of the more important figures of the 20th century. Hughes was truly one of the great aviation pioneers of his time. He held numerous aviation speed records. His record-breaking 1938 around-the-world flight in a Lockheed monoplane was celebrated by a million people in a tickertape parade led by Mayor Fiorella Laguardia in New York City. He defied death in a brutal plane crash in Beverly Hills after which doctors held little hope for his recovery. His tool company and Hughes Aviation became industrial giants. He was a movie pioneer who made numerous hits and turned relatively obscure actresses into Hollywood queens. His work for the CIA was top secret, but he was involved in some of the biggest projects ever undertaken by the intelligence agency, including the lifting of a sunken Soviet submarine from the depths of the Pacific.

By 1971 Hughes had gobbled up most of the big gambling casinos run by the mob in Las Vegas and settled down to a quiet life on the desert. He surrounded himself with a vanguard of Mormons because, he said, they were honest and he could trust them. He cloistered himself in his hotel room watching movies on TV night and day. When he didn't like the celluloid fare on one station, he simply bought it.

Our news director, Grant Holcomb, was of a mind to do an investigative special on the life of Howard Hughes. It was a great idea, I thought, when I was assigned to the project, not realizing that it was to be one of the most ago-nizing experiences of my journalistic life that most likely cost me my job at CBS. Holcomb told me money was no object. "Spend what you have to buddy," he told me, "I'll take care of the bean counters." To start the project I needed as much historical film of Hughes as I could get, his plane crash in Beverly Hills, an aviation speed record in Santa Ana, California; the ticker tape parade that greeted Hughes in New York City after his epic round the world flight, and the one and only flight of his controversial wooden transport plane, "The Spruce Goose." If we didn't have any pictures we didn't have a show.

*Howard Hughes at the controls of his wooden fly-ing boat, the "Spruce Goose," during its first and only flight, November 2, 1947.*

Along the way Hughes had purchased thousands of feet of newsreel footage about his career and locked it away in an Arizona warehouse. The only place I found to have any footage of Hughes was the Hearst Newsreel Library in New York City. So, for the tidy sum of $6,000, I purchased several thousand feet of film, paying in advance with a cashier's check. The video was delivered to me by special messenger and after screening most of it I put it in the film library for safekeeping. The next day when I returned to work the entire Howard Hughes film collection was gone. It had vanished and our security people had no idea who took it. We had no surveillance cameras in those days.

I was crestfallen and after spending a day waiting for the film to find its way back to me I called the Hearst people and told them what had happened. A voice on the other end of the line responded, "Howard Hughes strikes again. His people are everywhere." I was dumfounded.

The Hearst manager advised he would send me a duplicate version of the Hughes film collection, but suggested at the end of the work day I take the film home in my car for safekeeping. He said there would be no charge but if the film were lost again, it would be my tough luck.

I was ably assisted on the project by author James Phelan, who had written several books about Hughes. Jim got me an exclusive interview with Noah Dietrich, the business genius who was credited with making Hughes a very wealthy man. In exploring their relationship, Dietrich disclosed for the first time that Hughes had a terrible fear of germs and constantly washed his hands. By now an octogenarian, Dietrich proudly took credit for Hughes' success in the business world after inheriting the tool company from his father. He suggested that Hughes' desire for secrecy and privacy was a result of his germ phobia. So we decided to title the documentary *"The Anonymous Howard Hughes."* We were able to interview a number of other people associated with Hughes, including one of the many starlets squired about town by him during his motion picture days. She was Ida Lupino, who was 16 when she first dated Hughes, always in the company of her mother, she insisted. At the time of our interview Lupino had graduated from actress to director, one of the few women in Hollywood to achieve such status in those years.

Putting the documentary together was no easy matter. The editor broke some of the brittle film and restoring it took hours. Reporter Jerry Dunphy suffered a severe eye infection and was almost taken off the project. But finally after carting the film around in my car for over a month, the project was completed. It looked pretty good to me. I was in the editing room when a call was transferred to me from the front desk. "Is this Pete Noyes? the voice on the other end of the line asked. When I replied in the affirmative the man said, "This is Bob Johnson of the Bank of America. I understand you're producing a documentary about Howard Hughes." I was getting edgy at this point. The bank sponsored our special reports and it appeared something was up. Johnson told me in no uncertain terms, "...you're not going to put the show on the air." I asked why, and he said, "Mr. Hughes doesn't like it. And he's got $14 million on deposit in our bank. That's why." I told Johnson I wasn't killing the show regardless of what Hughes wanted, but he could talk to news director Holcomb. Once Holcomb got the call from Johnson he was outraged. But he knew what to do. Los Angeles *Times* gossip maven Joyce Haber was attending a party in Malibu that evening and Holcomb had been invited. He didn't intend to go, but the heavy handed bank meddling changed his mind.

The next day, February 2, 1971 Joyce Haber set off a firestorm of bad publicity about Howard Hughes and his banker friends when she wrote in her column:

*"Our local CBS-TV station, KNXT, has prepared a half-hour profile on Howard Hughes for airing a week from tonight on "KNXT Reports "The Anonymous Howard Hughes' was written and produced by Peter Noyes, who won the Golden Mike award for his investigative reporting in the Tate-LaBianca case. Among the people interviewed on Noyes' show are Ida Lupino, H.H.'s former friend, Noah Dietrich right-hand man to Hughes for 30 years, and Bob Maheu, the only-just fired right-hand man.*

*"The happenings behind the scenes at KNXT are more intriguing than anything that may be disclosed on the air. It has always been Hughes' custom to try to suppress or at least delay any stories being done about him.*

*"As is custom, then, last week the station received a call from one of the executives of Hughes Tool. The man demanded the show be cancelled. CBS refused. Next came a call from the sponsor, in the guise of a Bank of America official. The man explained that the bank, which has on deposit like millions of H.H dollars, would have to drop its sponsorship of KNXT Reports if the Hughes show wasn't cancelled. On Friday, the Bank of America suddenly dropped its sponsorship of KNXT Reports."*

That was the first time I heard about a call from the Hughes Tool Company which Holcomb refrained from telling me about so I wouldn't "blow a gasket." The station's sales manager, Bob Fairbanks, almost jumped with joy upon learning the bank had withdrawn its sponsorship. He pointed out that newspapers and industry trade magazines had picked up the story all over the country and within a few hours his sales people sold it out the at three times rate the Bank of America had been paying. The show was a giant in the ratings pulling in an audience of more than a million people in the Los Angeles area. It was syndicated nationwide by CBS, producing huge ratings everywhere it played.

Two weeks later one of my high school classmates, Joe Scott, called me and said the controversy over the making of "The Anonymous Howard Hughes" was so big he'd like me to talk about it at a meeting of the "Miracle Mile Businessmen's Association." I agreed without asking permission from anyone at CBS. I spoke for half an hour before 50 or so assembled guests. Little did I know that bank spies had hidden several tape recorders in the room and everything I said ended up on audio tape. It was the perfect way to set me up. I simply told the businessmen the truth and didn't hesitate to respond to their questions. I discussed the stealing of the film from our library, the problems we had in putting the story together, and the fumbling attempt by the Bank of America to kill a legitimate story.

I first learned of the secret tape recording of my comments when KNXT's new general manager, Ray Beindorf, summoned me into his office and started reading the riot act to me over my remarks. "Hey wait a minute Beindorf," I shouted. "I stand by everything I said. It's all true and you know it." The meeting ended on an abrupt note and I sensed that my days at CBS were numbered, as well as those of my immediate boss, Grant Holcomb. It wasn't too long before Holcomb was removed as news director and assigned to our bureau in Washington D.C. at a lesser paying job. When Holcomb was diagnosed with cancer he was fired by CBS. Someone at the network had the gall to send the dying Holcomb a potted plant to his room at Good Samaritan Hospital. With death only a few days away, he got out of his sick bed, donned a trench coat, and threw the potted plant out a window.

Holcomb's replacement, political editor Bill Eames, summoned me into his office and said I was being relieved of my duties because I was too old, at 42, to continue producing the Big News. He offered me a reporting job at one-half my salary which would almost place me at the poverty level. This in face of the fact that I had just picked up my second Emmy in two years for producing the most successful local news broadcast in the country, written and produced the highest rated documentary in the station's history and broken the Manson murder case. At first I took it like a death in the family.

It's amazing how fast news travels in our business. The next day Bill Fyffe, the news director at the local ABC station, called and offered me a job producing his hour-long news broadcast at twice my CBS salary. I didn't hesitate. I penned a note on the bulletin board saying I was leaving immediately along with this quote paraphrased from a Navy admiral in radio contact with a sinking warship in the Pacific during World War II: "Good luck, God bless you. Your picture is on my piano." The next stop would be, ABC TV, one mile to the east via the Hollywood Freeway.

# 11

## HOWARD HUGHES AND THE CIA

By 1974 I was fully entrenched at KABC Eyewitness News in Los Angeles, working as a news show producer. Things were going extremely well. My former colleague at CBS2, Jim Vinson, joined the writing staff, as did Don Bresnahan, one of the top writers in town at KTTV News. Gradually we began moving to the top of the ratings and when the meatheads at CBS2 fired Jerry Dunphy, we hired him immediately and the ballgame was over at what was left of Sam Zelman's creation, *The Big News*.

But before Dunphy was hired, News Director Bill Fyffe decided to beef up his anchoring staff and hired two brothers for our news coverage which was expanding to three consecutive hours starting at 4 p.m. Judd and John Hambrick were typical anchors who could do a pretty good job if the copy was well written, and they looked at the right camera. But Judd, the younger brother, decided he also wanted to be a producer and figured he could do the job better than me. Fyffe decided on a compromise and over my objections appointed Judd Hambrick my co-producer. The next day I asked Hambrick what he wanted to do and he promptly answered, "The entire Watergate story." So I handed him a mountain of wire service copy from the *Associated Press* and *United Press International*, as well as still photos and video tape of the day's proceedings in Washington D.C. It was about 30 minutes before air time when Hambrick handed me a ream of copy for the Watergate story. He did not use a single video tape, not even a photo. The entire script must have run seven or eight minutes with Judd Hambrick's face fully exposed on camera for the entire time.

I became so upset I went blind in both eyes for about two minutes. The next day the doctor told me what I had was an aneurysm, and treated me accordingly with advice to avoid stress which is next to impossible in any sort of newsroom. When I returned to work a week or so later Vinson and Bresnahan advised me they were certain Hambrick wouldn't get the Watergate story right and without telling me they put one together for broadcast that night. They said after I went blind they were sorry they hadn't told me in advance. That ended Judd Hambrick's career as a TV news producer and he returned quietly to the anchor booth. It was also the end of my producing career.

Bill Fyffe welcomed me back and said he had a different job for me, running his newly formed investigative unit. The reporter assigned to the unit was Dick Carlson who established quite a reputation for himself in San Francisco working alongside reporter Lance Brisson, the son of actress Rosalind Russell. It was Carlson and Brisson who penned an article for *Look Magazine* in which they linked San Francisco Mayor Joseph Alioto to the Mafia. The story resulted in a massive libel lawsuit against *Look* which eventually folded after Alioto prevailed in the courts. (Years later Mafia snitch Jimmy Fratianno gave the FBI detailed testimony about Alioto and his ties to organized crime figures.)

Carlson had worked as cop before turning to reporting and knew a lot of the tricks of the trade. He was excellent at interrogating people, knew how get his hands on critical public records such as search warrants, and even had expertise in picking locks, a skill not normally required of investigative reporters.

Before we barely got started the name of Howard Hughes surfaced once again in my reportorial life, and I must admit, I was a little squeamish about getting involved in another story about the shy billionaire. But I had to do the story handed me by my former classmate at Loyola University, Don Bowler, who left the District Attorney's office to take charge of security for Howard Hughes at his fortress-like headquarters in the 7000 block of Romaine Avenue in Hollywood.

I was quite surprised when Don called me with a mind blowing story, given the secret nature of the Hughes organization. He said in the early morning hours of June 5, 1974 a burglary team penetrated the supposedly impregnable security systems at the Hughes' Summa Corporation headquarters in Hollywood. Four armed invaders gained entry after they put a gun to the back of security guard Mike Davis. Then they ordered him to go inside and drop face down on the floor. They left him bound and gagged for five hours while they ransacked the huge complex. They used blow torches to knock open two of the 13 safes on the second floor as well as a huge vault, took art work, jewelry, a butterfly collection and numerous documents from the office of Summa executive Kay Glenn. In one safe they found $60,000 in cash, mostly in $100 bills, and Glenn's attaché case which was presumed to contain top secret documents including a contract with the CIA. The thieves also broke into a large conference room where Hughes aides were preparing an answer to a lawsuit by his former top aide Robert Maheu and scooped up numerous other files. They also took documents detailing Hughes dealings with Nevada Governor Paul Laxalt, who was later elected to the U.S. Senate. When Hughes was advised the burglars would probably make a ransom demand, Bowler quoted the Hughes as saying "they can go f... themselves."

In the days that followed police intelligence sources told me the story was much bigger than a simple burglary, and that the thieves may have made off with some top secret documents that linked Hughes and his wholly owned Summa Corporation (formerly Hughes Tool) to the Central Intelligence Agency. FBI Director Clarence M. Kelley decided that, if Hughes wouldn't pay the ransom demand, the bureau would go ahead and do it in the "interest of national security." The Watergate burglary in Washington had unnerved many federal officials, so much so that Watergate Special Prosecutor Leon Jaworski was on the phone to the LAPD almost daily, trying to sniff out details of the Hughes burglary.

Los Angeles Police Chief Ed Davis insisted the burglary was pretty much routine. But the truth was that the billionaire's press aides had instructed the LAPD to downplay the burglary because some of the stolen documents dealt with matters of "grave national security" and in the event they were recovered, no one was to look at them. The cops were told the documents must be returned immediately to the Summa Corporation.

There was good reason for higher ups in Washington to be worried. The Central Intelligence Agency, in a covert operation unknown to anyone in the Defense Department, commissioned the Hughes organization to build a salvage vessel to recover a four thousand ton Soviet nuclear submarine that had sunk to the ocean floor in the Pacific 750 miles northeast of Hawaii. The CIA dubbed it "Operation

Jennifer" and forked over $350 million dollars to the Hughes people to build the recovery vessel to be known as the "Glomar Explorer." Should anyone get wind of the operation, they were to be told Hughes was building a craft to mine minerals on the ocean bottom.

Two months after the burglary all hell broke loose at Summa Headquarters when top Hughes aide Kay Glenn went looking for the Glomar Explorer files and found they were missing from his attaché case. The panic stricken Glenn suspected the burglars had them. The CIA pondered its every move. Who on God's earth were they dealing with, and where were the documents?

Just 29 days after the burglary the Glomar Explorer lifted the Soviet nuclear sub off the ocean floor. But the sub broke in half. The operation was somewhat successful. Two nuclear tipped torpedoes were recovered from the broken sub along with the bodies of six Russian sailors who were buried at sea. The Glomar Explorer was scheduled to return to the area to retrieve the rest of the vessel in a mission cloaked in secrecy to avoid an international incident, which explained all the nervous phone calls from people in high places.

I was involved in a number of projects and after the initial story on the Hughes burglary put it aside. It did cross my mind that the White House "plumbers" had once planned to burglarize the office safe of Nevada publisher Hank Greenspun in search of documents dealing with Hughes' questionable political activities. But at first I simply dismissed the break-in at the Summa Corporation as just another burglary. Then I got a call from Donald Fried, co-author of the movie "Executive Action," mostly a fictionalized account of President Kennedy's assassination. Fried said he wanted me to talk to a man named Pat Repash who had considerable information about the

Hughes' burglary. My contact at the FBI, Roger (Frenchy) La Jeunesee, said I would be wasting my time getting together with Repash but I decided to check him out anyway.

When he came to our newsroom, Repash was about the most nervous informant I had ever met. He rattled off all sorts of information, repeatedly looking over his shoulder and chain smoked one cigarette after another. But he seemed to know what he was talking about. He said the burglary at Hughes headquarters was a "mob job" and the key man in the operation was a slick operator named Donald Woolbright who worked for the St. Louis Mafia. Repash said a lot of valuable government documents were taken in the burglary and Woolbright was holding them for ransom. At the time I was skeptical but almost everything Repash told me that day turned out to be fact. Several days later an investigator in the D.A.'s office called me to shed more light on another story. I asked him if he had ever heard of Donald Woolbright. The guy almost flipped out. He said this was a top secret matter, that the grand jury was about to indict Donald Woolbright for masterminding the Howard Hughes burglary. He said Woolbright was put up to the theft by Mafia figures in the Pipefitters Union in St. Louis, and had obtained files that were "political dynamite." He noted that Woolbright was a close associate of St. Louis Mafia kingpin Tony Giardino.

Standing 6 feet tall and weighing only 144 pounds, Woolbright was described as a perfect fit for a cat burglar, which was listed as his principal occupation in police reports. He had been arrested for burglary, possessing burglary tools, carrying a concealed weapon, possession of stolen property, possession of narcotics, counterfeiting and petty theft, impressive criminal credentials in view of the fact he had not served any hard time for those crimes.

Meantime the mood at the Hughes organization became more anxious day after day. President Ford was said to be very uneasy about the missing Glomar Explorer papers. So in cooperation with the LAPD, Summa Corporation ran an ad offering a reward in the Los Angeles Times and identified Hughes aide Nadine Hanley as the person to contact. A man positively identified as Donald Woolbright answered the ad. When the call came Miss Hanley was attending a dinner party in the Marina del Rey. She was put in touch with Woolbright who said his price was $1 million subject to conditions to be worked out with two of the underworld's best known lawyers, Morris Schencker and Sidney Korshak.

Woolbright and his three accomplices registered at the Sheraton Universal Hotel to begin the negotiations. But Hughes was still adamant about paying a ransom, and his reasoning was soon borne out. The Hughes negotiators learned that the stolen files had been sanitized, so to speak, and the burglars had removed a stash of material that would have been extremely embarrassing to Paul Laxalt, then running for a U.S. Senate seat in Nevada. The negotiations collapsed after the Hughes people decided that the ransom demand could go on indefinitely and the burglars could not be trusted. Howard Hughes did not want to play that game.

Despite his long arrest record, Woolbright was not your ordinary run of the mill hoodlum. He was articulate and gave the impression of being well educated. His home was filled with fine art and expensive China and furniture. Twice rebuffed in his ransom demands, he decided to sell some of the more interesting material taken in the burglary to Hollywood producer Leo Gordon. Gordon advanced Woolbright $4,000 for the purchase of some of the missing files. But then Woolbright disappeared from his home in Canoga Park, and Gordon hired Pat Repash, as his private investigator and together they took his story to law enforcement.

The existence of the Glomar Explorer and the six year project to recover the Soviet submarine from the depths of the Pacific was first disclosed in testimony before the Grand Jury that indicted Donald Woolbright. The story soon appeared in the Los Angeles *Times*, on columnist Jack Anderson's *Mutual Radio* broadcast, and on *KABC Television News* where we had been the first to report the burglary at the Hughes' headquarters. The *Times* story, written by reporter Jerry Cohen, was published in great detail on the front page of its evening edition. In the next day's morning edition it was greatly cut down and placed on page 23. Cohen told me after the night edition hit the streets several CIA agents walked into the managing editor's office and demanded that the story be drastically chopped in the interest of national security. Cohen was not one bit pleased. No one seems to know with certainty that the Glomar Explorer recovered the other half of the Soviet sub, although one Soviet publication claimed that the vessel's return trip was successful. It never became an international incident as far as we know.

Once again Donald Woolbright escaped a prison sentence. He was convicted at his first trial but the verdict was overturned by an appellate court. His second trial ended in a hung jury and he went free. It turned out Woolbright never got hold of that secret Glomar Explorer file. Hughes security guard Mike Davis confessed that after he worked himself free he found the file strewn on the floor near Kay Glenn's office. He admitted taking the files home to read them. So when the search began in earnest for the Glomar Explorer file, Davis said he got nervous and flushed the papers down a toilet.

Another chapter closed in the saga of America's bashful and very anonymous billionaire, Howard Hughes, the CIA's man in Hollywood.

# 12

## THE SLA KIDNAPS PATTY HEARST

During the same time frame as the Hughes burglary, one of the biggest stories in the nation was unfolding. It was about a band of ultra radical urban terrorists who called themselves the "Symbionese Liberation Army," best known by its acronym, the "SLA." They came to national attention on February 4, 1974 when they kidnapped newspaper heiress Patricia Hearst just two weeks short of her 20th birthday. She was the granddaughter of the legendary newspaperman William Randolph Hearst, and daughter of the old man's son, George Hearst, publisher of the *San Francisco Examiner*. Patty was a student at the University of California when she was taken at gunpoint from her Berkeley apartment while chatting with her fiancé, Stephen Weed whom she was scheduled to marry in a few months. Weed was beaten over the head with a wine bottle and tied up before the kidnapers fled with Patty.

The SLA demanded a ransom of $50 million to buy food to feed the poor and homeless in San Francisco. The Hearst family began complying by setting up food lines that fed thousands of people. But by that time Patty Hearst seemed to have embraced the SLA's radical philosophy and assumed the guerilla warrior name of "Tania." She sent a tape to a Berkeley radio station renouncing her parents and family riches while declaring that she had joined the SLA to take part in the "urban revolution." The SLA's professed goals were to overthrow the government and bring about the re-distribution of wealth, an idea right out of the Karl Marx handbook. And one of their plans to capture some of that wealth was quickly established.

On April 15, 1974 a security camera captured an iconic picture of a rifle toting Patty Hearst, just two months after her kidnapping, standing guard with a rifle as her new friends in the SLA robbed the Hibernia Bank in San Francisco of an estimated $10,000. After her capture, psychiatrists concluded Patty was a victim of the so-called "Stockholm Syndrome," apparently "brainwashed" by her captors. Later she concurred with that diagnosis and said she had been sexually abused in captivity. Thirty years later reporter Tony Valdez and I interviewed Patty Hearst after she filed suit to open up the financial books of the Hearst business empire. We found her to be extremely intelligent, and seemingly well adjusted despite the notoriety that once dominated her life and the nation's headlines.

The SLA first caught police attention on November 6, 1973 when its triggermen assassinated an African-American, Dr. Marcus Foster, the popular Superintendent of Schools in Oakland, California who was gunned down after he got out his car and started walking to his office. The SLA immediately took credit for the murder, saying Foster was executed because he wanted students to carry identification cards as a means of keeping the criminal element off of local campuses. A few years later SLA gunmen Joseph Remiero and Russell Little got life sentences for the crime, but the courts eventually overturned Little's conviction on a technicality and he went free.

The leader of the SLA was an escaped California prison convict, Donald De Freeze, an African-American with a long history of criminal activity, who changed his name to "Field Marshall Cinque" to honor the onetime leader of a slave rebellion. Cinque's gang was a mixed collection of radicals including several former convicts as well as a dozen or so fairly well educated white and Asian men and women, most with college degrees.

In 1974 a botched robbery was the first indication that the SLA was active in the Los Angeles area, and it wouldn't take long to find them. The robbers fled after they were overpowered by a security guard at Mel's Sporting Goods Store in Inglewood, their escape made possible by what appeared to be covering gunfire from Patty Hearst standing lookout across the street.

On May 17, 1974 the LAPD received a tip that some SLA members were holed up in a so-called safe house on East 54th Street in the heart of the black community of Watts. Soon the area surrounding the house became an armed camp and a score of reporters showed up at the scene. We assigned the story to KABC reporter Christine Lund, a striking statuesque blonde who would later become the city's first female anchor person. Everyone seemed to be just milling around the neighborhood so Christine decided to "door knock" the home to see if she could interview someone inside. So, much to the alarm of the cops, she pounded on the front door but a voice from inside told her to go away. Finally, she gave up and left. In no time at all a horrendous shootout took place after the LAPD fired tear gas projectiles into the house. The cops kept promising over bull horns that no one would be harmed if they surrendered, but the SLA guerillas were defiant to the end. After two hours a massive fire consumed the house and all six persons inside, including Field Marshall Cinque, were killed. Patty Hearst was not there. She had watched the entire episode on TV in another safe house a few miles away.

Christine Lund was widely criticized by her male counterparts in the news business for not abiding by the rules and boldly approaching the house in search of an interview. I had mixed emotions. I admired her courage but had qualms about the risks she took. Incidentally, a news special I wrote and produced that evening on the SLA shootout was awarded an Emmy by the Television Academy.

The SLA did not go away quietly after its leader and five comrades were killed in the shootout with the LAPD. Now led by Vietnam War protestors Bill and Emily Harris, the radicals resorted to robbing more banks and setting off bombs at public facilities.

On February 25, 1975 they robbed the Guild Savings and Loan in Sacramento of an estimated $3700. Then Bill and Emily Harris set their sights on an even bigger score at a bank in a well-to-do bedroom community. It was the Crocker National Bank in the city of Carmichael, a Sacramento suburb. On August 15, 1975 six SLA members drove up to the bank in a car with stolen license plates. Bill Harris directed operations outside the bank while wife Emily, armed with a loaded shotgun, and three others entered the bank, their faces hidden behind masks, and announced the holdup. Myrna Opsahl, a 42 year-old doctor's wife, had gone to the bank with two friends to deposit the weekend collection from the local Seventh Day Adventist Church. Suddenly Emily Harris let go with a shotgun blast, killing Mrs. Opsahl, the mother of four. Witnesses said Harris shot Mrs. Opsahl because she didn't move fast enough when she told to drop to the floor. Years later when tried for the woman's murder, Harris admitted her weapon killed Mrs. Opsahl, but said it went off by accident. But Patty Hearst later told investigators a different story. She quoted Emily Harris as saying the killing didn't matter because Mrs. Opsahl was "...a bourgeois pig married to a doctor." A witness inside the bank said another woman on the robbery team leaped over the counter and violently kicked a pregnant teller in the stomach, hurting her badly. That robber was believed to be Katherine Soliah, a former high school cheerleader who would eventually become one of the SLA's top commanders. Police estimated the robbers made off with nearly $15,000 from the Crocker Bank.

During the same period, April of 1975, the SLA was linked to a pair of attempted bombings in Northern California. Explosives were planted at the Emeryville Police Station and the Marin County Courthouse. Both bombs ignited but no one was hurt at either location. On April 25 Katherine Soliah and several accomplices planted bombs under two Los Angeles Police Department squad cars, seeking to exact revenge for the death of their six comrades in the SLA shootout. Both bombs were dismantled before they could go off. The cops found Soliah's fingerprints on the bombs and a warrant was issued for her arrest. Meantime Patty Hearst, Bill and Emily Harris and several other SLA members were arrested at a safe house in San Francisco.

That left only two SLA members at large, Katherine Soliah and her sometime boyfriend, Donald Kilgore.

Twenty-five years later in June of 1999, police in St. Paul, Minnesota, arrested Katherine Soliah. She was known to neighbors and friends as Sarah Jane Olson, a stay at home soccer mom married to a physician with whom she had three daughters. Part of her new identity was taken from Sarah Jane Moore, the radical middle aged woman sent to prison for trying to assassinate President Gerald Ford in San Francisco in 1975. The cops said Soliah was joined by Bill and Emily Harris in planting the pipe bombs under the cop cars. Soliah was also charged with complicity in the 1974 murder of Myrna Opsahl in the Carmichael bank robbery. Her parents and relatives in Palmdale, California were aghast at the developments. At Palmdale High School where her mother was a teacher and her father a coach, Katherine Soliah was described as an "All American" girl. She was a member of the pep squad, active in the Girl Scouts and regularly attended Sunday school. Friends said her former boyfriend, Donald Kilgore, talked her and brother, Steven Soliah, into joining the SLA. She was convicted on two counts of possessing explosives with intent to murder and served seven years in prison before she was paroled and returned to her home in Minnesota.

In 2002, more than a quarter of a century after the slaying of Myrna Opsahl in the Carmichael bank robbery, Bill and Emily Harris as well as Michael Borton were arrested on the basis of new evidence and charged with first degree murder. In a deal with the prosecution, all pleaded guilty to second degree murder and received prison terms up to eight years. All eventually went free.

The last of the urban terrorists still at large, James Kilgore was found teaching in Cape Town, South Africa in 2002. For 30 years he had been living under the name of Professor Charles William Pape. He had written a widely used text book in South Africa's schools, married an American woman and fathered two children. Kilgore was described as a brilliant student at the University of California's Santa Barbara campus where he was graduated with honors. Kilgore also played on the school's basketball team, and an acquaintance told me he was one of the greatest free throw shooters ever to play basketball on the West Coast. U.S. Marshals brought him back to California where he served less than six years in prison before being released.

Patty Hearst was given a seven year sentence for her role in the Hibernia bank robbery and spent almost two years in prison before President Jimmy Carter commuted her sentence. President Bill Clinton later gave her a full pardon on his last day in office.

She was one of 140 persons Mr. Clinton pardoned that day. Patty said she was "profoundly grateful."

# 13

## THE SHABBY CASE OF PRIVATE HAGELBERGER

He was an L.A. kid who escaped the hangman's noose with just hours to spare in a strange case of military justice in which a commanding general ignored the demands of a sitting president. It was a story that played out over 20 years of my career.

On April 15, 1952 Private Richard Hagelberger was just 19 years old when he and his Army buddy, Private Richard Vigneault, also 19, went AWOL in Diebach, West Germany, and got drunk on a combination of beer and cognac at a local tavern. During the drinking spree they struck up a conversation with two German civilians, whom they talked into taking them for a ride with the idea of killing them and stealing their car. Hagelberger gave a pre-arranged signal and Vigneault shot and killed the two Germans. They took off on a joy ride but seconds later crashed the car and were captured.

Both were sentenced to death by hanging after separate military trials at Nuremberg. The case came to my attention four years later when a young Army lawyer in the Judge Advocate General's office confided to me that a miscarriage of justice was about to take place. He told me about the case and said that Vigneault, the actual killer, had been granted clemency by President Eisenhower and his death sentence was commuted to 55 years in prison. But Hagelberger was scheduled to be executed by hanging at Leavenworth in just two months. The officer suggested that political influence had a lot to do with Vigneault's commutation. He said that Senator Styles Bridges of New Hampshire, Vigneault's home state, pressured the White House into granting clemency to the soldier. Hagelberger, on the other hand, had no advocate. When he was just four he was placed in an orphanage after his father died and shuttled from institution to institution. He joined the Army at 17 and went AWOL twice before being assigned to Germany. The two U.S. Senators from California took no interest in his case.

At the time I was working for Armed Forces Press Service and Pacific Stars and Stripes in Washington D.C. and neither organization was interested in the story. So I took it to Lloyd Norman, Pentagon correspondent for the Chicago *Tribune*. Lloyd told me he liked the story and would start working on it immediately. While we were chatting several other correspondents in the press room, chided me for getting involved in the case. "No one gives a damn about saving the life of a killer," one of them said. But Norman was not to be denied and we worked closely on the story from that day forward.

On July 4, 1956, he wrote in part:

"The Tribune learned May 30 that the Army was preparing quietly to execute Richard Hagelberger without public notice. It was learned that Hagelberger was going to die for the double murder although the death sentence of the actual murderer had been commuted to 55 years (by President Eisenhower)."

The major contention of the Army prosecutors who reviewed Hagelberger's death sentence was that he was a person of "high intelligence" and therefore should be put to death for his crime. Richard Vigneault, on the other hand, was a person of "low intelligence" and it was Hagelberger who convinced him to carry out the execution. Therefore Vigneault should not be executed.

On June 6, 1956, the official Army execution papers were signed. Hagelberger would die by hanging the following month at Fort Leavenworth. Now a sense of hopelessness hit those of us who had fought to save his life. But Norman kept pounding away at his keyboard about the injustice in the case. Just before the scheduled execution, Norman rushed up to my desk at the Pentagon with startling news. The commanding general at Fort Leavenworth, Kansas announced that Private Richard Hagelberger had been granted an indefinite stay of execution. The Pentagon and the Secretary of the Army quickly denied that a stay had been granted, but the damage had been done when the execution was halted. The only explanation we got for the stay of execution was that "it probably resulted from a clerical error." It appeared to some that the commanding general wanted no part in the execution.

White House Press Secretary Jim Haggerty told us the President was furious; that he had never seen the general so upset. He was especially angered by the suggestion that political pressure brought on the White House by Vigneault's family and Senator Bridges.

Meantime, Gerald D. Morgan, special counsel to the president, ordered a study of the Hagelberger case after inquiries from the Chicago *Tribune* presented the following facts which were ignored by military courts.

1. Hagelberger and Vigneault were apparently intoxicated before taking a ride with the two Germans.

2. An Army psychiatrist said Hagelberger was subject to "brain waves" similar to those preceding epilepsy and that small amounts of alcohol could affect his volition.

3. The death sentence was more severe than the soldiers would have received in a German court.

4. The court martial was prejudiced by the army command's effort to demonstrate to the German people that the U.S. would extract stern justice for the murders.

Perhaps Morgan presented the president with enough new evidence to call off the execution. Or perhaps it was the proclamation of the American Legion which urged the President to grant mercy to Hagelberger.

Mr. Eisenhower, his back seemingly to the wall because of the general's decision not to carry out the execution at Leavenworth and the subsequent negative stories about a miscarriage of justice, commuted Hagelberger's death sentence to 55 years in prison and specified in writing that he remain there always.

According to the U.S. Pardon Attorney, Lawrence M. Traylor, Mr. Eisenhower "expressed the hope that no future president would grant any further clemency to Hagelberger." as well as five other G.I's convicted of capital crimes during his tenure as president.

Now I was about to be discharged from the Navy, and I had a good feeling that we had advanced the cause of justice in the case of Private Hagelberger by help-ing stop his execution. Eighteen years later I was work-ing as a news producer at the ABC station in L.A. when I came across a wire service story announcing that the U.S. Supreme Court was about to consider Mr. Eisenhower's "life without hope" sentences for Richard Hagelberger and the five other G.I.'s. The appeal lawyers claimed Mr. Eisenhower acted in a way "completely foreign to our sys-tem of laws." They noted that there were roughly 23,000 persons jailed in the federal prison system, but just six, the soldiers named by Mr. Eisenhower during his presidency, were ineligible for parole. Hagelberger had been cited for only two offenses during his 22 years in prison, taking an extra piece of bread in a mess hall and betting on a foot-ball game. Year after year federal parole boards unani-mously voted that Hagelberger be paroled. But year after year the U.S. Pardon Attorney invoked the memory of one of the nation's most popular presidents, and each time Hagelberger was denied his freedom.

Clearing out the cobwebs in my mind, I decided to do something I should have done long before, a follow up story. I found Richard Hagelberger in a medium secu-rity federal prison in La Tuna, Texas near El Paso. In an exchange of correspondence, he told me he had obeyed all the rules during his long incarceration, and believed he deserved parole. The warden at La Tuna obviously agreed because he frequently allowed Hagelberger to spend weekends with his sister in El Paso and also let him visit local card clubs.

Fred Coughlin, former chairman of the Federal Clemency and Parole Board, became a staunch advo-cate for Hagelberger. He told me, "Hagelberger is being kept in custody for the simple reason that no one in authority has the intestinal fortitude to assert that President Eisenhower made a mistake in the type of commutation he handed down."

Ultimately the U.S. Supreme Court denied the appeal of Mr. Eisenhower's ruling,

But Chief Justice Warren Burger left the door open to another avenue of legal action to challenge the "life without hope sentences." He wrote that "...presidents have exercised the power to pardon under conditions that are not spelled out by statute." But he suggested that the prisoners might seek relief from a future president on the issue of clemency.

I wrote a lengthy opinion piece for the Los Angeles Times entitled, "The Shabby Case of Private Hagelberger," which appeared in the newspaper on July 8, 1974. There were the predictable letters calling me a "bleeding hearts liberal." But other readers expressed concern about a miscarriage of justice.

In July of 1975, while Gerald Ford was running for re-election against Jimmy Carter, reporter Dick Carlson and I were invited to the White House to interview the president. The interview was conducted in the Oval office. It was a far different scene from the 1957 interview with Mr. Eisenhower in the East Room when cameras were not allowed. We had to be careful not to trip over television cables. A Secret Service Agent told us his main job was protecting the President from falling down, a joking reference to Mr. Ford's undeserved reputation of being a "klutz." I recalled that Mr. Ford was an All-American football player in college so he had to have pretty good foot movement.

*President Gerald Ford welcomes Pete Noyes (left) and reporter Dick Carlson (center) to the Oval Office in 1976.*

The interview went extremely well and excerpts made the front page of the New York *Times* the next day. Afterwards the President took us into the side room of the Oval Office and showed us presidential memorabilia dating back to the time of Thomas Jefferson. Shortly after I returned home I received a large envelope from the White House containing an autographed picture of the President with me and Carlson. After Jimmy Carter won the election over Mr. Ford in November of 1976, I decided to do something that might subject me to criticism by my journalism colleagues. In the final days of his presidency I wrote Mr. Ford a letter urging clemency for Private Richard Hagelberger.

Mr. Ford did not grant Hagelberger clemency before leaving office. But his action was in line with the recommendations of Chief Justice Burger. He removed the "no parole" provision in the case of the "Eisenhower Six" and left the matter of freedom up to the discretion of federal parole boards. The U.S. Pardon Attorney had no objections and on June 6, 1977 Richard Hagelberger was the first of the group released from prison. It seemed obvious to me that Mr. Ford had ignored the recommendation of fellow Republican Eisenhower that "no future clemency" be extended to Richard Hagelberger. In my view that took a lot of guts on Mr. Ford's part. Just before his release from prison, Hagelberger sent me a letter of thanks for what I had done on his behalf. He concluded:

"It's going to be a new world out there. I have so many things I'll have to learn. I'll have to start from scratch. I don't have anything out there. All I have is what I leave here with. But I'll make it because I want to. I have a strong desire to stay out of these places." My long obsession with the case was finally at an end. When I last heard from Dick Hagelberger he was married and owned a Christmas tree farm in Oregon.

# 14

## THE DALE CAR, A DREAM OR A NIGHTMARE?

P.T. Barnum was probably right when he proclaimed "there's a sucker born every minute." So called "snake oil salesmen" have been thriving ever since the Serpent suggested that Eve persuade Adam to take that first bite of the apple.

The classic snake oil salesman in my lifetime was a husky guy who dressed up as a woman, topped his head with a wig consisting of shoulder length red curls, and said he had a solution for the energy crisis confronting the American public in the mid 1970s, a classy three wheel roadster that got 70 miles to the gallon of gas.

Jerry Dean Michael, who put on a dress and assumed the name of G. Elizabeth Carmichael, was well aware that if he called a press conference in Hollywood about his imaginary invention, hordes of reporters and photographers would show up. And they did. TV and newspaper stories about the "Dale Car" and the gutsy redhead riding out of the west who was going to challenge Detroit's "Big Three" automakers began appearing everywhere.

The stories were especially effective on television. A version of the Dale was on display at a showroom on Ventura Boulevard in the L.A. suburb of Encino. It provided a stunning image for the camera with its glistening yellow paint job and made for beautiful TV. Unfortunately, no reporter took the time to look under the hood. Had they done so, they would have learned the Dale had no motor. It was a sham. But because of the glowing press and TV accounts extolling the Dale's make believe aerodynamics and great gas mileage, investors began plunking down millions of dollars in option money to acquire the car once it went into production. And where was the car going to be produced? "Right here in Southern California," Carmichael said, "at the old Lockheed Aircraft plant in Burbank."

**G, Elizabeth Carmichael and her phony three-wheel car, the "Dale."**

We had been looking around for good investigative stories and decided there were some serious questions that should be asked about this so-called wonder car. An interview with Carmichael was quickly arranged. On arriving in the lobby of the showroom we noticed that of the men seated there was Frank Hronek, a legendary investigator for the District Attorney's office who had set up the wire taps on potential suspects during the Black Dahlia murder investigation. We both knew Frank quite well and asked what he was doing there. He said one of his mob acquaintances, Sammy Lisner, was working for the 20th Century Motor Car Company and had some information to share. That should have been the first thing that tipped us off that something was askew, but in all honesty it didn't. Later we found Carmichael had surrounded himself with a slew of ex-convicts. One of them was William Dale Miller who was shot to death in the Encino showroom by another ex-con, Jack Oliver a few months after we did our initial interview with Carmichael.

Carmichael cut an imposing figure as a woman. She stood 6 feet 2 inches tall, had fists like a boxer and weighed at least 210 pounds. To make a point to us during the interview, she got up from her desk, planted her right foot on an end table, and put her hand to her chin, a common enough gesture for men, but not for a woman. It got us to thinking. Could G. Elizabeth really be a guy? That became an overriding consideration as we proceeded with our investigation

In November of 1974 Elizabeth Carmichael's sales promotion was pretty much jump started by reporter Dan Jedlicka of the Chicago *Sun Times* whose story screamed with the headline: **THIS ONE JUST MAY BE THE CAR OF THE CENTURY.** You can't get much better press than that!

Jedlicka quoted Carmichael as saying her chief engineer was Frank McGuiness who worked seven years "on the Saturn rocket program." Carmichael added, "I wouldn't have employees like this if I wasn't determined to write a new chapter in automotive history" The yellow Dale mock-up on display in the showroom was described by Jedlicka as having a "sleek aerodynamic" look. He wrote: "Mrs. Carmichael tends to talk about the Dale as if it were an appliance. She points to its printed circuit dashboard, which eliminates the need for wires, just like a modern television set."

To quote Carmichael again: "All accessories, radio, heater and air conditioner, simply plug into the printed circuit dash. Everybody except maybe (billionaire) J. Paul Getty and some of his friends will be interested in the Dale. We're not ignoring the public's demand for good, low cost transportation. We're going to fill one hell of an important gap in the car market. We're going to revolutionize personal transportation." No one seemed to be paying attention to the old axiom, "If it sounds too good to be true it probably is."

Carmichael predicted she'd sell 88,000 cars during the first production year, a quarter of a million the second year. She claimed to have millions of dollars in backing from private parties. She predicted Detroit's Big Three automakers would try to "hurt" her project but the self proclaimed widowed mother of five said she was prepared to fight back. Invited to a guest spot on Johnny Carson's *"Tonight Show"* on the NBC lot in Burbank, she was repeatedly cheered and applauded by the studio audience as she vowed to slug it out with Detroit automakers.

So how was Carmichael going to do something no one else in the industry could do, get 70 miles to the gallon in her Dale car? Easy, Carmichael explained:

*"The Dale is 190 inches long and weighs less than a thousand pounds, the lighter the car the better the mileage. By eliminating a wheel in the rear we saved 300 pounds and knocked more than $300 off the Dale's price. The body is made from rocket structural resin, which is*

*stronger than steel. I drove it into a wall at 30 miles an hour and there was no damage. I didn't get hurt."*

And on and on she went. There were no gadgets on the car. The air conditioner had no moving parts. The power train assembly could be removed by simply taking off "four nuts." The Dale would run on a two-cylinder air-cooled engine, producing 40 horsepower which would account for its 70 miles to the gallon ride, all this at a cost of around $2,000.

Carmichael claimed she had a Bachelor of Science degree in automotive engineering from Ohio State University and an MBA in marketing from the University of Miami. She also described herself as one of the original participants in the Powder Puff Derby and described her occupation as "automotive engineer." None of this checked out and fueled our suspicions all the more.

When a story likes this appears in the newspapers, television news editors salivate. The story had everything, a beautiful and brainy woman battling Detroit with a dream that made economic sense. The Dale car came on the scene at the time of a major gasoline shortage with cars backed up for blocks waiting to buy gas. Just about every station in Los Angeles gave major coverage to G. Elizabeth Carmichael and her 20th Century Motor Car Company. It was truly one of the great scams of the 20th Century.

We ended up doing 30 stories on the Dale car fraud. Our initial efforts were somewhat tame because we knew little, if anything about the history of G. Elizabeth Carmichael. Our first story openly questioned the viability of the Dale car but missed its mark by quite a distance. The day after it appeared I was shocked to learn that two of our engineers on the ABC lot were so impressed with our Dale report they went out to the showroom and put option money down on the car. Perhaps our initial presentation was truly a failure to communicate our actual suspicion that the Dale car was a fraud. I guess our journalistic failing was that we tried to have all our reports evenly balanced and the stories somehow tilted in Carmichael's favor.

We interviewed a member of the Society of Automotive Engineers who expressed reservations about the Dale project and how it would be built. So we decided to see for ourselves, and simply walked in unannounced with a camera crew at a gigantic building abandoned by Lockheed Aircraft Company where Carmichael said she was going to mass produce the Dale. There were half a dozen men in white smocks standing around, doing nothing. There was no production line. We couldn't find as much as a wrench. It was strong evidence that Carmichael was strictly all hot air, and nothing more than a smart talking con artist. That was the story we told on KABC that night.

We learned our story triggered an assassination plot by Carmichael. Authorities in the District Attorney's office said she offered a hit man $6,000 to kill three people, prosecutor Bob Youngdahl who had started looking into the scam, reporter Carlson and myself. The hired gun reportedly told the D.A. he pulled out of the deal because $6,000 was simply not enough money to kill the three of us. And besides that, he wanted to clear up another case in which he was criminally charged.

Our TV reports on the scam were called, "The Dale Car: a Dream or a Nightmare?" The nightmare became apparent in our report on "The secret life of G. Elizabeth Carmichael." We flashed her picture on the television screen and then dissolved to a picture of man who looked very much like her – at least in the face. His name: Jerry Dean Michael, a convicted fraudster who had jumped

$50,000 bail in U.S. District Court 1960 and had been on the run ever since, scamming the public at every turn. Indeed Michael was married, had a wife and five children. News Director Bill Fyffe threw his arms around me the night we broadcast the story. "My God," he said, "your story is unbelievable."

Before Michael could be busted in L.A. he moved his scam to Dallas, Texas. I quickly notified my friend Earl Golz on the *Dallas Morning News*, but before he could get anything in print, Carmichael did more TV interviews and collected several million dollars in option money from gullible Texas investors. Then he skipped town again.

Finally Jerry Dean Michael was indicted by the Los Angeles County Grand Jury. I was the lead-off witness. A nationwide search for the fugitive began. And in a matter of days he was arrested hiding out in women's clothing in a Florida motel. He was strip searched after being taken into custody. A local reporter asked the sheriff if Michael were a man or a woman. "Boy," the sheriff drawled, "that's a man. Make no mistake about it." So Jerry Dean Michael was returned to L.A., all the time insisting he was a woman, thanks to a "partial" sex change operation. Justice was swift. Michael was found guilty, but allowed to go free on $50,000 bail posted by a perfume company whose bosses apparently believed she was a gutsy woman wronged by the justice system and had a great story to tell.

It was hardly a surprise to me that Michael jumped bail causing the perfume company to forfeit its $50,000 investment. Eight years later Michael was finally arrested, on a fugitive warrant in Arkansas. He was brought back to L.A. and sentenced to 10 years in an all male prison on his fraud conviction. I had trouble tracking Michael in the California prison system. In fact I couldn't find him listed anywhere.

Then I learned that the day before he was sent to the big house he contacted a notary public who came to county jail and provided the paper work that legally changed Michael's name to G. Elizabeth Carmichael. It boggled my mind. How do you go serve time in a men's prison with a name like that? But somehow G. Elizabeth Carmichael alias Jerry Dean Michael survived. After his release from prison he retired to a small town. Would you believe the name of the town? It was Dale, Texas where his death was reported with virtually no fanfare in 2006. A footnote: Our story about the Dale Car fraud was given television's highest honor, the Peabody Award.

# 15

## TENNIS ANYONE?

It goes without saying that television news is a strange business, one in which virtue is seldom its own reward. My colleague, Dick Carlson, who shared the Peabody award with me, was fired despite the overwhelming good will and publicity he brought to the station. Carlson figured his days were numbered when reporters were summoned to a dressing room to pick up their new blue blazers with the number 7 (for KABC-TV Channel 7) emblazoned in gold on the upper left pocket. When Carlson got to the front of the line the tailor said he didn't have a jacket for him. "Why?" demanded Carlson. The tailor shrugged his shoulders and advised Dick that he didn't make jackets for those who were about to be sacked by the station.

Meantime, I was offered the job of news director at the CBS station in San Diego and my ego got the best of me. News Director is the prime position in a television newsroom because that's where the money is. I knew I could do the job. I had a great run at the CBS station in Sacramento in the same position, so why not? Since Carlson was out of work I persuaded him to join forces with me and he became my anchorman.

Talk about nightmares, KFMB, the CBS affiliate in San Diego, was one of my worst. I reported for work on the Friday after Thanksgiving in 1975 and virtually the entire station went out on strike that day. Teenagers who had absolutely no experience with a commercial camera were running around taking pictures. Anyone who walked in off the street could qualify as a reporter. Management types were working as engineers, with very little knowledge of what they were doing. Getting a filmed story on the air was akin to a miracle. Ray Wilson, the dour former station anchorman, was put back on the air after a long absence, and he relished reading the news despite the lack of skilled technical people and professional writers.

It didn't take me long to figure out what was happening. Station General Manager Robert L. Meyer intended to bust the union that represented most of his employees, IBEW, the International Brotherhood of Electrical Workers. Meyer apparently had the blessing of the man who owned the company, August L. Meyer (no relation), the octogenarian president of Mid-West Broadcasting. The plan to oust the union was simple. After a hundred days or so several "good" engineers would be enticed to cross the picket lines and go back to work. When that happened, Bob Meyer predicted, the rest would follow. Then he would slam the door on those union employees he considered trouble makers.

The reporters and anchormen and women, members of AFTRA, stayed out of work less than a week. But the cameramen, engineers and technicians picketed day after day. After several months, as Meyer had foretold, several members of their union crossed the picket lines and went back to work. Then the strike collapsed and Bob Meyer had a field day padding the payroll with the sons and daughters of his corporate buddies. Meyer's young son was given a top engineering position. One of those hired to work in the newsroom without my knowledge was Eric Sorenson, the son of one of Meyer's college class-mates. Sorenson went on to become a CBS news pro-ducer. Years later when he became a news director at the CBS station in L.A. he apologized to me for the way he was hired behind my back.

Our intent to turn the station into a news powerhouse was pretty much put on hold by the strike. San Diego, one of the most beautiful cities in the world, was also one of the most corrupt. One of its leading citizens, C. Arnholt Smith, teamed up with a major organized crime figure, Tony Alessio, to buy the San Diego Padres baseball team with no money down. Mafia figure Morris (Mo) Dalitz, head of Cleveland's notorious "Mayfield Road Gang," found a friendly atmosphere in San Diego and set up shop at the La Costa Country Club which usually was crawling with mob figures.

When I got there I was shocked to learn San Diego did not have paramedics. There was a measure on the election ballot to create a paramedic system, but there appeared to be considerable opposition. So I decided to produce a series of special reports on the subject. The leader of the opposition, a La Jolla businessman, told me "If we do get paramedics they'll spend 90 per cent of their time picking up old people who'll soon be dead anyway. So who needs paramedics?" Despite such incredible cyn-icism San Diego voters approved the use of paramedics in 1976, and I truly believed that our stories were instrumental in the passage of the ballot measure.

Meantime, after little more than a year on the job I heard from several newspaper reporters that my days were numbered at the San Diego station along with those of Dick Carlson. I truly believe we were hired simply because of our experience and the belief that we could get the news on the air if there were a strike. Bob Meyer made all sorts of promises to me including one not to hire Dr. Frank Magid, the television guru who consulted with station managers about the quality of their news broadcasts, and was widely detested by working journalists. Shortly after the strike Meyer retained the Magid organization, and when I reminded him of his promise to me he said, "So I lied." Almost after walking in the door Magid decided I was trying to undermine his efforts to "modernize" the newsroom. Magid assigned a young guy named Jim Schwinn to meet with various members of my reporting staff. Schwinn first wanted to meet with Bob Dale, an off-beat reporting type who was loved by the people of San Diego. "Bob," I said, "this is Jim Schwinn of the Magid Company. He'd like to sit down and chat with you." Without missing a beat Dale responded, "Magid, Magid. I thought that was something you found on the bottom of a garbage can." That set the tone for the meeting and I quickly fell out of favor with Schwinn who seemed convinced I had scripted Dale's remark.

As our days were winding down in San Diego, Carlson and I came across one more story that attracted nationwide attention. It was the strange tale of Renee Richards who was featured in a newspaper story after winning an invitational tennis tournament at the La Jolla County Club. There was a picture of the 33-year-old Richards in *The La Jolla Light* standing a good head taller than the tournament favorite she whipped, a 16-year-old high school girl who had been shut out 6-0, 6-0. Richards entered the tournament using a bogus name as a representative of a Newport Beach tennis club. We got the impression she looked more like a guy than a gal. "Here we go again," I said to myself.

We established quickly that Renee Richards was the person participating in the La Jolla tournament. She was a practicing ophthalmologist. So our next check was with the California Medical Board. Yes, a board spokesperson said, Richards was qualified to practice medicine in California. "That is all we can tell you." Unfortunately board officials lied. We went directly to Governor Jerry Brown who after considerable soul searching informed the medical board it must abide by the California Public Records Act and give us all the vital information it had on Richards.

We learned that Dr. Renee Richards was actually born Richard Raskind on August 19, 1934 in New York to Josephine Raskind, a psychiatrist, and Dr. David Raskind, an orthopedic surgeon. That was a solid starting point. Now there was much more to find out about him. Raskind started playing tennis at eight and became one of the top junior players in the country, captain of his school team, and later a standout performer at Yale. After a stint in the Navy in which he reached the rank of lieutenant commander, Raskind returned to New York, and married a young woman. They had a son named David. But apparently Raskind felt overwhelmed by the urge to become a woman. So in 1975 he had a sex change operation and moved to California where he began the practice of medicine under the name of Renee Richards.

Before the sex change Raskind was rated one of the top male amateur tennis players in the state of New York. Now as a woman she aimed her sights on the U. S. Open and the La Jolla tournament would be a tune-up. Carlson called Renee Richards and told her we were prepared to do a story about her deception in San Diego, and would she comment? Richards had nothing to say. Two days later when we were preparing to broadcast the story, Richards called Carlson and she said she would kill herself if we put the story on the air. It was an extremely difficult decision to make, but I instructed Carlson to go ahead with the story. After the broadcast Richards called Carlson and thanked him for the tasteful way he told the story. I was roundly criticized by CBS commentator Bill Stout for invading Richards' privacy. I could stand the brickbats but I was taken aback a week later when the new NBC comedy, "*Saturday Night Live*," satirized the story with the title, "*TENNIS WITHOUT BALLS*."

Richards was initially denied permission to play in the U.S. Open for Women, but the New York Supreme Court overturned that decision, and in 1977 Richards and Betty Ann Stuart reached the doubles finals of the U.S. Open before losing. At one time, Richards was ranked 20th among women tennis players throughout the world. In later years she twice coached Martina Navratilova while she was winning successive singles championships at Wimbledon.

The Renee Richards story won a local Emmy for investigative reporting, but I wasn't around to accept it. I had long since been unceremoniously booted out of the CBS station, and had gone to work for NBC in Burbank, California where I would spend the next 20 years of my life in a professional organization that meant business when it came to covering the news.

It was a shame but the San Diego job was Dick Carlson's swan song as a TV news reporter and anchorman. He moved on to Washington and ran the Voice of America for six years. After that he was named Ambassador to the Seychelles, a group of 100 islands off the coast of East Africa, followed by an appointment as chief of the Corporation for Public Broadcasting in Washington D.C.

# 16

# THE COVER UP OF A MADMAN'S CRIME

James Warren Jones, the self-styled prophet better known as the Reverend Jim Jones, founder of the so-called "People's Temple," certainly ranks as one of the greatest madmen in the history of the United States. The story has been told over and over again of how Jones' armed guards assassinated a U.S. Congressman and half a dozen others on a fact finding mission in the jungles of South American country of Guyana. Then Jones with hypnotic like persuasion induced hundreds of his followers to swallow Kool Aid laced with cyanide resulting in the largest mass suicide in the history of the western world. In the horrible grand finale Jones was shot to death by one of his guards who then killed himself. The date was November, 18, 1978. Jones was just 49 years old.

There were 918 victims including 226 children at the encampment known as "Jonestown." Most of the youngsters were foster kids placed in Jones' care by state agencies in California, ignorant of the fact that he was a sexual deviate. The adults who died had followed their prophet to Jonestown from his temples in San Francisco and Los Angeles for what he promised would be a better life in a communal environment. Representative Leo Ryan, a Democrat representing South San Francisco, had flown to Jonestown with members of his staff and a NBC television crew in response to complaints that Jones was holding some people against their will.

After inspecting the encampment the congressman, staff members and reporters, were about to depart from the nearby Port Kaitani air strip when a group of gunmen rode up to their plane in a truck trailer and began firing. Ryan was killed as were two of my colleagues at NBC, reporter Don Harris and cameraman Bob Brown. Also slain were San Francisco Examiner photographer Greg Robinson and Jonestown defector Patricia Parks. Among the survivors was Ryan's legal aide, Jackie Speier who was shot five times and left in critical condition at the air strip. (Eventually she recovered and was elected to Congress from the San Francisco area.) Other survivors included reporter Tim Reiterman of the San Francisco Examiner, who was hit by several gunshots, and two other NBC employees, soundman Steve Sung, who suffered a severe bullet wound in an arm and producer Bob Flick who was not hurt. Ryan was the first and only member of Congress to be killed in the line of duty.

The bodies of 400 Jonestown victims went unclaimed and were buried in a common grave in Oakland, California. The vast majority of the dead were African-Americans But this is not a story about the human massacre at Jonestown. Rather it's about what I'm convinced was a cover up that allowed Jim Jones to escape registration as a sex offender and set up his house of horrors in Jonestown at what was supposed to be an agricultural commune governed by socialist principles on 3,000 acres of land leased from the Marxist leaning government of Guyana.

Our investigative unit at KNBC in Burbank, California was the first to tell the story of Jones' infamous sex crime arrest. On December 13, 1973, five years before the massacre, Jones was arrested at four in the afternoon by two LAPD plain clothes vice officers in the restroom of a run-down movie house on South Alvarado Street, about a mile from the L.A. branch of his People's Temple Church. The officers had gone to the Westlake Theater in response to complaints from neighborhood residents about vagrants who were engaged in lewd conduct.

The officers said they were seated in the balcony when Jones made a "homosexual overture." Jones then led them to a restroom. One of the officers went inside and saw Jones enter a stall. He said Jones emerged from the stall "...masturbating with his right hand" and pointing directly at them to join him.

Officers Larry Kaegle and Lloyd Frost arrested Jones and booked him at the Rampart Police Station for violating Section 647a of the California Penal Code, known commonly as "lewd conduct." Jones was released on $500 bond.

Several days after his arrest Jones and several of his aides showed up at the Rampart Police Station and offered to donate $5,000 to the station fund which was used for various programs not financed with taxpayer money. Captain Jim Marchessano was so incensed he ordered Jones and the others to get out of the station. Lieutenant Bob Macintosh, commander of the vice squad, declared: "It was a veiled bribe. They were talking about a lewd charge and the amount of the donation, but it didn't meet the definition of bribery." I found that conclusion difficult to accept.

On December 20, 1973 Jones appeared in court for his arraignment before Judge Clarence (Red) Stromwall, once a member of the LAPD's legendary "Hat Squad," a team of four tough homicide cops known for their fancy suits and wide brimmed hats. But he was anything but tough when attorney David Kwan brought his client before the bar of justice. Judge Stromwall dismissed the charge against Jones on grounds of insufficient evidence after there was no objection from the young city prosecutor assigned to the case. The arresting officers were not even called as witnesses. Jones did stipulate through his attorney that the cops had "probable cause to arrest him."

A more astonishing event took place in the same courtroom the following February 1 when Judge Stromwall ordered all records in the Jones case "sealed and destroyed" on a motion by defense attorney Kwan.

The lawyer had a reputation in legal circles as a guy who could get things done at the courthouse. Two years later in 1975, he was acquitted on felony charges that he took $8,500 to guarantee immunity from prosecution to a man targeted in a medical fraud investigation.

All of the legal chicanery in the Jones case remained out of public view until the mass suicide at Jonestown. I had just taken on new duties in the investigative unit at the NBC station when I received a call from officer Kaegle. He told me about the cover up of all the sordid details involving Jones' arrest in 1973 and his futile attempts to bring the situation to the attention of his superiors. Kaegle said he was convinced political influence had a hand in scuttling the charges against Jones and he had brought the matter to the attention of the FBI.

I immediately sent my researcher, Don Ray, to the various city and state offices where criminal records are kept to determine if there was any physical evidence of the arrest of James Warren Jones on Dec. 13, 1973. To Ray's surprise a clerk at one of the offices handed him the Jones criminal file which was clearly marked "Seal and Destroy" on the order of the court. For whatever reason, the people working in the clerk's office had declined to obey the judge's order.

We were told it was illegal in California to seal a sex crime file, much less destroy it. The state attorney's general's office had a special unsealing detail that regularly went to court to open the records of those involved in sex crimes, and we learned that the unit was already investigating the Jones case.

The file handed over to Ray had just about every necessary detail for an all inclusive story including the original police report and the court docket which included a final notation to "seal and destroy" the entire record.

**The unsigned court document dismissing charges against Jim Jones and ordering records in the case "sealed and destroyed."**

Much of the legal heavy lifting to keep Jones' arrest away from the news media was done by Timothy Stoen, an assistant district attorney in San Francisco. Deputy State Attorney General Mike Franchetti told me that Stoen approached him directly about purging Jones' file. He said "certain people" wanted to "get" Jones and it would be a terrible thing if they discovered his arrest. Franchetti added, "I told him what the law was and that we would not comply." But Franchetti acknowledged that some unknown person in his department had flagged Jones' file with the possible intention of removing it.

Stoen, a Stanford law school graduate, took Jones' case to the highest levels of the LAPD He apparently persuaded an aide to Deputy Chief Ed Davis to write a letter of support for Jones. Stoen even arranged a meeting with another deputy chief, Dale Speck. I called Speck and he seemed surprised that I knew about the meeting. He said his recollection was that he told Stoen "it was not our affair, that it was an issue between Jones and the courts."

All this, of course, took place five years before the madness at Jonestown. Eventually Timothy Stoen turned into one of Jones' harshest critics when he also became a victim of the tragedy. Stoen's six-year-old son was one of those who died at Jonestown.

After the furor erupted over the dismissal of the lewd charge against Jones, the besieged Judge Stromwall issued a three page memorandum in which he answered questions from his critics. Stromwall wrote in part:

*"During 1973 and for a period of approximately five years as judge at the Metropolitan Misdemeanor Arraignment Court, I handled in excess of 1,000 cases per week. I have no independent recollection of handling a case over five years ago involving a Jim Jones among*

*the, many thousands of cases appearing in court during that period."*

Judge Stromwall also defended his order to destroy the record of Jones' arrest. He said since Jones had been found factually innocent, the state did not have a compelling interest in keeping the arrest record. California Attorney General Evelle Younger disagreed and challenged the ruling, but a local appellate court upheld Stromwall's decision in this specific case.

But the burning question remained, why was the charge dismissed in the first place? The city attorney's office conducted an investigation but failed to determine who made the decision not to prosecute Jim Jones. A juvenile official in Mendocino County in Northern California said he would never have allowed more than 100 foster children to be turned over to Jones had he known about the sex crime allegations. At the time Timothy Stoen was an assistant district attorney in Mendocino County and, of course until their falling out, he was one of Jones' most trusted advisors. It's believed he recommended the foster kids be turned over to Jones.

Our discovery of Jones' arrest in 1973 only seemed to compound the tragedy at Jonestown five years later. Our parent employer, NBC News, which lost two excellent employees in the slaughter at Jonestown, never once reported on its national broadcasts our story about the cover up of Jones' arrest for a sex crime in Los Angeles. I was told the bosses at NBC News just didn't want to hear anything more about Jim Jones; that they were "tired of the whole ugly story." Truthfully it was an ugly story but so was the Holocaust.

# 17

## SILENCE ABOUT A NUCLEAR MELTDOWN

When I went to work at NBC's west coast headquarters in Burbank, California I didn't realize that one of my first investigative stories would be tied to an event in my life almost 20 years before. The date was July 12, 1959. I was working the night city desk at City News Service when City Hall reporter Ridgley Cummings called me and told me about "...a major story in the works." The city's radiation monitor at City Hall has just given off an extremely dangerous reading, about ten times above what's considered the safe level. Cummings said he checked and rechecked the figures with the people in charge of reading the radiation monitor and he strongly advised me to go with the story. So I went with it, and soon the story was all over the Southern California air waves.

The next day, the dayside editor ran a retraction stating that the radiation story was based on faulty information. When I got to work that afternoon boss and owner Joe Quinn, a colonel in the U.S. Army Reserve, walked up to me in the city room and said he had just fired Ridgley Cummings, and that I must be more careful in checking copy from reporters. Truthfully Cummings was an excellent reporter and I had never seen him make a factual error in one of his stories. But now everyone at City Hall was damning him as a "tabloid crazy" who spun out of control on a "scare story." Cummings set up his own business reporting from City Hall for community newspapers, but his career was effectively ruined. He was the same reporter who a few years later tipped me to the lack of drinking fountains in the L.A. Dodgers new baseball stadium in Chavez Ravine. Not long after that he choked to death while eating pistachio nuts.

In 1979 I learned much to my surprise that Ridgley Cummings had been vindicated, and what had happened 20 years before was part of a deadly government cover up. At the time he reported the radiation danger there had been a partial nuclear meltdown of a sodium reactor at the Santa Susana Field Laboratory in an isolated foothill area northwest of Los Angeles. There was great fanfare when the reactor went on line in 1957. Edward R. Murrow, the legendary CBS newsman, did a special segment on the reactor in his program, "See It Now." Murrow told how the reactor was capable of lighting up and powering the city of Moorpark in the Conejo Valley. The film showed street lights turning on and a small boy reading from a lamp, the result of nuclear energy from the sodium reactor. I had the greatest respect for Murrow but in all honesty his story seemed to be a propaganda message on behalf of the Atomic Energy Commission.

There was not one word anywhere, not in the newspapers, radio or television, when the nuclear meltdown took place. Years later it was determined the damage to the rods in the sodium reactor unleashed many more times the radiation than the widely reported nuclear disaster at Pennsylvania's Three Mile Island in 1979. It was learned that after the initial meltdown officials kept turning the sodium reactor on and off in the hope of solving the problem. Finally, 14 days later they ordered the reactor shut down and dismantled.

The cover up that went on for 20 years until a group of UCLA students led by Michael Rose and Professor Daniel Hirsch learned what had happened and then proved it by going straight to the archives of the old Atomic Energy Commission. It had been the policy of the AEC to send cameramen to the site of a nuclear accident to film the damage and subsequent cleanup. The UCLA students and Dr. Hirsch, formed an organization called "Bridge the Gap," filed for the AEC film under the Freedom of Information Act and to their surprise, got just about everything in the government archives.

They brought the film to our investigative unit at KNBC where I viewed it with reporter Warren Olney, son of the famed California special prosecutor. We were stunned by what we saw. The film showed workers cleaning the top secret Field Laboratory, most with no protective covering on their faces. A study by UCLA's School of Public Health released in 1997 found 100 cancer deaths among workers at the facility who were exposed to high levels of radiation. At the time of the accident in 1959 there were very few people living in the foothills near the lab first operated by Atomics International, then later by the Rocketdyne Corporation. The area built up quickly during the Southern California housing boom. The disclosure of the meltdown and two subsequent nuclear accidents caused widespread apprehension among people living in the area. Repeated demands for a "superfund cleanup" were ignored by the federal government. Apart from the nuclear problems, there was continuous rocket testing at the facility and the chemicals used to wash the rockets poisoned virtually all the underground water in the area.

We were allowed to take our NBC cameras into the field laboratory. Suddenly we noticed a giant hole in the ground – it looked about 50 feet deep – and there were workmen down deep doing something. I got chills up my spine when our guide told us the hole was the site of the old sodium reactor and it was expected to remain "hot" for another 20 to 30 years. "But not to worry," she said. "We're taking care of the problem."

One of those who disagreed vehemently with that conclusion years later was State Senator Sheila Kuehl. Rocketdyne had sold the 2,850 acre site to the Boeing Aircraft Corporation which announced plans to turn it over to housing developers. Senator Kuehl warned that families who purchased homes could be exposed to such deadly elements as Strontium-90 and Cesium-137, nuclear elements that have a life span of 200 to 300 years according to the best scientific estimates. I knew that to be a fact. About 10 years previously the Santa Monica Mountains Conservancy had obtained a plot of land adjacent to the field laboratory, the so-called Sage Ranch, where cattle once grazed. After the meltdown it was more than a coincidence that the cattle started dying.

In 1996 I planned to do another story on the meltdown and asked the Conservancy to see a copy of their environmental impact report on the land. I was given a flat turn down. So I filed for the report under the California Public Records Act, and won a ruling that I must be given access to it. The conservancy lawyer's begrudgingly let me read the report but would not let me copy it. It showed there were elements of Strontium-90 and Cesium-137 throughout the area. Strontium-90 and Cesium-137 were critical elements of the atomic bombs dropped on the Japanese cities of Hiroshima and Nagasaki during World War II that led to Japan's surrender to the Allied forces.

For years I failed to understand why there was little, if any reaction to our stories describing the dangers inherent in a nuclear meltdown so powerful it twisted the reactor rods like putty and posed a clear and present danger to the surrounding community. From the start the Department of Energy had given the impression that it was protecting the Field Laboratory, one of its prime contractors, from public scrutiny, and not once did it ask that the area be declared a superfund site. In January of 2008, almost 50 years after the meltdown, Governor Arnold Schwarzenegger signed into law a bill sponsored by Senator Kuehl requiring that the 2,850 acre site be placed on the state's superfund list requiring a cleanup meeting the strictest standards in the nation. And until that is done the current owner, the Boeing Corporation, won't be able to sell it to developers as planned.

The credit for uncovering the government's 20-year blackout on the nuclear accident must go solely to Professor Daniel Hirsch and his UCLA students who unlocked the box containing those secrets through the Freedom of Information Act. In this particular case we in the news media simply acted as conduits when we should have been doing our job way back in 1959 when the meltdown took place. Professor Hirsch doggedly kept the story before the public for many years and won acclaim from both Democratic and Republican legislators for acting in the public interest. To me the bottom line on the story is determining how many people died as the result of the nuclear contamination. One woman whose husband was involved in the early cleanup after the meltdown told me her husband died a horrible death from three different types of cancer. We were told nearly everyone involved in the cleanup suffered radiation poisoning. One scientific survey estimated the nuclear accident may have caused as many as 1,800 cases of cancer within 62 miles of the site "over a period of many decades." Jim Arness, the veteran actor who starred in one of TV's biggest hits, "*Gunsmoke*," joined in a class action suit seeking damages for the radiation poisoning that engulfed the area. Arness owned property close to the nuclear facility.

Thinking back to that period when the meltdown took place, I have to admit I was asleep at the switch along with the rest of the reporters in L.A except for Ridgley Cummings, who wrote the truth and got fired for it.

POSTSCRIPT 20013

In January of 2013 the U.S. Environmental Protection Agency completed a three-year study that showed hundreds of sites in and around the area of the nuclear meltdown were still badly contaminated. More than half-a-century later scientists found the area strewn with chemical and radiological contamination. The EPA confirmed there was a strong presence of Strontium-90 and Cessium-137 among the cancer causing elements found at the site,. These, of course, were key elements of the first atomic bombs that devastated the Japanese cities of Hiroshima and Nagasaki during World War II. Still undetermined, who will pay for the cleanup, the federal government or the state of California? The feds appear to be backing off even though the meltdown occurred on their watch under the aegis of the old U.S. Atomic Energy Commission.

# BERYLLIUM-DEADLY WONDER

The nuclear age was born in the U.S, on Dec. 2, 1942 at an indoor squash court under the grandstands of an abandoned football stadium, Stagg Field, at the University of Chicago, named for the school's legendary football coach Amos Alonzo Stagg. It was there that a team of scientists led by famed Italian scientist Enrico Fermi touched off the first sustained nuclear chain reaction, giving birth to the development of the atomic bomb which would ultimately bring a halt to World War II in the Pacific with its devastation of the Japanese cities of Nagasaki and Hiroshima.

Much has been written about the U.S. crash program called the Manhattan Project which led to the development of the A-Bomb. It was there that scientists and metallurgists worked round the clock, knowing all the while that their counterparts in Nazi Germany were involved in a similar race to harness nuclear energy and give Adolf Hitler the ultimate weapon of mass destruction.

In 1986 a source in the administration of President Ronald Reagan told me I should investigate the cause of a mysterious disease that afflicted many of the scientists who worked on the Manhattan project. The disease was beryl-liosis, also known as chronic beryllium disease. Beryllium is a most unusual metal. It is lighter than aluminum and stronger than steel. Early in the 20th century it was found to be the critical ingredient for building lightweight bicycles. At the start of the Manhattan Project scientists concluded it would be the perfect metal to house the deadly components of the first atomic bombs.

But the scientists and metallurgists who worked with beryllium apparently knew little about its toxic effects. Interviews with several of those involved in the Manhattan Project revealed that in their haste to develop the atomic bomb they shaved the beryllium ore right at their work place without any protective covering. We know now that they exposed themselves to beryllium dust. Just a few particles inhaled in the recesses of the lungs can provoke a fatal dose of berylliosis..

Probably no story I was involved with in my half-century as a journalist had a more telling impact than our series on the dangers of beryllium. I put together a news team at KNBC-TV led by veteran network correspondent David Garcia and producer Paul Skolnick and I took on the job of executive producer. During the course of our four month investigation we interviewed more than 50 persons across the country and read hundreds of government documents obtained through the Freedom of Information Act.

The story was really brought home to us when Garcia interviewed Dr. Herbert Anderson, who as a graduate student studied under Fermi at Columbia University. When Dr. Fermi became the chief architect of the Manhattan project Dr. Anderson was one of his first hires.

Garcia and Skolnick caught up with Dr. Anderson at the Los Alamos National Library in New Mexico where he was named a senior fellow following a distinguished career at Columbia University. Dr. Anderson was obviously a very sick man, suffering from acute beryllium poisoning. He breathed with an assist from an oxygen canister, and his words were labored. He was not angry about his plight and insisted he and the others working with beryllium had no idea it was so toxic. Dr. Anderson told us: *"I was grinding the stuff by hand without any protective covering. I didn't know there was anything wrong with beryllium. It looked like a perfectly reasonable material. We saved the lives of hundreds of thousands of young men. We were taking a risk and it was worth taking. We took it because we thought of ourselves as heroes."*

Two years later Dr. Anderson, one of America's great scientists, died as a direct result of his work on the atomic bomb.

The government picked up all of Dr. Anderson's medical bills because he was a federal employee. Larry Kellman, a metallurgist who worked on the Manhattan Project, wasn't so lucky. Kelman was employed by the Argonne National Laboratory, a property of the University of Chicago, which refused to accept responsibility for the beryllium poisoning that ravaged his body. Said Kellman, "Nobody ever told me what we were working with was beryllium. It was just another material." He accused the government of a cover up which he said was "bigger than Watergate."

Long before the A-Bomb came crashing down on Hiroshima, beryllium was widely used in hundreds of products, particularly household appliances. For a time it was a deadly ingredient in fluorescent lights. At the prodding of scientist Harriet Hardy, manufacturers found a way to eliminate beryllium from the makeup of fluorescents. But there is no doubt a number of people who handled broken fluorescents before the manufacturing change were exposed to the poisonous dust.

The United States is one of three countries that mines beryllium ore and exports it throughout the world. Combined with a copper alloy it is used in everything from television sets to missile guidance systems. As of 1986, when our stories were broadcast, a leading health authority, Dr. Nancy Spince, estimated as many as 800,000 Americans may have been exposed to workplace beryllium dust which sometimes takes 10 to 15 years to detect in the human body when the lungs start shrinking.

Following our reports the Reagan Administration moved quickly to tackle the beryllium problem, setting up a national registry to track down every government worker exposed to beryllium dust.

The House Subcommittee on Health and the Environment led by California Democratic Congressman Henry Waxman began an immediate campaign to track down private companies where beryllium was used in the manufacturing process to be certain workers had adequate safety gear to protect them from exposure to the metallic dust.

Our reports on NBC 4 won a Television Academy Emmy for investigative reporting. The judges said our story was one of those that truly "made a difference."

In 1999, a dozen years after our story was broadcast, President Bill Clinton and his Energy Secretary, Bill Richardson, approved an agreement to pay damages to those government workers whose bodies had been damaged by beryllium poisoning. There was one stipulation. They could not sue if they accepted the settlement.

# 19

## THE D.B. COOPER MYSTERY

"D.B. Cooper," became an instant legend when he leaped from a Northwest Airlines Boeing 727 with a huge stash of cash on Thanksgiving Eve, November 24, 1971. Beer drinking D.B Cooper fan clubs sprang up in many cities to toast the man who seemingly eluded the FBI with his daring escapade, the only unsolved skyjacking in U.S. history. Cooper boarded the plane in Portland, Oregon, and once it got off the ground he handed a stewardess a note demanding $200,000 in cash and four parachutes, then opened a suitcase that appeared to contain a bomb.

During the negotiations, which were radioed to Northwest Airline officials on the ground, the man who had purchased the airline ticket under the name of Dan Cooper, downed several shots of bourbon and chain smoked cigarettes. (No one seems to know how Dan Cooper became D.B. Cooper although it may have due to a miscommunication by the FBI.)

When the plane landed at the Seattle Airport, Cooper's demands were met. The 36 passengers and two stewardesses were allowed to get off the plane. The pilot and two crewmen remained on board as Cooper enjoined them to "get this show on the road."

The plane took off for Reno, Cooper the only person in the passenger section. About 35 minutes later the captain noticed a big drop in the cabin's pressure. Cooper parachuted out of the 727 from the cabin's rear door in freezing weather, clutching the $200,000. The plane was traveling at a speed of about 200 miles an hour. (Because of the Cooper incident, by federal decree it is now impossible for a passenger to open the back door of an airplane in flight). No trace of Cooper was ever found. But in February of 1980 an 8-year-old boy at a family picnic on the Columbia River west of Vancouver, Washington, found a packet of rotting $20 bills while digging in the sand. The boy kept digging and found 11 more packets of twenties for a total of $5,880. The FBI said serial numbers on the money showed it was part of the $200,000 in cash turned over to Cooper.

Most of the FBI agents who worked the case believed Cooper was killed in the parachute jump and his body swallowed up by the Columbia River.

In 1979 my investigative unit received information that the FBI was investigating a suspect in Stockton, California who might be the real D.B. Cooper. His name was Robert Rackstraw, a decorated Vietnam veteran. At the time of the Cooper skyjacking he would have been 26 years old. Cooper was believed to be in his thirties, or so the FBI reported. When we first got wind of the story just about everyone in law enforcement was looking for Bob Rackstraw. The FBI wanted him for stealing explosives, and for a check kiting scheme that netted him about $75,000 from three banks. He was also wanted by local police for stealing a small airplane and reporting by radio that he was ditching it after it caught fire over Monterey Bay. Later the plane was found at an Orange County airport. It had been repainted.

The FBI finally got their man after Rackstraw was returned to the United States from Iran where authorities gave him a one-way ticket home after learning he was wanted on a variety of charges including the murder of his stepfather. Rackstraw was ultimately acquitted by a jury of the murder but the other charges stuck and he went to prison.

During the Vietnam War Rackstraw served as a lieutenant in the Army's Green Berets where he worked with explosives and also spent time as a paratrooper, doing dangerous "halo jumps" behind enemy lines. Halo jumps were made at night with the parachute opening at a very low altitude to escape detection by the enemy. This was certainly enough to interest the FBI in the possibility that Rackstraw might be D.B. Cooper despite the slight age difference.

Reporter Warren Olney and I traveled to Stockton, California to interview Rackstraw in jail and determine if he could actually be the legendary D.B. Cooper. The man was a genuine war hero. He had been awarded the Silver Star, the Air Medal with 36 clusters, and the Paratrooper Good Conduct Badge. He also claimed that he was awarded five Purple Hearts for wounds suffered in combat, but proof of that could not be found in the public record. His background as a paratrooper and munitions expert certainly qualified him for official scrutiny. Bob Rackstraw told us he was not D.B. Cooper, but laughed when he said it and there seemed to be a knowing smirk on his face. That's as far as we got. The Rackstraw story made for "good copy," as reporters like to say, and Olney went on the air to report the many bizarre elements of the case and the possible link to D.B. Cooper. We found Rackstraw well educated and articulate and his daredevil reputation well deserved.

For several years I received a flurry of letters from Bob Rackstraw, berating the judicial systems and the probation officers he dealt with after his release from custody. Then the letters stopped. Many years later I picked up the phone and Bob Rackstraw was on the other end of the line. "Pete, guess what I'm doing for a living these days?" he asked. I told him I didn't have a clue. "Working as a probation officer in Orange County, dealing with all these bad guys," Bob said. I congratulated him and told him to keep up the good work now that he's on the right side of the law. In retrospect, Bob Rackstraw was just one of many tormented Vietnam veterans who searched desperately to regain a foothold in the United States after the war, sometimes at the expense of others

# 20

## MAYOR FOR SALE

Corruption has long been a way of life at the Los Angeles City Hall with the exception of a few "reformist" mayors who promised cleanups that usually failed to materialize. Sam Yorty was a mayor who led the voters to believe he was on the up and up. But his dark side proved otherwise.

Yorty's reputation as a hard line radical was just one of things he tried to suppress in his image as a conservative voice at the Los Angeles City Hall. Running as a Democrat, he was first elected to the California Assembly in 1937 and the little man with the twangy Nebraska accent quickly established himself as a left-wing social advocate and a staunch supporter of author Upton Sinclair's campaign to "End Poverty in California" (EPIC). After serving as an Army officer during World War II he moved on to Congress, eventually changing his political stripes to that of a populist Republican. He was elected mayor of L.A. in 1961 after a relentless attack on the incumbent, Norris Poulson, and his City Hall crowd, claiming they were trying to make life miserable for housewives with their proposed recycling program which would require them to separate trash into three containers. It was the same Norris Poulson who engineered the deal to bring the Brooklyn Dodgers to L.A. But Poulson lost his voice for some unexplained medical reason and couldn't be heard uttering a single word to defend himself against Yorty's attacks during the race for mayor.

One of the best kept secrets at the time was Yorty's dirty linen while attending the USC School of Law. Yorty got his girlfriend pregnant and took her to an abortionist in Hermosa Beach, California, where she died on the operating table. Local police did an extensive report which years later fell into the hands of an ex-LAPD cop who defeated Yorty for re-election in 1972, the city's first African-American mayor Tom Bradley. When Yorty learned Bradley supporters had the police report, he seemed to lose his fighting spirit. A debate with Bradley became a one sided affair with Yorty's bellicose nature subdued, and his opponent making one critical allegation after another, Yorty barely responding. Yorty lost the election.

But Sam Yorty's twelve years at City Hall were fruitful financially. He enjoyed the perks of office, taking numerous trips to promote L.A. at home and abroad, and, more importantly, promote Sam Yorty. He often beat the traffic by flying to work from the San Fernando Valley in a city helicopter. Some said his honor had illusions of grandeur when he made an aborted run for presidency of the nation. The mayor somehow became a bosom buddy of one of the richest men in the world, billionaire Armand Hammer, chairman of the Occidental Petroleum Corporation. Dr. Hammer was raised in New York City where his father was a major figure in the American Communist party and was briefly imprisoned during World War I for subversive activities. The younger Hammer earned a medical degree from Columbia University, but barely put it to use. He was always too busy courting the world's powerful people in his never ending quest for oil. Hammer grew into an international figure, respected equally by capitalists and communists alike. In the Soviet Union he was welcomed with open arms by Dictator Nikolai Lenin and given valuable art treasures from the days of Czarist Russia. Sheiks in the Middle East entrusted Dr. Hammer with their huge oil reserves. He was a power broker, an unmitigated bully who got his way at every turn. God help the politician who tried to cross him.

In 1984 our investigative unit at KNBC Television was informed by FBI sources that a major investigation was underway to determine if some members of the Los Angeles City Council accepted bribes from Dr. Hammer so he could obtain an oil drilling permit in the Pacific Palisades, a coastal enclave seven miles south of Malibu. At that time the oil reserves there were valued at five to ten billion dollars. Ostensibly the bribes were paid in the form of campaign contributions and were part of the public record. One of Dr. Hammer's biggest boosters was Councilman Art Snyder who took $33,000 from Hammer. Snyder once took a wild punch at one of my colleagues after the reporter questioned him about a letter he had written to motion picture studio bosses. In the letter Snyder suggested that if the film studios wanted to continue getting tax breaks from the city it would be a good idea to hire his teen-age bride, Michelle, as an actress-singer.

Now Dr. Hammer had been in trouble before for his political gift giving. In March of 1976 he was convicted of making an illegal $54,000 contribution in four years before to Richard Nixon's presidential campaign. When it came time for sentencing, Hammer showed up in federal court in a wheel chair, hooked up to a heart monitoring device and escorted by several male nurses. The judge was obviously sympathetic to Hammer's poor health. He gave him probation rather than a jail sentence and fined him $3,000, chump change to the billionaire. Hammer was

wheeled back outside the court. He then startled onlookers as he unhooked the heart device, leaped out of the
wheel chair and hopped into a waiting limousine which
sped away from a mob of reporters, curious to know what
miraculous cure they had just witnessed.

As for drilling in the Palisades, Dr. Hammer had an ally at
City Hall in Mayor Sam Yorty. In 1966 a test core hole author-
ized by the Office of the Los Angeles Zoning Administrator,
gave Dr. Hammer a good inkling of the vast oil reserves
below the Palisades. It was so promising that Chevron Oil
began bidding for property in the same general area. The
land in question, a vacant two acre plot, was owned by
the State of California. So Mayor Yorty had his Recreation
and Parks Department apply to the state to acquire the
land for badly needed beachfront parking, a seemingly
logical and legal request. The state complied and then
Yorty got down and dirty with Dr. Hammer. The Recreation
and Parks Department designated the land for "oil drilling
only," ignoring anything to do with public parking. Then,
without competitive bidding, the city sold the oil rich land
to Hammer for just $44,000. Yorty was rewarded with 1,000
shares of Occidental stock, and picked up a $4,500 cam-
paign contribution from Dr. Hammer. There were reports
that Hammer even offered Yorty a seat on the Occidental
Petroleum board of directors.

A grand jury investigation described the events as
"bewildering" but failed to return criminal indictments
against Dr. Hammer and the mayor. It was a corrupt a deal
as anything envisioned by Fred Howser or Big Bill Bonelli,
and it stank up the whole fabric of city government. It was
like old times at City Hall, Mayor Sam taking his cues from
the ghost of very corrupt Mayor Frank Shaw of yesteryear.

But the battle over oil drilling had just begun, and the residents of the sleepy village of Pacific Palisades awakened

ready for an all out fight with one of the world's richest men, and his sidekick, Mayor Sam. A group of house-wives formed an organization called "No Oil Inc." With a legal assist from the Center for Law In the Public Interest headed by Kennedy family confidant McGeorge Bundy, a court was persuaded to halt the drilling. But it was only temporary. The anti-Yorty forces at City Hall were quick to warn that the Pacific Palisades and its huge bluffs over-looking the Pacific Ocean were vulnerable to major land-slides. Dr. Hammer vowed to pay for any damage drilling might cause. But the opposition was adamant. Hammer then called the Center for Law In the Public Interest and warned Bundy he would ruin the organization financially if it continued to support No Oil Inc. Bundy was said to have angrily rebuffed Hammer.

So Dr. Hammer decided to do battle with the ladies of No Oil Inc. He hired a notorious mob lawyer from New Jersey, Herb Itkin, to do his dirty work. Itkin became a fed-erally protected witness after he provided the FBI with a list of all his Mafia clients rather than go to prison. He moved to Los Angeles where he changed his name to Herb Atkin, not very much of a disguise, and hired himself out as a private eye. I once interviewed Itkin/Atkin at NBC about his life as a protected witness on condition we not show his face or identify him by name. After the story was broadcast, Atkin called me and complained that none of his friends recognized him on TV.

By 1978 Dr. Hammer's plans for drilling in the Palisades were still in legislative limbo, stalled by the city coun-cil, and his buddy Sam Yorty was no longer in office. Dr. Hammer suggested that Atkin hire a woman to infiltrate No Oil Inc., telling him money was no object. So Atkin's girl-friend took the job. He leased an expensive condo for her in the Palisades and then furnished it lavishly. Dr. Hammer had suggested Atkin buy her a home but the P.I. said it wasn't necessary. The girlfriend was then equipped with a recording device which was strapped to her stomach. She advised the people at No Oil Inc. that she was pregnant, said she very much opposed to drilling and wanted to attend their regularly scheduled meetings. For almost a year Atkin would report to Dr. Hammer time after time that nothing insidious happened at the meetings; that the recordings brought to him by the girlfriend were of little, if any, value. But Hammer insisted that the spying continue.

The battle over the Palisades dragged into the 80s with Mayor Tom Bradley running the show at City Hall. Bradley had made his opposition to oil drilling in the Palisades a key issue in defeating Yorty's bid for re-election in 1972. But Dr. Hammer still had his share of supporters in the city council.

Some council members did a slow burn when the bribery charges were leaked by the FBI in 1984. Our researcher, Meera Cheryian, poured through public records at the U.S. District Courthouse where she found evidence that Dr. Hammer had paid $8,000 to mob enforcer Joe Hauser to bribe public officials so he would get his way. All told, Hammer had paid $100,000 to the city's elected representatives, insisting the money was intended as campaign contributions. His lawyers said it was simply a way of doing business. Many others said what happened was a crime. But no one in the justice system had the guts to take on Dr. Hammer in this instance. Occidental's Board of Directors formed its own investigating unit. One of its first discoveries was that their chairman had $1 million in potential bribe money stashed in a deposit box at a branch of City National Bank below Occidental headquarters. The deposit box was in the name of Dr. Hammer's secretary.

Before our first investigative report was broadcast Dr. Hammer got wind of what we were doing and was on the phone to our new station manager, John Rohrbeck trying to kill the story. It was Rohrbeck's first day on the job. I insisted the story was libel proof, that it had been vetted by the NBC Legal Department. Rohrbeck was obviously shaken by the call from the billionaire but said he saw no reason to yank the story. Reporter Patrick Healy proceeded to tell the story and followed it up with two more investigative reports.

Hammer needed 10 votes in the Los Angeles City Council to win permission to drill in the Palisades but he never got them. Time after time he could only muster nine votes with the six other council members voting no or abstaining. Our investigative stories at the NBC station were credited with being a large factor in scuttling the oil drilling plan.

But two years later we learned oil drilling in the Palisades was not a dead issue. The Grand jury investigation was long forgotten and, for the first time, the council quietly approved a measure calling for two exploratory wells to be followed by drilling on coastal land. Mayor Tom Bradley, a longtime drilling foe, shocked his aides when he signed the measure. But the final say belonged to the California Coastal Commission which said no to immediate drilling but yes to the exploratory wells. The issue dragged on for three more years until a city council loaded with new environmentally minded members voted overwhelmingly to withdraw the drilling plan pending before the Coastal Commission. The issue was then placed before the electorate and Los Angeles voters rejected big oil's drilling plans once and for all.

Dr. Hammer died on Dec. 10, 1990, just six years after our disclosures about his attempts to buy off City hall so he could drill in the Palisades. He was 92. And the Occidental

Board of Directors abandoned all of Dr. Hammer's original drilling plans.

Likewise shocking were allegations against Yorty's successor, Tom Bradley, the city's first African-American mayor who had spent many years on the LAPD. Shortly after Bradley's election to a fifth term in office, the city attorney's office confirmed reports that his Honor was involved in two major conflicts of interest with local banks. Bradley admitted that for two years he received an annual stipend of $24,000 for serving as a director of Valley Federal Savings and Loan at a time the bank was seeking zoning variances from the city. He also admitted accepting $18,000 for serving as a consultant to the Far Eastern National Bank in L.A.'s Chinatown. The bank received $2 million in deposits from the city after Bradley put in a few good words with the city treasurer.

Bradley told reporters his involvement with the two banks was "an error in judgment.

But just as in the case of Sam Yorty and his raging conflict of interest with Occidental Petroleum, Bradley was never prosecuted. The only elected official who dared to speak out was Councilwoman Gloria Molina who said that Bradley's employment by the two banks "compromised" the city. Bradley was elected mayor five times, but lost two races for the governor's seat.

Across the street from City Hall at LAPD Headquarters, one of the city's top cops likewise escaped prosecution in a major corruption scandal. In 1992 Deputy Police Chief Maurice Moore, an African-American and veteran of 40 years on the force, was implicated in a major drug money laundering scandal involving his son, Kevin. Investigators alleged Moore took part in two real estate transactions with his son in which drug money was used to pay $260,000 for a residence and $800,000 for an apartment house. The younger Moore was sentenced to federal prison in 1989 after pleading guilty to smuggling 1,000 pounds of cocaine into the country. When Kevin Moore got out of prison he claimed ownership of the home which was in his father's name.

Bernard Parks, the city's African-American police chief, was informed of the allegations against his deputy chief but took no action against him. Moore was allowed to retire gracefully on a pension of more than $200,000 a year by Chief Parks who said Moore's long career with the LAPD "was distinguished by a remarkable commitment to public service." And once again crimes by the people's leaders in the City of the Angels went unpunished.

# 21

# THE MOB KNOCKS OFF AN "L.A. GUY"

It was probably the biggest organized crime "hit" in Los Angeles since "Bugsy" Siegel was knocked off by the mob in 1947. The victim was 52-year-old Victor J. Weiss whose resume gave him almost legendary status in the L.A. sporting community. Vic wore tailored suits, drove around town in a $75,000 Rolls Royce which he didn't own; sported a ring with five big diamonds and an expensive Rolex watch. An affable glad-hander, he was well known for picking up the tab for his friends at local bars and restaurants. He managed a stable of boxers including Armando Muniz who lost a title fight to welterweight champion Sugar Ray Leonard when Weiss, who doubled as manager, threw in the towel. Muniz, who later became a school teacher, told me Weiss never took a cent from his boxing paychecks. Weiss was reported to be a big time gambler who wagered heavily on the outcome of his boxers' fights, sometime betting on them to lose if that appeared likely.

He was one of those flashy L.A. guys who lived beyond his means, trying to impress people by carrying a big wad of money. He was on a first name basis with some of the biggest names in the Los Angeles sporting community, people who gathered frequently at Monty's restaurant, agents, pro ballplayers, a scattering of mob figures and bookies. LAPD intelligence officers, several of them friends of mine, frequently went undercover at Monty's. Vic was a confidante of Carroll Rosenbloom, then the owner of the Los Angeles Rams, who mysteriously drowned while swimming off the coast of Florida despite having a reputation as an excellent swimmer. But it was Vic's relationship with his old high school pal, Jerry Tarkanian, one of the most successful college basketball coaches in the nation, that some thought may have led to his demise. Tarkanian and Weiss had grown up in Pasadena, California and went to high school together. Tarikanian was known in the sports world as "Tark the Shark," a guy who would do anything to win. His recruiting techniques were under constant scrutiny by NCAA investigators and stories about his errant ways while coaching the top ranked "Running Rebels" of the University of Nevada Las Vegas were legendary. But he was  great in his line of work and the soon to be owner of the Los Angeles Lakers, Dr. Jerry Buss, dearly wanted him as his head coach and put out an overture. As a favor to Tarkanian, Weiss agreed to negotiate a coaching deal with Dr. Buss and Jack Kent Cooke, the current owner who was selling the team to Buss for $67 million.

On June 14, 1979 Weiss took off in the Rolls Royce for the Beverly Comstock Hotel in Beverly Hills to sit down at the bargaining table on Tarkanian's behalf. According to Buss and Cook the meeting went smoothly and after an hour went by they clinched a deal.  Cooke wrote down terms of a contract on his personal stationery and handed it to Weiss who put in his brown suede Gucci briefcase with red stripes for delivery to Tarkanian. They shook hands and Weiss drove off from the hotel in the Rolls Royce and a rendezvous with death. Tarkanian sat nervously in a Long Beach hotel waiting for Vic to call with the terms of the coaching contract. But the call never came.

Four days later on Father's Day, a security guard in the parking garage at the Sheraton Hotel in Universal City notified the LAPD that he had found a red and white Rolls with a foul odor emitting from the car trunk on the second level of the four-story structure. Vic's wife, Rose, first reported him missing on June 15 after he failed to come home the previous night. She said they had planned to go out to dinner to celebrate her birthday.

At the time the Rolls Royce was found Homicide Detective Leroy Orozco had just concluded a Father's Day dinner outing with his family when his beeper went off. He called headquarters and was dispatched to the hotel parking garage. Orozco told me, "It was eerie. When I got to the second floor of the garage it was all lit up and the Rolls was the only car there. I knew Vic's body was inside the trunk because I could see body fluids seeping from it."

Upon Orozco's arrival the car trunk was forced open and it was readily apparent that Vic Weiss had been murdered. His body was wrapped in a yellow bed sheet and his hands were tied behind his back. There were ropes over the bedspread around his neck, legs and ankles. The 51-year-old Weiss was believed to be carrying a large sum of money. One source close to the 51-year-old Weiss said he believed Vic was carrying $60,000 in laundered money to be delivered to the "boys" in Las Vegas." No money was found at the scene.

Weiss wallet was gone along with his credit cards. So was his Gucci briefcase which investigators determined contained the contract offer to Tarkanian, a checkbook, and a Hughes Air West flight saver ticket to Las Vegas scheduled for June 15, the day after he vanished. (Later I learned from Hughes Air West that the ticket was actually used by someone on the day scheduled but the only name to show for its ownership was Vic Weiss.) The killers left behind Vic's Rolex watch which had stopped running at 4:30 a.m. on June 15, and the diamond ring, which friends said was worth anywhere from $50,000 to $100,000. There were surveillance cameras in the garage, including one directly above the Rolls Royce. But someone had tampered with it as well as the other cameras in the garage and nothing was captured on video. There were lots of fingerprints on the Rolls, but it turned out that most of them were left by potential car buyers. Weiss was a limited partner in a Rolls/Ford new car agency owned by his friend, Gerald Cutter, who allowed him to use the luxury car when it was not being shown to customers. Cutter said Vic's role at the agency was solely "promotional.

Almost immediately Orozco and his partner, John Helvin, began getting phone calls from people who reported seeing Weiss in the very distinctive Rolls the day he disappeared. From what the witnesses said they ascertained that Weiss drove from Beverly Hills to Ventura Boulevard in the San Fernando Valley and west to the suburb of Encino. There the trail seemed to end.

But it was picked up again with a major break in the case. An eyewitness came forward, a woman, assigned the alias of Carol Smith, who had an appointment with Weiss in the late afternoon on June 14 after Vic's meeting with Buss and Cooke. Smith was identified as the girlfriend of Vic's boss, Gerald Cutter who was giving her a new Mustang and asked that Vic have her sign the motor vehicle transfer of ownership papers. The woman told Orozco she was looking out a window when she saw Weiss pull up to her apartment, and park the Rolls. Suddenly a late model white Cadillac drove up behind the Rolls. Two white men wearing business suits and dark glasses got out of the Cadillac, and a third man remained inside. One was a huge blond man about 6 feet 6 inches tall and built like a football player. The witness said the big man confronted

Weiss, angrily pointing a finger in his face. Carol said he was left handed because she spotted a watch on his right wrist. After a short conversation, Weiss got back behind the wheel of the Rolls. The large man sat in the right front passenger seat; the second man was in the back seat. Weiss took off in the Rolls with the Cadillac and the third man following closely. The witness said the Cadillac had orange license plates. In 1979 Arizona had orange plates, a possible indication that the killers were from out of state. Carol said she did not get a good look at the driver of the Cadillac, nor could she clearly see the faces of the two men who accosted Weiss.

Carol said she was moving into a new apartment and couldn't call police immediately because she didn't have a phone. (Again, this was in the days before cell phones). Five days later she called Gerald Cutter at the car agency where Weiss worked, told him what had happened, and asked if she should contact police. Cutter told her to do so. She was then directed to Orozco and Helvin in the LAPD Robbery-Homicide unit.

The detectives asked the good looking young woman if she would consent to hypnosis  or take a lie detector test, but she declined to do soon the advice of her attorney. The detectives wrote in their report: *"Her refusal to submit to hypnosis is understandable when you consider that perhaps the killing came from an organized crime source. Her background and education seems to be of a higher caliber and she seems to be of a stable nature (at this point). Based on all of this information detectives have little choice except to vigorously pursue her observations."*

The day after Vic's body was recovered Orozco and Helvin interviewed his widow, Rose, at her home in Encino. Gerald Cutter, the car dealer was at her side. Orozco told me every time she was asked a question she turned to

Cutter who seemed to be controlling her answers. She knew of no reason anyone would want to kill Vic. He had promised her a big birthday celebration at Monty's and she was stunned when he never came home. It turned out the house where they lived was owned by Cutter and that Vic's main job was to promote the car dealership. Weiss wasn't really a big money man after all. As part of his deal at the Ford/Rolls agency, Cutter provided him with a house and a car as needed, but apart from the wad in his wallet he was almost penniless. He had a $50,000 insurance policy on his life but owed $80,000 as the result of a bankruptcy at another car dealership.

Gerald Cutter's involvement in the entire affair was bothersome to the detectives. Cutter was known to have associated with organized crime figures from his home town of St. Louis including the brothers Donald and Jerry Woolbright who were sales associates at Cutter's car dealership. It was the same Donald Woolbright who was accused but never convicted of the infamous "Glomar Explorer" burglary at Howard Hughes' headquarters in Hollywood.

The detectives learned that the car dealer's wife, Geraldine Cutter, had died the year before when she apparently lost control of her car in the driveway of their home and it plunged over the side of a hill. At the time she was in her bathrobe. No alcohol or drugs were found in Mrs. Cutter's blood and traffic cops listed it as an "accidental traffic death."

Orozco and Helvin were dogged in their pursuit of the killer or killers. But their investigation was hampered by rumors, speculation and informants with all sorts of theories. A TV investigating team from Chicago claimed that Weiss was part of a nationwide gambling ring that paid National Football League referees $100,000 to fix pro and college games. They said Weiss made huge sums of money which he deposited in a bank in the Grand Caymans. Don Bowler, the man who put Mickey Cohen in prison, told me Vic Weiss ran the biggest booking layoff operation in the West. Frank Hronke of the L.A. District Attorney's office said Weiss was suspected of dealing in stolen jewelry and cocaine. John Gier of the Orange County District Attorney's office advised me that someone close to Weiss had a $1 million insurance policy on his head.

A newspaper reporter in Riverside, California called me to say that Weiss was involved in a partnership with San Diego mob figures Frank (the Bump) Bompensiero and Chris Petty in the operation of a restaurant in Imperial Beach. (Bompensiero was later murdered in a mob execution because he been an FBI snitch). Helvin and Orozco got calls from several tipsters who insisted Weiss was involved in a money laundering operation and carried large sums of money from local gambling operations to Las Vegas on a frequent basis. One organized crime informant had a very specific version of what happened. He said Weiss dropped $60,000 at gambling tables in Vegas. He said as part of the pay back Weiss agreed to take laundered cash to Las Vegas once a week. He said money was brought to Weiss weekly in a brown paper bag and placed in the trunk of his Rolls. He said Weiss then drove to the Burbank Airport where he boarded a plane to Vegas with the money. He said Weiss was killed because he skimmed the laundered money on a regular basis, and was warned to stop, but didn't. The informant even gave the cops the name of the suspected hit-man, a member of the Teamsters Union. But the detectives had an excellent description of the hulking hit man from their own eyewitness, and the Teamster was ruled out as a suspect.

There were three other murders in which informants linked the victims to Vic Weiss. Ronald Launius, a professional hit man believed responsible for 30 killings in Northern California, was said to have been associated with Weiss. The 37-year-old Launius was one of four druggies beaten to death in the so-called Wonderland Avenue murders on July 1, 1981. One of those who took part in the killings was porn star John Holmes, who later died from AIDS. No substantial link between Launius and Weiss was ever established by the cops.

The name of Jeffrey Rockman, a convicted jewel thief and bank robber, surfaced on a scrap of paper the detectives found on the desk in Vic's home office. The detectives believed that Rockman had sold Vic stolen goods. Rockman was shot to death in his beach townhouse on April 29, 1980. His real name was Anthony Starr, but after testifying for the government in a bank robbery case in Detroit, Starr was given the identity of Jeffrey Rockman and placed in the federal witness protection program. There was nothing the cops turned up to link his death to the Weiss murder. But it certainly showed the feds weren't very good at protecting their witness.

The cops also received information that Weiss was involved with Horace McKenna, a former California Highway patrol officer who operated several nude bars in Orange County and had links to a ring of luxury car thieves. McKenna was killed March 9, 1981 when a burst of machine gun fire rocketed through his limousine at the gates of his Orange County estate. But no definitive links to the Weiss murder were ever established.

Orozco and Helvin started checking the phone records of Weiss and some of his cronies, and established that Vic had been calling a number of organized crime figures. They obtained a search warrant for a home in Las Vegas where a possible suspect lived. But when they got to the house it was empty, and they figured someone had tipped the guy off.

Another stop was in a small burg in central Florida, New Port Richey, where one of the calls was made to a mob enforcer for an organized crime family. From the time they checked into a motel they found themselves under surveillance by a man in a black Mustang. He was there when they went to bed and he was there when they got up in the morning. It appeared he was following their every move. They tried to get a warrant to conduct a search of the suspect's home but were turned down for lack of evidence. They kept looking over their shoulders as they got out of town.

At this point Orozco and Helvin were getting somewhat paranoid. When they returned to L.A. they stopped talking to other cops about the case. One of those rebuffed while trying to pump them for information on the Weiss case was a private investigator known to work for the mob. To compound their paranoia, someone fired a number of shots at Helvin's home in suburban La Mirada. No one was hurt, but Helvin and his family were scared stiff.

Helvin finally retired, but Orozco stayed on the LAPD for another 10 years until 1993 when he went to work for me in my investigative unit at the NBC station in Los Angeles. But he never forgot about the Weiss case. One of things Orozco discovered along the way was the existence of an FBI wire tap in Las Vegas on Anthony (Tony the Ant) Spilotro, the mob boss for many years in the gambling city. The wire tap done in 1979, not long after the Weiss murder, had a person telling Spilotro over the phone: "The Vic situation has been taken care of." It simply reaffirmed Orozco's thinking that the Weiss murder was a mob hit ordered by "Tony the Ant," who for some reason didn't like the idea of people skimming off his laundered money. Spilotro himself was soon to be the victim of another mob hit. He and his brother, Michael Spilotro, disappeared on

June 14, 1986 after being summoned to Chicago by the mob hierarchy. They were beaten and burned alive, then buried in an Indiana corn field where their bodies were eventually found. Eleven years later five Chicago gangsters were convicted of the murders. Their motive: Spilotro had broken the Mafia code of honor when he slept with the wife of another "made man."

I retired (temporarily) in late 1999 after working with Orozco for five years at the NBC and CBS stations in Los Angeles. Orozco decided to go back into law enforcement and was hired by the District Attorney's office in Orange County as a welfare fraud investigator. In 2006 he was meeting with his last LAPD partner, Paul Tippin, when the Weiss case came up again from a most unexpected source. Lt. Rick Morton, an intelligence officer in the Orange County DA's office, approached Orozco and asked if he had worked on the Vic Weiss murder case. Orozco replied that he had, and Morton said that the FBI had a man in protective custody named Frank Randazzo who identified the killers in the Weiss case as Glenn Donald Stewart and Anthony Mercado, a couple of ex-cons. Stewart's name immediately rang a bell with Orozco. A blond haired man with the sound alike name of Glenn Steward and one Anthony Mercado had been accused of an organized crime murder in South Los Angeles three years previously. They were acquitted because the court ruled the cops had a critical witness illegally hypnotized.

For almost 10 years Frank Randazzo had been sequestered by the FBI while awaiting sentencing in Rancho Cucamonga, California on charges of receiving stolen property. One of the stolen items was actor Burt Reynolds' sports car. No one seemed to know why Randazzo was important to the FBI, and the Orange County Sheriff. Lieutenant Morton refused to give Orozco any more information on Randazzo's whereabouts. I was now working in the investigative unit at the local Fox station where Reporter Chris Blatchford and I did a follow up story on the case which paid off immediately. Specifically we mentioned that a mystery man named Frank Randazzo appeared to have critical information about the Vic Weiss murder 27 years before, but apparently was a federally protected witness. Not long after our story was broadcast on the 10 p.m. news Attorney Roger Remlinger called our assignment desk and reported that Randazzo was his client. He said Randazzo was no longer a federally protected witness and had been turned back to local authorities. He said when the story broke the 63-year-old Randazzo was in the jail lockup watching the news on television. When his name was mentioned, several other prisoners asked, "Is that you Frank?" Randazzo called Remlinger who immediately arranged to have him transferred to a safe location in the jail area reserved for informants.

It turned out Randazzo was about to be sentenced on a 10-year-old felony conviction for receiving stolen property, a Mercedes Benz. He was already a three-time loser and now that he was no longer of any use to the feds Superior Judge Barry Plotkin wasn't about to let Randazzo linger in legal limbo any longer. The judge sentenced Randazzo to a term of 25 years to life.

I asked Judge Plotkin for permission to interview Randazzo in front of a television camera, and he agreed, telling the bailiff to bring Randazzo back to court. I wanted to know if Randazzo drove the Cadillac that followed Weiss and the two other men in the Rolls Royce. But the pint-sized Randazzo refused to talk about the Weiss case. He complained about the long sentence and his failing health. He was confident he would get out of jail on appeal. He said Burt Reynolds better not testify against him at a second trial about stealing the actor's stolen sports car or there would be "hell to pay." I had been cautioned by

Randazzo's attorney not to ask any questions that might incriminate Randazzo, and then, after the interview, Roger Remlinger, a former homicide cop, asked why I didn't ask Randazzo if he were the driver of the Cadillac. In subsequent correspondence with me from prison Randazzo admitted his ties to organized crime. He wrote that he had introduced Mafia killer Michael Rizzitello to Joe Morgan, the Anglo leader of the notorious Mexican Mafia. He said that was when the Mexican gangsters started doing a lot of the Italian mob's dirty work. An LAPD cold case detective interviewed Randazzo about the Weiss murder and came away convinced that he had quite a gift of gab but wasn't directly involved in the case.

So from all that the only information we had to go on were the names of the Weiss murder suspects Randazzo gave to the Orange County intelligence officer, Glenn Donald Stewart and Anthony Frank Mercado. Both had long criminal records, but even more interesting was that both had been involved in a murder three years earlier that resembled the Weiss killing. So again I turned to public records for information. I quickly established that the Glenn Steward in the L.A. murder case and Glenn Stewart identified as a possible suspect in the Weiss murder were one and the same person.

In 1976 in what seemed to be a practice run for the Weiss murder, Stewart and Mercado were charged with fatally stabbing a drug-dealing associate, Amelio Beltran, then dumping his body wrapped in a blanket in the victim's own car trunk in predominately black South Los Angeles. The dead man had been stabbed seven times. With his blond hair Stewart stood out like a sore thumb in the predominately black area and several witnesses provided police with good descriptions of him and his car spotted at the murder scene. But the charges were kicked out after the judge ruled the cops acted illegally when they had their most important witness hypnotized. Up to this point in his life Stewart had a record of seven arrests, six of which were drug related. In 1973 he was sentenced to five years to life in state prison for the sale of narcotics. He was paroled after just two years in prison and was back on the streets dealing big time in narcotics, according to intelligence sources. His sidekick, Mercado, had a long record of arrests going back to 1953, assault with intent to commit murder, three busts for auto theft, five arrests for robbery, five arrests for narcotics charges, like Stewart, a habitual criminal. But the big difference between the two men was that Stewart was out of prison when Vic Weiss was killed while Mercado was in the big house, serving a five year sentence for dealing in drugs and forgery.

I called Lieutenant Morton at the Orange County District Attorney's office and asked if he knew Stewart's whereabouts. He said Stewart had died a few years before in Florida, but he could not tell me exactly where. Morton's story just didn't sound right to me.

So I checked the Social Security death index and found that a Glenn Donald Stewart had died on July 25, 1996 in Hermosa Beach, California. I was positive it was the same guy. Then I obtained a death report from the Hermosa Beach Police Department. The report by officer Bill Clawson said the 48-year-old Stewart had collapsed while jogging, and may have struck his head on the curb when he fell. He was taken by ambulance to the South Bay Medical Center where he was pronounced dead. He was almost a perfect match to the description provided by eyewitness Carol Smith shortly after the Vic Weiss murder. Stewart had long blond hair. He weighed 272 pounds, and was six feet six inches tall. Relatives said there was a long history of heart disease in his family and that his father and other relatives died at a relatively young ages. They said Stewart ran about six miles daily and didn't use drugs, didn't smoke and was a social drinker. But the writer of the police report observed that Stewart had a long drug related history and had been accused of "multiple capitol crimes." Leroy Orozco told me Stewart was a perfect match to the eyewitness description in the Weiss murder.

"The Weiss killing had nothing to do with Jerry Tarkanian coaching the Lakers," Orozco said. "There was reliable evidence that Vic was carrying laundered money to Vegas on a weekly basis. And when he got caught skimming, he signed his death warrant for the mob. So they hired a guy the size of a football player to get the job done." In all probability the left-handed Stewart (with a watch on his right arm) was very likely the guy eyewitness Carol Smith saw confronting Weiss in front of her apartment. I wondered if Glenn Donald Stewart really died from a heart attack. There was a deep abrasion on the left side of his forehead that could have been caused by a blunt instrument. "We'll never know," said Orozco. Stewart's body had been cremated. Case closed. All the principals are dead.

There was a tragic footnote to the Vic Weiss murder case. In 2007 his son, Wolfe, a Marine hero in the Gulf War, was killed by a sniper while working as a security guard in Iraq. One year later Vic's wife, Rose, was stabbed to death by their mentally disturbed adopted daughter in Thousand Oaks, California.

# 22

# THE "BLACK DAHLIA" MURDER

Covering the news in Los Angeles has been an incredible adventure. In my lifetime there has been one big story after another. Two of the more memorable stories that seemed to obsess me occurred in 1947, almost 10 years before I went to work as a reporter at the cop shop. The first was the mutilation murder of the so-called "Black Dahlia," the beautiful aspiring actress Elizabeth Short. The Dahlia case probably sold more newspapers, books and movies than any crime story in the history of L.A. Five months later the assassination of pretty boy mobster Benjamin (Bugsy) Siegel, known as the man who invented Las Vegas, shocked the citizenry of upscale Beverly Hills which prided itself on keeping the criminal element out of town. I believe I've found credible evidence that might help solve both murder mysteries.

In 1991 The Dahlia and Siegel murders figured prominently in my plans for a 30 minute television show called "Murder One" which I had been given the go-ahead by NBC to write and produce after I put together a pilot. Determining just who killed the "Black Dahlia" was one of my first projects.

The severed body of 22-year-old Elizabeth Short was found January 15, 1947 in a vacant lot at 39th Street and Norton Avenue in an area known as Leimert Park. Her body had been cut in half with surgical-like precision, and the blood drained from her torso, which had been scrubbed clean. Reviewing old documents in the case I recently learned that the killer had carved the letter "D" in her pubic area, something never disclosed by the cops in their initial investigation.

I was 16 at the time and worked at my dad's drug store, just eight blocks from the murder scene. The next day I inspected the area but there was nothing much left in the way of evidence other than car tracks in the dirt lot where the body was dumped and something resembling a spot of blood on the sidewalk. From that day forward I was as curious as the next person to learn who killed this beautiful young woman from Medford, Massachusetts who, according to local legend, was labeled the "Black Dahlia" by patrons at a Long Beach drug store soda fountain where she once hung out. Elizabeth wore her black hair in a striking bouffant and her wardrobe was usually solid black if the newspaper reports of that era can to be believed. The inspiration for her nom de plume may have also come from a film playing at local movie houses at the time called "The Blue Dahlia." It starred Veronica Lake and Alan Ladd and was written by Raymond Chandler, the noted mystery writer who used L.A. as a locale for many of his crime stories.

Elizabeth Short might best be described as a beautiful wandering vagrant, at least in the two years leading up to her murder. People remembered seeing Elizabeth at the Florentine Gardens night club in Hollywood, a magnet for young actresses; at the broadcast studios on the Sunset Strip, in Santa Barbara, San Pedro, Long Beach, Camarillo, Berkeley, San Diego and Pacific Beach. She frequently traveled out of state, spending time in Miami and Jacksonville, Florida, Chicago, Indianapolis, Indiana and her home town of Medford, Massachusetts. She never stayed very long in any one place, but her looks were something special, perhaps unforgettable. She reportedly had bit roles in two movies, and had an occasional waitress job. But no one seemed to know how she supported her life style. A few of the hundred or so men interrogated by the cops suggested she was a prostitute. But her best friend, Ann Toth, insisted Elizabeth was always a lady who didn't drink or smoke, not a lady of the evening.

*Photograph of Elizabeth Short, the so-called "Black Dahlia," found in her possessions by police after her murder in 1947.*

There was an unconfirmed reported that she couldn't engage in sex because of an oddly- shaped vagina. But there were also reports that Elizabeth had a score of lovers. Reading the old reports it was difficult for me to determine where the truth ends or begins.

In the week leading up to her death Elizabeth and Ann Toth spent several days at the home of Mark Hanson, the impresario of the Florentine Gardens night spot. Ann insisted it was strictly an innocent visit, that Hanson was a perfect gentleman and gracious host.

The cops later considered Hanson a suspect in Elizabeth's murder but he insisted there was no love interest on his part and remarked that Elizabeth had unappealing "bad teeth." She was last seen alive a few days later making a call at a pay phone in downtown L.A.'s Biltmore Ho Heirens dietel after she was dropped off there by a married man named Robert (Red) Manley who had spent the weekend with her in San Diego. Manley was also considered a potential suspect. He insisted they never had sex. He said Elizabeth complained of feeling ill during their excursion.

Also fitting into the time frame around her murder was another aspect of Short's life in L.A., her fascination with the national radio shows broadcast from the CBS and NBC studios on Sunset Boulevard in Hollywood. Jack Egger, the chief usher at the CBS studio at Sunset and Gower, said Elizabeth attended live radio shows there at least 20 times. He said the last time she was there was the first Wednesday in January of 1947 (six days before her murder) accompanied by a man she introduced as a "Chicago cop." Elizabeth said they were there to see the "Jack Carson Show," The man displayed a Chicago police badge and Egger, who wanted to be a cop, admitted them without tickets. Egger described her companion "...as a well dressed dapper sort of person with penetrating eyes." The ex-cop was also considered a potential suspect but LAPD detectives were never able to identify him.

Chicago police told the LAPD they could find no officers on assignment or vacationing in Los Angeles at the time of the Dahlia murder. But they reported 69 retired Chicago cops lived in the L.A. area. The word "retired" was engraved only on the badges of former cops. Egger said the badge he saw had no such wording. What intrigued the County Grand Jury was a report that Short lived in Chicago the year before she moved to L.A. Two Chicago newspapermen who knew her well said Short was obsessed with the so-called "Lipstick Murders," particularly the 1946 slaying of a kidnapped six-year-old girl whose body was sliced in half in almost identical fashion to the way Short would die the next year. The reporters said Elizabeth struck up an acquaintance with a Chicago homicide cop but they didn't know his name .Eventually a young college student. William Hieriens, pleaded guilty to the "Lipstick Murders." Later he insisted he was drugged by the cops and forced to confess. He died in 2012 while serving his 65th year in prison, .maintaining his innocence to the end. Jack Egger, the CBS usher who saw the "Chicago cop" with Short became a wire tap expert for the D.A. and later a Beverly Hills police captain. (This was the same Jack Egger who 12 years later had me arrested in Beverly Hills while I was investigating the slaying of mobster Johnny Stompanato. (See Chapter Two.)

During the first stages of the LAPD investigation nearly 100 men and women confessed to murdering Elizabeth Short, but all were ruled out, most for psychological reasons. Hardly a year goes by that the story of Short's murder isn't told with a new twist. "Who is the Black Dahlia?" was the subject of a 1975 TV movie starring Lucie Arnaz. Critics called it "terrifying." In my opinion the most entertaining

Black Dahlia film (but not the most accurate) was the 1981 release of John Gregory Dunne's *"True Confessions"* in which the killer was a wealthy developer with ties to the city's political elite played by Charles Durning. In 2005 Director Brian de Palma gave the movie going public his version simply titled, *"The Black Dahlia."* It was pretty much a dud and did poorly at the box office with its mix of fact and fiction. There have been at least a dozen books on the murder.

Over the years there have been many suspects, some real, some imagined. An Orange County house-wife, Janice Knowlton, wrote a book entitled, *"Daddy Was the Black Dahlia Killer."* Knowlton said for years she suppressed the memory of seeing her father dismember "Aunt Betty's body." Knowlton claimed her father had buried other murder victims on the grounds of their home. Law enforcement officers conducted a giant dig there but found nothing. That prompted Knowlton to remark, "...that shows they took me seriously." Former LAPD homicide cop Steve Hodel also claimed his father killed Elizabeth Short in his book, *"Black Dahlia Avenger: a Genius for Murder."* A degree of credibility was given the book after the District Attorney's office made public its investigative files in the Short case shortly after Hodel's book went on sale. The files revealed that the author's father, Dr. George Hodel was one of 30 medical doctors whose activities were seriously scrutinized following the Short murder. Considering the crisp surgical cut that severed Short's body, the cops felt the killer had to be a surgeon or a medical student.

Dr. Hodel was far from being a model citizen. His wife was quoted as telling her teenage daughter that her father had been partying the night of the Short murder and later told her, "they'll never be able to prove I did that murder." The District Attorney strung wire taps throughout Dr. Hodel's home. Some of the recordings indicated Dr. Hodel was well aware of the wire taps and was taunting investigators about the Dahlia case. In one recording he says, "*Supposing I did kill the Black Dahlia. They couldn't prove it now. They can't talk to my secretary anymore because she's dead.*"

I was surprised to learn that my good friend Frank Hronek of the District Attorney's Bureau of Investigation had placed the "bugs" in Dr. Hodel's home since he had never once mentioned anything about the case to me. At one point Dr. Hodel had been accused of having an incestuous relationship with his teenage daughter. An informant told an investigator that Dr. Hodel bragged that he paid $15,000 to attorney Jerry Giesler which was used to influence the District Attorney and that's how the charge against him was dropped." Knowing Giesler's reputation as a Hollywood fixer, it didn't surprise me. Dr. Hodel eventually left the country and lived in the Far East until the late 1980s when he moved back to Los Angeles.

The younger Hodel first began to suspect his father of the Short murder following his death in 1991. He found among his father's possessions two pictures which contained images he thought were those of Elizabeth Short. However, many students of the original crime could not see any resemblance to the Black Dahlia in the two pictures. Hodel was methodical in his approach, and greatly impressed Stephen Kay, the co-prosecutor on the Manson murders. Short's killer had mailed a cryptic message to the Los Angeles *Examiner* nine days after the murder in a package that contained her social security card, birth certificate, address book and other possessions. A handwriting expert surmised that the block printing on the envelope resembled the handwriting of Hodel's father, and also the lettering on the body of another murder victim, Jean

French. From the start police suspected the Short and French murders were connected.

I have a great deal of respect for Steve Hodel and prosecutor Kay. After years of investigation my findings run along the same lines, but I have concluded that Short's killer may well have been a different surgeon. I've also concluded it probably wasn't Dr. Walter Bailey, a suspect advocated by several journalists who have spent considerable time researching the case. Dr. Bailey lived on the same street where Short's body was discovered. He had his share of mental problems and died several years after the murder. For a time a Hollywood tour bus took visitors on a tour of the places that figured in Short's death and one of the stops was in front of Dr. Bailey's old home.

In 1991 a newspaper in Arizona, the *Mesa Tribune*, carried an interview with 90-year-old Paul Freestone, thought to be one of the last surviving officers of the Dahlia investigation. At the time of the slaying Lt. Freestone was a command officer at the University Police Station, the jurisdiction in which Elizabeth Short's body was found, but not necessarily where she was murdered. In the early stages of the probe Freestone worked closely with the lead homicide cops, Harry Hanson and Finis Brown. Freestone assigned his men to scour the area for clues and possible suspects. Reporter T.M. Shultz's story in the *Mesa Tribune* quoted Freestone as saying that the top of Short's lips had tiny razor like cuts. "They almost resembled a tic-tac-toe deal," he said. "I often wondered just what that meant. It must have some meaning but I could never figure it out."

I found Freestone's name in the Mesa phone book and called him in the hope of getting an interview. "Sure," he said. "Come out here and we'll talk. Bring a camera." He asked if I had the crime scene photos and I said yes. "Bring those too," he said. A half hour later he called me back and said, "Skip the pictures. I forgot for a moment that I'm blind." So I flew to Mesa with a cameraman, not knowing exactly what to expect but well aware a successful interview would greatly enhance my television story on the Black Dahlia case.

I never met Paul Freestone while he was on the force, but we had a number of mutual friends, including former LAPD chief Daryl Gates and a lot of small talk ensued before we got around to discussing the Dahlia murder. Freestone really opened up with me when the camera began rolling, going far beyond his interview in the Mesa newspaper. After Short's body was found, Lieutenant Freestone led the search for evidence in the surrounding community and was involved in many details of the investigation. Over the years he said he remained in close contact with Detective Finis Brown and they regularly discussed the Dahlia case. Ten years after the murder, "Brownie" as Freestone called him, said he was going to review all the evidence in the case, including Elizabeth Short's address book which was mailed to the Los Angeles Examiner by the killer. Brown told Freestone he found an error in a phone number for a doctor listed in Short's address book. The error was made by a clerk assigned to transcribe the numbers to the official police report. The wrongly transcribed number had been checked by an investigator, who tried calling it and when he didn't get an answer, dropped the matter. So in 1957 Finis Brown went to the offices of the phone company, and checked a so-called "reverse directory" which listed phone numbers first, then the name and address to which they were registered. Freestone quoted Brown as saying the 1947 reverse book identified the phone number in Short's address book as belonging to a doctor, a known abortionist who committed suicide a month after the Dahlia murder. Freestone said Brown told him the investigation was over and there was nothing more to talk about since the killer was dead.

Freestone said he could not remember the name of the doctor. I played a tape of the interview for former LAPD Chief Gates and he said it was the most plausible explanation he had ever heard as to who killed Elizabeth Short.

After ex-cop Steve Hodel's book came out in 2006 linking his father to the murder of Elizabeth Short, the D.A.'s office made public its long secret files on the Black Dahlia case, and it gave me an excellent opportunity to see if I could further validate Paul Freestone's story. He had died in Mesa, Arizona shortly after I interviewed him in 1991. There can be no doubt about his credibility and his knowledge of the case. His name was one of the first investigators mentioned in a 1951 "Final Report" on the Dahlia murder prepared by D.A.'s Lieutenant Frank Jemison, a special advisor to the grand jury. Jemison listed 22 possible suspects in the Dahlia case, including the "unkown Chicago Cop," and Dr. George Hodel. All told, seven physicians and one dentist were named in the report. Six of the suspects were men. One was a woman, a surgeon. Despite putting Dr. Hodel's name on the list, Jemison wrote that the available evidence tended "to eliminate" him as a suspect.

A name that caught my attention immediately was that of a doctor, a known abortionist, whose name was in the Jemison report. The doctor's name was Paul De Gaston, who was listed in Elizabeth Short's address book under the alias of "Dr. C.J. Morris." The Jemison report said De Gaston was accused of murder in 1934 in Los Angeles, but did not specify who he was accused of killing and if he was convicted. The report said he served prison time in the state of Washington for performing abortions, but did not say when. Jemison added that De Gaston was arrested once again in L.A. in 1951 on an abortion charge and indicated someone would be questioning the doctor soon about the Black Dahlia case. But as far as I could determine no one ever did.

So what I had was confirmation of a portion of the Paul Freestone story attributed to the case's lead detective Finis Brown. The phone number of a doctor who performed illegal abortions was indeed found in Elizabeth Short's address book along with several hundred other names. But there was no way of determining if it was the wrongly transcribed number Brown was talking about. And just as Brown said, the name in the book was an alias keeping with the fact that abortionists never listed their real names for fear of arrest. But part two of the story went unconfirmed. Dr. De Gaston did not commit suicide a month after the murder. A search of public records indicated that a Paul De Gaston died in Mission Viejo, California in 1963. After I first broadcast the story of the Black Dahlia in 1992 I received a letter from an elderly woman who identified the killer as a medical doctor who performed abortions at his office above the Torch Club in Hollywood, a place sometimes frequented by Elizabeth Short. The letter writer also said the abortionist committed suicide a month after the murder. I phoned the woman, who appeared quite credible and she gave me the name of the doctor. I spent months trying to find out who he was and where he died with no success. The best available information in police files indicates that Dr. De Gaston used the alias of "Dr. C.J. Morris" while also operating out of an office on Hollywood Boulevard. The calling card of one more doctor was found among Short's possession. It was that of Dr. A.E. Brix who told the cops Elizabeth Short came to the office to see what his fee would be for treating her for "female trouble." Apparently the price was too high because she left without treatment. Incidentally, Short's critically important address book disappeared from the police evidence locker sometime in the mid 1990s.

It was difficult for me to challenge Paul Freestone's version of Detective Finis Brown's take on the Black Dahlia murder. It's as close to the truth as anyone can come based on the available evidence. An abortionist killed the Black Dahlia, Elizabeth Short, on the operating table. Then he carved up her body, drained her blood and contorted her face to cover up his crime. Stricken with guilt, he may or may not have killed himself weeks later. And what was labeled another "crime of the century" had been solved, maybe. But perhaps I shouldn't be overlooking that mysterious Chicago cop. I'm certain of one thing. The story will be told in some fashion over and over again, the beauty from Medford, Massachusetts, one of five daughters of Phoebe and Cleo Short who came out West, like so many others, hoping her star would shine in Hollywood. It did, but only after her death.

# 23

# THE ASSASSINATION OF "BUGSY" SIEGEL

Five months after the "Black Dahlia," murder, Benjamin (Bugsy) Siegel, perhaps the most notorious gangster in the history of Hollywood, was assassinated by a rifleman as he sat on a sofa reading the Los Angeles *Times* in front of a picture window at his girlfriend's rented home in upscale Beverly Hills.

Siegel was a killer but also a man of vision. He left his wife, Esther, and two children behind in the East and moved to L.A. when the opportunity arose to become a player in mob activities in Hollywood. But opportunity really knocked when he visited Las Vegas, a dusty, wide open town populated with street walkers, cow pokes and tin horns who gambled their money away at run down poker parlors and drank themselves into stupors at cheap saloons.

Bugsy liked what he saw in Nevada's virtually unrestricted gambling policies and loose prostitution laws so he convinced the mob hierarchy to finance his plans to build a million dollar hotel, the Flamingo, which would cater to customers with loads of money. Handing out the start up dollars for the project was Meyer Lansky, the intellectual and financial leader of the so-called "Jewish Mafia." Bugsy," a name he bitterly resented that was hung on by his mob rivals, built himself a spacious two story apartment on the grounds of the Flamingo. Years later, before the building was torn down, I inspected it with a cameraman. There were escape hatches everywhere. As an example, all Siegel had to do was open his closet, flip up a floor board, then slip down a fire ladder to a basement hideaway.

Bugsy sensed someone might try to kill him and took every possible precaution including surrounding himself with heavily armed bodyguards in Las Vegas. That's why his assassination in front of a picture window in Beverly Hills seemed so out of character.

It was a balmy evening in Beverly Hills on June 20, 1947 when Siegel met his fate. Bugsy's girlfriend, Virginia Hill, supposedly a "bag lady" for the mob, was out of town, partying somewhere on the East Coast. In the living room with Siegel was hoodlum Allen Smiley, a mob underling who was an errand boy for Bugsy. Upstairs were Virginia Hill's brother and his girlfriend. Siegel and the others had returned home following dinner in Santa Monica. Everyone seemed to have a good time at dinner and Bugsy decided to catch up on the news of the day in the *Times* evening edition. The house at 810 Linden Drive was illuminated with bright street lights. The exterior sparkled with a plush green lawn and lots of trees. The Beverly Hills cops patrolled the area every 30 minutes to protect the privacy of the rich and famous.

The killer apparently was well versed on the cops' timetable. He set his rifle on a picket fence on the south side of the home, then unloaded a flurry of shots that killed Siegel instantly and shattered the Venus de Milo replica next to where Alan Smiley was standing, shaken but unharmed.

The rifleman jumped into a waiting car and fled moments before the Beverly Hills cops made their rounds.

*Mobster Benjamin (Bugsy) Siegel, executed in Beverly Hills by a "hit man" on June 20. 1947.*

So what was the motive for the mob assassination of one of their own? For one thing, moneyman Meyer Lansky and his cohorts in the Mafia hierarchy didn't share Bugsy's vision. He was breaking the mob bank with his repeated requests for more money to get the job done. And girlfriend Virginia Hill wasn't helping anything with her big spending ways, which included lavish parties costing as much as $25,000 and $500 tips to waiters. So they decided Bugsy had to be eliminated and asked his chief rival in the L.A. Mafia, Jack Dragna, to get the job done. If the mob ever misjudged one of its own, Bugsy Siegel was the case in point. The Flamingo Hotel was the first big money maker in Las Vegas turning into a monumental cash cow for Meyer Lansky and his crowd just as that man of vision, Bugsy Siegel, had foretold.

For years police were unable to pin the murder on anyone. Jimmy (The Weasel) Fratianno, a mob executioner turned FBI informant, claimed Brooklyn born hit man Frankie

Carbo killed Siegel. But Fratianno was regarded as both a liar and braggart who would do anything to curry favor with FBI agents, and his version of the Siegel murder was generally discounted. The most believable version of who killed Bugsy Siegel was supplied by two of the top investigators in the Intelligence Division of the Internal Revenue Service, John Daley and Marty Philpott. They identified the killer as an affable man who loved animals, Eddie Cannizzaro.

Eddie was born Gesulado Cannizzaro in Vizzini, Sicily on Nov. 25, 1922. The family moved to New York in 1924 and then on to Chicago a few years later where Eddie eventually took up with organized crime figures. He served with distinction as an Army medic in the Pacific Theater during World War 11 and qualified as an expert marksman. When Eddie was discharged and looking for work he said his mob connections in Chicago put him in touch with the Jack Dragna gang in L.A. Dragna liked what he saw and soon Eddie was working as a driver and bodyguard for the old man.

*Eddie Cannizzaro, the Mafia "soldier" who confessed to the murder of Benjamin "Bugsy" Siegel in 1947.*

In the mid 1980s Eddie, seriously ill with a heart problem, told the federal agents he wanted to come clean before he died. He said he killed seven people for Dragna, including Siegel. The agents quoted Eddie as saying Bugsy was his "retirement hit." And as far as the federal agents could tell, Eddie never worked another day in his life after killing Siegel. He said he was treated like royalty whenever he visited the mob-run casinos in Las Vegas, that he "never paid a dime for anything." Eddie devoted countless hours in his long retirement to animal rescue operations in the community of Agoura on the Western edge of the San Fernando Valley. His reputation as an animal lover was widespread, earning him the sobriquet, "The Cat Man of Agoura."

According to the federal agents Eddie said he was picked for the hit "...because he knew Siegel and wouldn't make a mistake." He said five men in two cars were involved in the operation. One of the cars let Eddie out near the Siegel residence. Then the car moved to the end of the block. The second car remained in front of the house to protect the shooter and lead police on a false chase if problems arose. Eddie said he had a semi-automatic with a full magazine. He told the agents it was a "clean hit," and he ran down the street and made his getaway in the tailing car. He said he was never questioned by police. Eddie Cannizzaro was 66 when he died from his heart problems at a hospital in Thousand Oaks, California, less than a year after he confessed the Siegel murder to the federal agents. A newspaper obituary said Cannizzaro was an "accountant" and "active in animal rescue efforts." His only accounting, as far as I know, was counting up the cash from Jack Dragna's bookmaking operations.

Benjamin Siegel would have surely loved his burial site, a crypt at the Hollywood Forever Cemetery where many tinsel town celebrities are entombed. The words on the crypt describe the philandering Siegel as a "Loving Husband and Father." And there are lipstick smudges all over it. A small tribute indeed to the hoodlum credited as being the man who invented Las Vegas.

# 24

## THE COLUMNIST'S DAUGHTER

A story that attracted little attention because of the assassination of President Kennedy in Dallas, Texas was the murder of a beautiful young starlet with a "can't miss" reputation among Hollywood movie makers. Karyn Kupcinet was the daughter of the man known as "Mr. Chicago," newspaper columnist and TV commentator, Irv Kupcinet of the Chicago *Sun Times*. The 23-year-old actress was strangled in her West Hollywood apartment on November 28, 1963, six days after the Kennedy slaying. Karyn's death went virtually unnoticed because the newspapers and TV stations were so focused on the tragedy in Dallas.

Eventually Penn Jones, editor of a small newspaper in Midlothian, Texas, advanced the theory that Karyn was killed because she might have had advance knowledge of the JFK assassination. For one thing, he claimed her father once knew Jack Ruby, the killer of Presidential assassin Lee Harvey Oswald. In his book, "*Pardon My Grief II*," quoting the Associated Press, Jones wrote that a few days before the assassination a long distance operator in Oxnard, California overheard Karyn Kupcinet scream over the phone that President Kennedy was going to be killed. There may have been such a call, but I found not one iota of truth in Penn Jones' claim that it was made by Karyn Kupcinet. There was no mention of her name in the AP story. A telephone company supervisor acknowledged that such a call had been made, but he said there was no way to trace it and no one knew the name of the caller. Irv Kupcinet angrily denounced Jones and said there was no basis for his daughter to have any knowledge of such a conspiracy, that it was simply "...a product of his imagination."

At one time or another Penn Jones seemed to involve scores of people in the plot to kill the President and apparently just picked Karyn's name out of the blue. He wrote that she was killed two days after JFK when, in fact, her death certificate stated she died six days later. But Jones was never one to let the facts get in the way of a good story.

Karyn, a brunette with deep dark brown eyes, was already a modest success by Hollywood standards. Her career had taken off with appearances in such TV hits as "Wagon Train," "The Donna Reed Show," "Hawaiian Eye," "Perry Mason," "The Beverly Hillbillies," and "The Andy Griffith Show." She also landed a featured role in a new Gertrude Berg show only to see it cancelled. She also had small but fairly good roles in several movies including "Ladies Man" with comedian Jerry Lewis, "Wild and Innocent" with Sandra Dee and Audie Murphy, and Roger Corman's hit comedy, "Little Shop of Horrors."

Actress Karyn Kupcinet and actor Robert Conrad on the set of the ABC television show "Hawaiian Eye" circa 1961

Like many another Hollywood starlet who preceded her, Karyn, known as "Cookie" to her family and friends, had her share of problems. There were reports of drug abuse, and of being hooked on diet pills. There had been an arrest for shoplifting and a broken romance with actor Andrew Prine that apparently ended with bitterness on both sides. After their breakup, she was said to have stalked the actor and his new girlfriend, although that may have just been idle gossip, according to investigators.

The original detective on the case, Bob Chandler, told me that Prine was considered a suspect at one point and was given a lie detector test which was inconclusive. The detective said he knew Prine had been to Karyn's apartment recently because he found one of the actor's shirts there. Chandler said a great deal of work was done attempting to eliminate Prine as well as another possible suspect, David Lange, a movie technician who lived in the same apartment building, and was the brother of actress Hope Lange.

Karen's partially clothed body was found two days after her death by her best friend, Marsha Ross, who had invited her to Thanksgiving dinner, and became alarmed when she didn't show up. "We just drove over to her place, walked up the stairs. I opened the door and I knew something was wrong," Ross said. Karyn was strewn on a couch with the TV turned on. She added that a brandy snifter filled with cigarette butts was upside down on the floor. And there was half a cup of cold coffee across the room on a table. Apparently robbery wasn't a motive since nothing of value was taken. Miss Ross said she could think of no reason why anyone would kill Karyn.

On Thanksgiving Eve, Karyn had gone out to dinner with two friends, actor Mark Goodard and his wife, Marcia. Mark Goodard told detectives Karyn "was happy and vivacious" at dinner and said she was not the sort of person who would commit suicide.

Later that same evening, Karyn was visited by two other friends, actor Robert Hathaway and writer Edward Stephen Rubin. The two men said they watched TV with Karen until she excused herself, saying she was sleepy and wanted to go to bed. The two men said they left the apartment around 11 p.m. That was the last time anyone reported seeing Karyn alive.

Karyn was not sexually assaulted according to the police file on the case. Dr. Harold Kade, the autopsy surgeon, said Karyn died as the result of a broken bone in her throat caused by "manual strangulation." Crime writer James Elroy suggested that Karyn broke her neck from a fall in the shower. If that were the case, how did she make her way to the living room sofa where her body was found?

Sheriff's detectives spent hundreds of man hours on the case questioning everyone who had been involved with Karyn in the days leading up to her murder. I did two comprehensive television stories on Karyn Kupcinet's death, one on the NBC reality show "Murder One," and the other as a news segment on KCBS-TV some years later. Each time detectives hoped the TV reports might produce someone who might shed light on Karyn's murder. But not one person came forward.

Year after year Irv Kupcinet and his wife, Essee, traveled to Los Angeles to see what if anything investigators had found out about Karyn's death. And year after year they returned to Chicago, crushed by the lack of progress.

Equally crushing to the Kupcinets was a 1992 report on NBC's *Today Show* that listed Karyn's murder as one of the "mystery deaths" linked to the JFK assassination. Irv Kupcinet went on the attack in his column in the Chicago *Sun Times* on Feb, 9, 1992 when he wrote:

"The NBC Today Show on Friday carried a list of people who died violently in 1963 after the death of President John F. Kennedy and may have some link to the assassination. The first name on the list was Karyn Kupcinet, my daughter. This is an atrocious outrage. She died violently in a Hollywood murder case still unsolved. That same list was published in a book years ago with no justification or verification.

"The book left the impression that some one on the list may have been killed to silence them because of knowledge of the assassination. Nothing could be further from the truth in my daughter's case. The list apparently has developed a life of its own and for 'Today' to repeat the calumny is reprehensible. Karyn no longer can suffer pain by such an inexcusable moment, but her parents and her brother Jerry can."

The Kupcinets' yearly trips to L.A. stopped when Essee died in 2001. They had been married 62 years. Two years later the man known as "Mr. Chicago" died at 91. His last column appeared in the *Sun Times* the day before his death.

Their Academy Award winning son, Jerry Kupcinet, became one of Hollywood's more successful producers and directors. The Kupcinets kept Karyn's memory alive by financing a playhouse in her name at Shimer College in Waukegan, Illinois.

Can the murder ever be solved? It seems unlikely since there apparently is no substantial DNA evidence. Perhaps someone will come forward and confess. But other than that, Karen Kupcinet will remain just another name in the yellowed pages of the long list of unsolved L.A. homicides.

# 25

# GETTING AWAY WITH MURDER

One of the most unforgettable stories of my early days as a newsman involved the murder of a colleague, a veteran Hollywood columnist who had fallen on hard times and was in the midst of a comeback. The year was 1960 and the victim was 38-year-old Roby Heard. For many years I had no idea that the names of billionaire Howard Hughes, and his wife, actress Jean Peters, would be major talking points in solving the case.

Heard was a long time celebrity reporter for the Los Angeles *Herald Express* whose beat included the Academy Awards. He was fired for imbibing a little too much to suit his boss, Agnes Underwood, the only woman working as a city editor at a big city newspaper. Roby was considered a brilliant writer and my boss, Joe Quinn, decided to take a chance on resuscitating his career at City News Service.

I found Roby Heard to be a top flight rewrite man with a remarkable knowledge about sprawling Los Angeles County. Nine months after he was hired, on Nov. 12, 1960, Roby failed to show up for work. I reported him missing to the LAPD. Hours later I got a call from a homicide investigator.

He said Roby had been murdered in his Hollywood apartment, bludgeoned on the back of his head with a claw hammer while eating a breakfast of bacon and eggs at a desk in his living room. He was fully clothed but one of his pants pockets was turned inside out. His billfold was found in another pocket but there was no money in it. Roby had been paid on Nov. 11 with a check for $95 but it was missing. The bloodied claw hammer was found in a small dressing room.

Apartment house residents said the hammer belonged to Clarence Best, a 60-year-old handyman who had been working at the Lido apartment house for several months. But when the cops started looking for him he was nowhere to be found. Roby Heard's murder was front page news. His burial at Forest Lawn was attended by scores of reporters who had worked with him over the years.

The LAPD issued a warrant for the arrest of Best, who was described as a white male with gray hair, five feet eight inches tall and weighing 185 pounds. No one seemed to know much about Best. He had no criminal record in California, and finally the LAPD consigned the case to its unsolved file. Thirty one years later, in 1991, I was working at NBC when a former City News Service writer asked me if anyone had ever been arrested in Roby's murder. No arrest had been made, but there was an old arrest warrant for one Clarence Best, and I decided to track him down.

Searching through public records I found a Clarence E. Best who lived in East Canton, Ohio, and was married to one Elizabeth Peters, who had a daughter named Jean by a previous marriage. Could Jean, I wondered, be the beautiful actress Jean Peters, the former Miss Ohio who captivated Hollywood with her good looks and dazzling dance performance in "*Captain from Castile*" with Tyrone Power? Could it be the same Jean Peters who was brought to 20th Century Fox at the suggestion of billionaire Howard Hughes after he saw her in a screen test? The same Jean Peters who married the bashful billionaire in Tonopah, Nevada in 1957? Indeed it was. A source inside Howard Hughes' empire told me the story. Clarence Best, a burley, semi-literate handyman was, in reality, the stepfather-in-law of Howard Hughes. Upon meeting Best, Hughes declared him persona non grata at his Bel Air estate. Jean's mother was free to come and go as she pleased. But Hughes was adamant. He did not like Best. He didn't trust him, and there would be no welcome mat laid out for Clarence Best in Bel Air. In retrospect, Hughes' instincts were pretty good.

So in 1960 when Mary Elizabeth (Peters) Best came to Los Angeles for an extended visit with her daughter, Clarence Best trudged along, but was forced to find another place to live. So when he saw an ad for a jack of all trades at the Lido apartments in Hollywood he took the job with its offer of free rent. He told his friends in East Canton he had a well-paying position managing Hughes' apartment houses in L.A.

Then, for some unknown reason, he killed Roby Heard, and skipped town. The motive was unknown. Checking the Social Security death index, I found that the Clarence E. Best who lived in East Canton, Ohio had died in 1972.

But I wondered, did we have the right Clarence Best? I decided to find out. Reporter Bill Lagattuta flew with me to Ohio to gather information about Clarence E. Best. When we got to the small burg of East Canton, Best's former neighbors told us he had been dead for many years. We found his grave in a local cemetery and took a picture of it. The grave marker stated Best was born in 1900 and died in 1972. We were 20 years late. But we knew we had the right man after talking to townspeople who said Best was regarded as a local celebrity because of his frequent trips to Hollywood with his wife, Mary Elizabeth, mother of actress Jean Peters, and wife of Howard Hughes. Jean Peters was listed as one of Best's survivors at the local mortuary which handled his funeral arrangements.

In 1992 after our story about the Heard slaying on "Murder One," cold case detectives gave us credit for solving the case, and pronounced it closed. The sad part of all this was that Clarence Best got away with murder.

Jean Peters was not pleased with our story and told me so in a letter. She had never publicly discussed her marriage to Hughes after they divorced in 1971. I completely understood her embarrassment and pain at our story. But unfortunately she was very much a part of it as was Howard Hughes. Miss Peters died on Oct. 13, 2000 at 74, a onetime farm girl who left her imprint on Hollywood's galaxy of stars. Cardinal John Henry Newman once wrote that "a gentleman is one who never inflicts pain." For that I apologize to the memory of Jean Peters.

# 26

# IT'S WHO YOU KNOW IN HOLLYWOOD

It's been often said in Hollywood to get ahead "it's not what you know but who you know." I obviously didn't know the right people when I became part of a package deal that my bosses at NBC worked out with a relatively new Hollywood entity, Rysher Entertainment. A show I had created, "Murder One," dominated the Saturday night ratings at 7 p.m. in the Greater Los Angeles area week after week starting in October of 1991 and was awarded an Emmy by the Television Academy. After spending all my adult life as a newsman, I was about to venture into show business, Hollywood style. My boss, John Rohrbeck, a rising star in the corporate galaxy at NBC, put the show up for sale to the highest bidder and Rysher, emerged the winner.

I retired from NBC and stayed on as executive producer for Rysher but much to my surprise I soon had little or nothing to do. My original anchorman, Bill Lagattuta, was fired when he asked for a raise and replaced with a San Francisco feature reporter named Mike Hegedus. And it wasn't long before they replaced me.

The bosses at Rysher didn't like *"Murder One"* as a title, and changed the name to *"Prime Suspect"* which was already being used by a British production company. Their wisdom became suspect, particularly after the ABC Network picked up the name *"Murder One"* and launched a very successful crime show which enjoyed a long run on TV. I was already out in the cold and felt abandoned by the folks at NBC where I had spent nearly 20 years. But that's show biz. John Rohrbeck, who persuaded me to retire from NBC and sign on with Rysher, moved up the corporate ladder to a high paying job with General Electric, the new owners of the NBC television network. I was told by corporate types the success of *"Murder One"* and its sale to Rysher had a lot to do with Rohrbeck's promotion to president of the NBC Stations Division. Later he fell from grace after he admitted to a bad cocaine problem, and went into rehab. He died at a Los Angeles Hospital in 2002.

Back on the street, I accepted an offer from Rupert Murdoch's fledgling Fox network to work as an investigative producer on a new national program. It was called *"Front Page"* and Murdoch envisioned it as a rival to the very successful *"60 Minutes"* on CBS. The show's executive producers included my friend, Dave Browning, who would later end up with *"60 Minutes,"* and Dave Corvo, who went on to become the executive producer of NBC's *"Dateline"* show. I told them I had a good story in mind for their first broadcast.

For some time I had wanted to do an investigative report on Bob Evans, the star crossed motion picture producer who made some of Hollywood's biggest hits in the 1960s and 70s. After a fling as an actor in several films, Evans, at age 36, was named chief of production at Paramount Studios. His box office successes included such hits as *"Rosemary's Baby"*, *"Love Story,"* *"The Godfather,"*

*"The Odd Couple," "Goodbye Columbus," "Chinatown," "The Saint" and "Barefoot in the Park."*

In some circles Evans was credited with saving Paramount Studios from bankruptcy with his production of *"Love Story"* which starred Ryan O'Neal and Evans' future wife, Ali McGraw. His was one of the most impressive resumes in Hollywood. Box office success led to a 12 bedroom mansion in Beverly Hills and five different wives. But it was pretty safe to say that Bob Evans was down and out in Beverly Hills by the time the 1990s rolled around.

In 1980 Evans was busted for cocaine possession and the court ordered him to make a television documentary on the dangers of drug abuse as a condition of his probation Evans did the job at the NBC studios in Burbank with help from some of his Hollywood buddies. The program was entitled *"Get High on Yourself."*

Then in 1983 Evans became involved with director Francis Ford Coppola in making *"The Cotton Club."* One of his partners on the project, promoter Roy Radin, was murdered and his body dumped in the mountains. Evans was named a material witness in the case which eventually ended in the murder conviction of his former lover, cocaine dealer Lani Greenberger. The motive apparently was a dispute over profits from *"The Cotton Club."* Strangely, despite his status as a material witness, Evans was never called to testify. He was represented by attorney Robert Shapiro, a man who knew his way around the District Attorney's office. *"The Cotton Club"* was a box office flop and Evans ended up broke, down and out in Beverly Hills, his reputation shattered.

Those were hard times for the once high flying Evans. But rehab in the movie colony usually resulted in a quick comeback for the fallen. In 1991 Evans was reinstated as a producer on the Paramount lot by the corporation's president, Stanley Jaffe. That's where I picked up the story. Evans' first project was the movie "*Sliver*" starring actress Sharon Stone in a story about voyeurism and neighbors spying on each other at a New York City apartment house. Stone at the time was engaged to Bill McDonald, Evans' partner on Sliver. I learned through various sources that Evans was having trouble financing the movie and that he and McDonald were involved with several shady operators in raising money through an investment scheme.

Several detectives in the Los Angeles Police Department Organized Crime and Intelligence Division (OCID) told me if I wanted to know more about the Evans project I should meet them at a San Fernando Valley restaurant. After lunch they took me to their police car and opened the trunk. One of the cops pulled out a large carton and said, "...here's the Evans file. We can't do anything with it. No one at the DA's office wants to prosecute the guy." So I took the file and opened up what amounted to Bob Evans' "Pandora's Box."

It was obvious the cops felt a deep sense of frustration with District Attorney Gil Garcetti's office when they gave me their files on Evans. The thrust of the story was that two notorious con men known as the "Two Daves" were working out of Evans' office on the Paramount lot in Hollywood. David Knight and David Bryant had a previous record of civil fraud involving an oil drilling scam. Their company, Parker Bryant, Inc. was suspected of bilking 8,000 investors out of $200 million. The California Department of Corporations initiated a criminal investigation against Parker Bryant but dropped the ball after the two Daves put their company into bankruptcy. But that didn't stop Evans' partner in the movie, Bill McDonald, from letting the two Daves set up shop right in the middle of Evans' huge studio office with a new company known as Axiom Entertainment. It was another scam launched by "Dave and Dave" in which they promised investors, mostly senior citizens, huge profits from investing in Bob Evans' films.

One elderly man in Nevada told me he lost $75,000 in the oil drilling scam and another $10,000 in Axiom Entertainment. A 76-year-old grandmother in Orange County said she lost everything she had, $325,000 in the various investment schemes. Yet the District Attorney and the California Corporations Commission sat on their hands and did nothing. Small wonder the LAPD officers were frustrated and turned their files over to me.

There was a police informant in the case, Bob Evans' executive assistant, a woman named Laura Matook, who suddenly skipped town and my producers at "Front Page" insisted that I find her. Eventually I traced her to Chicago where she had moved, apparently frightened for her role in revealing details of the scam only to have the authorities ignore her story. I knocked on her door and asked for an interview. She politely turned me down, but I told her to call me at the hotel where I was staying if she changed her mind. My producers told me not to come back to L.A. until I got an interview with her. The next day Miss Matook called me and said she wanted to tell her story on camera. She said the truth had to come out. A Paramount official denied that two Daves took up space in Evans office, although admitting they may have visited McDonald once or twice. Not true, she said, adding that the two Daves conducted business right out of Evans' office, peddling investments in Axiom Entertainment. Matook said several times the ever present Daves handed out envelopes filled with cash to people in the office as sort of a good will gesture. She said she declined to accept one of the envelopes at least twice.

To celebrate their success the "Two Daves" threw a Malibu beach party for their friends and associates with a "Conan the Barbarian" theme, which was filmed. I managed to get a copy of the film and on it Dave Knight evokes a gale of laughter when he proudly tells his cronies about "...the barbaric nature of the work we do for a living."

The Axiom Entertainment scam wasn't as big as the oil drilling scheme. But state investigators told me that it netted Bob Evans own company at least $1 million which he used to help finance "*Sliver*" and "*The Two Jakes,*" the latter a sequel to "*Chinatown.*" Both movies were box office flops in the United States although "*Sliver*" did fairly well overseas.

McDonald insisted he was not responsible for the con. But we came across a check for $15,000 to McDonald written on the "Two Daves" own company letterhead two years earlier. McDonald insisted that money was simply paid him to provide an introduction to Bob Evans. Incidentally, Sharon Stone never married McDonald. Instead she when went to the altar with a newspaperman, Phil Bronstein, executive editor of the San Francisco Chronicle.

My report on the Bob Evans affair was broadcast as the first story on the debut of "*Front Page*" on the Fox network June 26, 1993. The reviews were favorable. But the programmers kept searching for an audience at different time slots and the show was cancelled after a few months because of low ratings.

Shortly after the first broadcast a private investigator asked me to meet with him. He said he had a tape he wanted me to hear. It was a wire tap on the phone of Hollywood madam Heidi Fleiss and the party on the other end of the line was Bob Evans. He was angry with

"Front Page" and my presentation of the story. "Why," he demanded "did that guy Noyes have to run the story about me as the first thing in the show. They never give me a break." "Bob," Heidi responded, "you should be ashamed of yourself for stealing all that money from those old people who really need it." Evans seemed taken aback by the madam's rebuke and the conversation came to a halt.

The only people punished for the scam were the investors who hoped to make a buck off Bob Evans' movies. If anything the Evans case illustrates the true nature of corruption in Los Angeles, the cozy relationship that exists between the power brokers and the elected officials which allows crimes against the public to go unpunished. Why is it, you have to ask, that the little guys always get stiffed? Despite his various pitfalls, Bob Evans seems to lead a charmed life. Evans was invited to a dinner party at the home of actress Sharon Tate on August 9, 1969. He wasn't feeling all that well and at the last moment called the actress and said he couldn't make it. But some uninvited guests showed up-- the Charles Manson family. And Bob Evans counted his blessings. He always has.

After "Front Page" folded, NBC asked me to return as a news consultant in late 1993. I was there for about six months when CBS offered me an incredible contract to rejoin the station where I first began my TV news career in 1961. NBC was quite unhappy that I left right in the middle of the O.J. Simpson case. I would have stayed but they refused to come close to matching the CBS offer. Former LAPD homicide cop Leroy Orozco joined me as part of my new investigative team.

# 27

## O.J. - RUNNING WITH THE MOB

Then, there was another case of "who you know, not what you know." It involved Orenthal James Simpson, better known as O.J., one of the greatest running backs in the history of both college and professional football. And for those who knew him best, he was probably one of the worst human beings who ever graced the face of the earth. Despite his acquittal by a jury, I don't have any doubt that the man they called "The Juice" used a knife to kill his estranged wife, Nicole Brown Simpson, and her friend, Ron Goldman, shortly before midnight on June 12, 1994,

I was at the murder site the next morning, a horrific scene with blood splattered in front of his wife's home in the upscale community of Brentwood. It was hard to avoid stepping on the evidence despite the police cordons thrown up all over the area. Later in the day I talked to a homicide investigator who had been searching for evidence inside Simpson's $2 million home a short distance away. He said there was blood in the bathroom sink next to Simpson's bedroom, and also on some socks that were strewn about on the floor. Simpson claimed the blood came from a cut on his finger but subsequent DNA testing said in all likelihood the blood was that of murder victim Ron Goldman.

After Simpson's arrest he was held without bail at the L.A. County Jail. One of his first visitors was the Reverend Roosevelt Grier, a former football star with the Los Angeles Rams. Grier was seeing Simpson in his capacity as an ordained minister. He left the jail in a virtual state of shock after Simpson was overheard by jailers to scream at the minister, "Yes, I killed the f........bitch." But of course testimony from the jailers could not be used because it was the classic case of a "priest-penitent" relationship, which is not admissible testimony under the law.

There was a lot of blame to go around for Simpson's acquittal. The case should have been tried in the Santa Monica courthouse because Simpson and his murdered wife both lived in that jurisdiction. But District Attorney Gil Garcetti knuckled under to his buddies in the legal system, including Robert Shapiro who had joined the Simpson defense team, and allowed the case to be transferred to the downtown courthouse where the jury wound up with eight black members. Moving the trial downtown produced widespread negative reaction because Simpson lived in the jurisdiction of the Santa Monica courthouse where the jurors would have been his "peers." It was probably the reason Garcetti was voted out of office at the next election.

The prosecuting team of Chris Darden and Marcia Clark was clearly outwitted by Johnnie Cochran, a former D.A.'s prosecutor himself who performed brilliantly. How can you forget Simpson trying to force his hand into that once bloodied glove during the televised trial and Cochran responding, "If it doesn't fit, you must acquit." This despite testing that showed the glove contained traces of blood from ex-wife Nicole, Ron Goldman and O.J. himself. DNA testing also strongly indicated that O.J.'s blood was found at the murder scene. The odds of it not being O.J's blood were placed at one in 170 million.

Obviously there were other factors in O.J.'s acquittal including sloppy handling of the blood evidence by LAPD crime lab workers. Much of the critical forensic evidence was gathered by LAPD detective Mark Fuhrman who, under questioning on the stand, insisted he had not used the "N" word within 10 years of the trial, testimony quickly contradicted. The prosecutors seemed barely prepared for a case of such magnitude. I was the only reporter present at the Criminal Courts Building the first day of the Los Angeles County Grand Jury investigation. Suddenly prosecutor Clark stormed out of the grand jury chambers and went face to face with a young woman who was about to testify that she spotted Simpson fleeing from the murder scene. Clark asked her, "Is it true you accepted $5,000 from the National Enquirer for your story." When the woman replied "yes," Clark screamed at her to get out of the building and the witness was never heard from when the case came to trial. Apparently Clark thought she had a slam dunk case and could ignore a critical witness who happened to sell her story to the tabloid press. Simpson, of course, was acquitted by the jury of all charges at a trial in a courtroom in downtown Los Angeles.

Later at a civil trial in suburban Santa Monica, where the trial rules are not as strict as those in a criminal case, a jury agreed there was a preponderance of evidence that Simpson killed his former wife and Ron Goldman and awarded surviving family members millions of dollars in damages.

When O.J. Simpson attended USC in 1967 as a highly touted running back, he brought with him a reputation as a guy with a violent streak who had problems with young women. In fact, reporters on the campus newspaper, "The Daily Trojan," tried without success to track down reports that O.J. had beaten up several cheerleaders. Shortly after the murders our investigative unit at the CBS station in Los Angeles received information that mob money had been used to pay off three women who had been assaulted by Simpson while he attended USC. Two of the women were described as cheerleaders; the third as a pretty Asian student. An informant told us each was paid $25,000 for their silence with money raised from the mob in Chicago and Las Vegas. I was somewhat skeptical at first until the informant said the man who arranged the payoffs was the late Jack Catain, a major underworld figure from Chicago who had become a successful industrialist in L.A and a counterfeiter at the same time. Catain was known as a USC booster and contributor to the university's football program. For years Catain had been identified by intelligence sources as being deeply involved in organized crime.

So why were the "boys" suddenly squealing on what seemed to have once been a major mob investment in O.J. Simpson, everybody's All American at USC and star running back for the National Football League's Buffalo Bills for 10 years, now an actor of lesser magnitude? The answer was quick and to the point. "We don't like a guy who goes around beating up and killing women." The informant said that before Simpson murdered his wife and her friend, he nearly killed an actress who was living with him in his trailer on the Paramount lot where they were both appearing in a "Naked Gun" movie." He said the actress, whose name I am withholding, was beaten so severely her jaw was broken. The informant said she was taken to the UCLA Medical Center where she was treated for multiple injuries under a bogus name. At this point Jack Catain was presumed to be dead and the mob hierarchy said there would be no more payoffs.

For many years Jack Catain's activities were heavily scrutinized by the FBI, Secret Service and the Internal Revenue Service's Intelligence Division. Catain had moved from Chicago to L.A. in the 1950s and founded an aluminum company, according to the Los Angeles *Times*. The company was acquired by a conglomerate, Rusco Industries, which at the time had annual revenues averaging $100 million. Catain soon became president of Rusco. He was also involved in construction, a cosmetic business and a company that sold exotic cars. He even got mixed up with a notorious con man named Barry Minkow who apparently took him for lots of money. Catain gave big bucks to a number of worthy causes, but the feds insisted beneath his high profile as a charitable benefactor was the face of a crook who dealt in counterfeiting, money laundering, extortion and ticket scalping.

On November 7, 1986 Catain was found guilty by a federal court jury of taking part in a scheme to distribute $3.5 million in counterfeit $20 bills, his first conviction although he had been considered a major organized crime figure for many years. Allowed to remain free on bail, Catain was reported to have died less than four months later from a heart condition at a hospital in suburban Encino. A hospital supervisor said Catain died in the cardiac intensive care unit, but gave no other details. There were rumbles by some federal investigators that Catain might not be dead; that a "stiff" may have taken his place at the hospital and the body was cremated so there could be no identification. And Jack Catain, they speculated, could have skipped town for a hideout in South America.

There are many other missing details in the life of Jack Calain. Just why did he come to the aid of O.J. Simpson time after time, as the mob source claimed? Did the mob hierarchy want to have the football great under its control? Could he have been used for point shaving purposes?

And what other secrets did Catain take to the grave with him if he actually went to his grave? O.J. Simpson isn't talking. As of this writing he's locked up in a Nevada prison, appealing a nine-to-33 year sentence for participating in an armed robbery at a Las Vegas hotel with a gang of thugs. Simpson claimed he was only trying to recover some valuable memorabilia that had been stolen from him. This time the jury didn't buy his story.

USC wasn't the only university in L.A. to have a booster with big time mob connections. Sam Gilbert, known to basketball players at UCLA as "Papa Sam," was reported to have died of a heart attack a few days before he was indicted on drug money launderings charges by a federal grand jury in Los Angeles.

Jerry Tarkanian, then coach of the University of Nevada basketball team, was quoted as saying that during the 1960s and 70s "the only team with a higher payroll than the UCLA Bruins was the Los Angeles Lakers of the National Basketball Association."

Gilbert made a fortune in the contracting business and donated huge sums of money to UCLA. He took a big interest in the basketball program when legendary coach John Wooden arrived on the scene and guided the Bruins to 10 national championships in 12 years. Some of the greatest players in the game such as Lew Alcindor (later known as Karem Abdul-Jabbar) and Bill Walton made UCLA the marquee college basketball program of all time.

"Papa Sam" reportedly took care of the athletes, buying them new clothes and providing them with lots of expense money. There was even a report that Gilbert paid for an abortion for a basketball player's girlfriend. Coach John Wooden, a scholarly man almost universally recognized as one of college basketball's greatest coaches, seldom said anything about Gilbert's relationship with his players. But on one occasion he told Basketball Times he confronted two of his stars, Sidney Wickes and Curtis Rowe, and demanded to know if the costly new clothes they were wearing were purchased by Gilbert. The soft spoken Wooden said when the players admitted Gilbert was their benefactor, he told them, "I don't like this."

During Wooden's tenure the NCAA never took any punitive actions against UCLA. But that all ended when Wooden retired. In 1981, the NCAA placed the UCLA basketball program on probation and ordered the school to dissociate itself from Sam Gilbert.

In 1987 a federal grand jury indicted Gilbert for helping launder $126 million in drug money as part of a joint organized crime venture to build the Bicycle Club, a huge 100,000 square foot draw poker palace in the Los Angeles suburb of Bell Gardens. As the principal contractor, Gilbert reportedly turned a profit of $36 million. After the indictment came down, federal agents immediately went to Gilbert's palatial home in Pacific Palisades, where he often entertained UCLA athletes, only to be told he had died two days previously. There was a lot of head shaking in the U.S. Attorney's Office. Apparently the "Grim Reaper" had once again had beaten them to another major figure in Southern California's organized crime network, or so it appeared.

# 28

# EVERYONE LOVES A
# HOLLYWOOD MYSTERY

For years I'd been a student of the Hollywood genre, something I probably acquired from the late columnist Florabel Muir during my days as a young reporter on the police beat. When I produced the show "*Murder One*" for NBC, stories about real life movie town mysteries were a big part of the presentation. Now a dozen years later my news bosses at CBS wanted me to revive the genre because the audience loved Hollywood mysteries.

There were plenty to choose from starting in the 1920s with the death of party girl actress Virginia Rappe at the hands of comedian Fatty Arbuckle; the slaying of mobster Johnny Stompanato in actress Lana Turner's bedroom in Beverly Hills; the strange death of blonde and beautiful comedienne Thelma Todd who died in the garage of her Malibu home, ostensibly from carbon monoxide poisoning. Andy Edmonds, a colleague, did extensive research and wrote a book that was turned into a movie linking the notorious mobster Lucky Luciano to Todd's death. Director Roman Polanski became fair game after he fled to Paris rather than go to prison for molesting and drugging a 13-year-old girl in the spa at the hillside home of actor Jack Nicholson. Then there was the beating death of actor Sal Mineo in an underground parking garage after he apparently made a homosexual advance to his killer. All Hollywood was abuzz at the strange drowning death at sea of the beautiful actress Natalie Wood, whose first picture as a child, "*Miracle on 34th Street*," charmed the nation. Then, too, there was the bizarre death of film colony beauty queen Marilyn Monroe, who, according to the official record, which I believe to be correct, died from a drug overdose, perhaps accidentally.

In 1995 I had the good fortune to take a call from screenwriter Peter Brooke who said he wanted to pitch a couple of stories that the studios wouldn't touch. Brooke was a charming guy who knew just about every old timer in Hollywood and he seemed convinced that I was one person who wouldn't shy away from vintage show business mysteries that seemed too hot for the studios to handle. His first story concerned the death of famed silent screen director Thomas Ince who once produced a movie that ran six hours. Ince and William Desmond Taylor were considered the two greatest directors of the silent movie era, and like Ince, Taylor died prematurely, murdered in a case that was never solved.

As Peter Brooke narrated the story, in the fall of 1924 Ince was a guest aboard a yacht owned by the legendary newspaper magnate William Randolph Hearst whose seagoing party included his mistress, Marion Davies, comedian Charlie Chaplin, and Louella Parsons, then an unknown writer but soon to become a nationally syndicated Hollywood gossip columnist, often referred to by her detractors as "Miss Lollipop." According to the official version of what happened on November 19, 1924, Thomas Ince died of acute indigestion. Ince supposedly became quite ill aboard the yacht which docked in San Diego after cruising near Catalina Island. He was taken to a hospital, then released and driven to his home in Beverly Hills where he died. The next day the *Long Beach Press Telegram* came out with the headline: **MOVIE PRODUCER SHOT ON HEARST YACHT**. That was the only mention of a shooting. The next day the two Hearst newspapers in Los Angeles, the *Examiner and Evening Herald*, both reported that Ince died of "acute indigestion." Case closed or so it would appear.

But according to Peter Brooke the scenario was much different. Hearst had long suspected that Chaplin, a known philanderer, was having an affair with Miss Davies. And when Hearst caught them embracing in a cabin he went off and grabbed a pistol he reserved for scaring off sharks and seagulls and started firing at Chaplin who was running for cover. According to witnesses interviewed by Brooke, Hearst fired two shots which missed their intended mark and struck Thomas Ince in the back.

Brooke led me to several old time Hollywood producers who provided virtually the same yarn with a few added frills. They said Ince's body was unloaded from the yacht in San Diego and driven back to Los Angeles. The old timers said the wife and children of Thomas Ince were provided with a handsome trust by the Hearst organization and never had to worry about money as long as they lived. There was no love lost for Marion Davies in the Hearst family. The day Hearst died his sons cancelled her free subscriptions to the *Examiner* and *Evening Herald* as well as an assortment of magazines the old man owned. As for Louella Parsons, Brooke said she was rewarded for her silence with a lifetime job as chronicler of the Hollywood scene for the Hearst newspaper empire.

Our television report on the Thomas Ince case generated considerable interest and I was at a loss to understand why Hollywood wasn't interested in Peter Brooke's story lines. Brooke died in 1999 and a few years later the story Brooke laid out for me was captured in a movie called *"The Cat's Meow"* produced and directed by one of Hollywood's great talents, Peter Bogdanovich.

Another story pitched me by Peter Brooke was that of George Reeves, the actor who starred in the TV show *"The Adventures of Superman"* from 1952 to 1958, and was one of the nation's most highly recognized TV personalities. Reeves was just 45 when he died from a gunshot wound to the head on June 16, 1959, at his suburban home in Benedict Canyon one year after his TV show was cancelled. Some of the actor's friends said he was depressed, but others, including Reeves' former wife, Eleanora Rose, were convinced he would never have committed suicide. For one thing at the time of his death Reeves was engaged to wed a New York socialite the following month. No suicide note was found at the scene. There was a gun between Reeves' legs but it was never dusted for fingerprints by the cops.

Reeves' family hired the Nick Harris Detective Agency to investigate the actor's death and the lead investigator, Milo Speriglio, concluded that George Reeves was murdered. Said Speriglio, *"...the trajectory of the bullet to his brain was such that he would have to have been standing on his left hand with the gun five feet away in his right hand if he indeed committed suicide."*

According to Peter Brooke, the most plausible explanation for Reeves' murder was his illicit 15-year romance with Toni Mannix, wife of high powered MGM studio executive Eddie Mannix. He said the word on the street was that Mannix hired a hit man to kill "Superman." It was much the same scenario as the 2008 film "Hollywoodland" released by Miramax Pictures. By then Brooke had been dead seven years. It was also the same story line we presented on television as one of "Hollywood's Greatest Mysteries" twelve years earlier. Brooke was a major contributor to that presentation.

But the one case Brooke told me about that I never got around to putting on TV was perhaps even more intriguing of all, one that involved some of Hollywood's biggest names including a future president. Brooke's girlfriend, a gorgeous Hollywood honey blonde movie bit player, vanished off the face of the earth about a month after they started dating. The disappearance of 27-year-old Jean Spangler on Friday evening, October 7, 1949 was indeed one of Hollywood's greater mysteries. The year before the monstrous murder of another aspiring actress, Elizabeth Short, the so-called "Black Dahlia," shocked the people of Los Angeles. There were plenty of people who thought Jean's disappearance might be linked to the Dahlia murder.

Jean Spangler was divorced from her first husband and had a 5-year-old daughter, Christine Louise. They lived in an apartment with Jean's mother, Florence, and wid-owed sister-in-law, Sophie Spangler. Jean had worked her way up from a chorus lines at the Florentine Gardens and Earl Carroll's night club to bit player at Columbia Studios where she had roles in seven movies and was on a first name basis with such actors as Robert Cummings, and a future president, Ronald Reagan.

A lady friend of Brooke on the Columbia lot introduced him to Jean and they had a whirlwind romance. "At this time in his life," Brooke said, "I was a naïve romanti-cist and I became totally infatuated with her." Actor Bob Cummings later told police that Jean visited his dressing room between takes, and mentioned how she had just met a young writer. "Not one of those Hollywood boobs," Cummings quoted Jean as saying, "but someone genu-ine, someone I could see myself marrying." That someone was Peter Brooke.

Brooke said he planned a date with Jean on Friday night, October 7, around 9 p.m. at the Black Watch, a bistro across the street from the landmark Schwab's drug store on Sunset Boulevard. Jean warned him that she might be late because she first had to meet with someone about "a problem." Brooke waited patiently for Jean to appear, spending much of the time with actor Dane Clark and director Sobey Martin. Jean was scheduled to get her big break shortly when she was scheduled to co-star with Clark in a stage play. Brooke had just sold his first screenplay, "A Killer's Toy," to a British producer and Sobey Martin was scheduled to direct the movie. After waiting several hours Brooke became convinced something was wrong, that Jean would never have stood him up. Finally, Brooke gave up and went back to his apartment at midnight. He called Jean's home and talked to her sister-in-law, Sophie who was caring for Jean's child. She too was worried because Jean always returned home in time to look after her daughter. Sophie told the cops that around 5:30 the evening of October 7 Jean came downstairs, looking slim and gorgeous in her white jacket and slacks. She told Sophie, "I'm going to work. Wish me luck." Sophie said she nodded and Jean crossed her fingers and said goodbye. Several hours later Jean called Sophie and told her she'd be working late at the Columbia lot and "not to worry." But when Peter Brooke called Sophie and said Jean had not shown up for their date, it seemed obvious that something had happened to her.

Accompanied by Brooke, Sophie filed a missing persons report at the Wilshire police station. Detectives told them Jean was probably out "partying all night" and would be home soon. But the next day newspaper headlines blared out that Jean Spangler's purse with two broken handles had been found in Griffith Park north of downtown L.A. A guard was making his rounds and opening the gates to the park when he found the handbag on the edge of the road. The purse had no money. It contained Jean's driver's license, house key, address book and member-ship card in the Screen Actors' Guild plus some cosmetics. Inside the purse was a note that read: *"Kirk, can't wait any longer. Going to see Dr. Scott. It will work best this way while mother is away."*

The note was unsigned, and now the cops were taking Jean's disappearance seriously. The presumption was that someone named "Kirk" was the father of her unborn child and that she planned to have an abortion. Dr. Scott was believed to be a phony name since abortionists seldom used their real names in those days because abortion was a crime. Family members and Jean's personal physician insisted she wasn't pregnant. But detectives interviewed a showgirl who had worked with Jean at a local club and quoted her as saying she was three months pregnant.

**Actress Jean Spangler and the note found in her purse after she vanished.**

Among those questioned by the cops were Kirk Douglas and Bob Cummings, both of whom worked on the Columbia lot, and boyfriend Brooke. Douglas was personally interviewed by Chief of Detectives Thad Brown at the Beverly Hills office of the actor's attorney. Prior to the meeting detectives learned that several times Jean mentioned to acquaintances that she was a friend of Kirk Douglas. One person quoted her saying she attended a party with the actor on September 24. But Peter Brooke told the cops he was the one who took Jean to the party and insisted Douglas wasn't present.

Douglas told Detective Chief Brown he was surprised that his name had surfaced in the case because he did not know Jean and never dated her. But he promised to check some more to determine if he had ever worked with Jean. The next day Brown returned to the attorney's office where Douglas told them he checked with his producer and found that Jean had been in one scene with him in "Young Man With a Horn." Said Douglas, "I think I stopped and talked with her while she was with a group of extras." Chief Brown and his detectives bought Douglas' story. Some days later, Jean's mother, Florence, who had returned from a trip to Kentucky, told police a man named Kirk picked up Jean twice at their home. But she said she could not identify him because he never got of his car.

Bob Cummings told the cops about that conversation in which Jean confided how happy she was with new boyfriend, Peter Brooke. The detectives also learned that Jean was a good friend of Ronald Reagan. There was a photograph of them together at a Hollywood film preview and Jean visited the future President when he was in the hospital. The record indicated the cops never talked to Reagan in person, but instead interviewed his mother.

According to Reagan's mother, her son had not seen Jean for some time.

Before Jean disappeared she told her sister she planned to see her former husband, Dexter Benner, a well-to-do chemist and plastics manufacturer, about child support. But Benner told police that never happened; that Jean had never asked for such a meeting. Benner gave what police described as an "iron clad alibi" to his whereabouts the night of Jean's disappearance. Benner said they were married in 1942 and divorced in 1946 after he learned she had a lover while he was in the armed forces.

For several years the L.A. newspapers hammered away at the story of Jean's disappearance, keeping it on the front pages with the Black Dahlia and Bugsy Siegel cases. They learned that Jean had been linked romantically at one time with Johnny Stompanato, the Mafia bad boy who some years later was stabbed to death in actress Lana Turner's bedroom. About the time Jean vanished, Davey Ogul, a member of mobster Mickey Cohen's gang, also turned up missing. Ogul's abandoned car was found near Cohen's clothing store in West Los Angeles. There was an intelligence report that Cohen might have crossed the El Paso border to Juarez, Mexico with Jean Spangler, and Davey Ogul but nothing came of it. Days later Cohen returned to the states from Mexico but he was alone.

Two years after Jean's disappearance the Fresno Police Department notified LAPD that a woman and man resembling Jean Spangler and Davey Ogul had been spotted at a motel and night club in the Central California city. LAPD Homicide cop Ed Jokish went to Fresno and picked up the trail of the two persons sighted there. But his search came to a dead end in Yosemite National Park. And so it went. What happened to Jean Spangler? Was she killed by an abortionist who botched the operation and got rid of her body? Were she and Davey Ogul rubbed out by the L.A. mob? Was she living in Mexico with a lover? Peter Brooke went to his grave many years later, not knowing the fate of the love of his life. To this day it remains one of Hollywood's greatest mysteries.

# 29

# THE ROMAN POLANSKI SAGA

When director Roman Polanski was arrested in Switzerland on an extradition warrant from Los Angeles on September 27, 2009 it almost seemed as if the notorious Dreyfus affair of the 1890s was being relived all over again with the roar of protest from the Hollywood film colony. Captain Alfred Dreyfus, the only Jewish member of the French Army's high command, was convicted of treason for giving military secrets to the Germans, and exiled to Devil's Island. He won his freedom after the crusading writer Emil Zola proved the charges were fabricated and the result of virulent anti-Semitism.

Polanski, a Polish Jew by birth, likewise became the focal point of an international incident, particularly in France where he lived. The charges of anti Semitism began atter he was arrested while preparing to attend the Zurich Film Festival where he was to receive a lifetime achievement award. He had fled from Los Angeles 31 years before after pleading guilty to having unlawful sexual intercourse with a 13-year-old girl and possibly facing hard time in prison. Actress Debra Winger, who was scheduled to present the award to Polanski, charged the film festival was "unfairly exploited by his arrest."

Hollywood's luminaries closed ranks behind Polanski. Movie producer Harvey Weinstein issued a clarion call to every Hollywood filmmaker to fight Polanski's forced return to the United States, saying the director had served his time for what he described as "a so-called crime." There was an immediate avalanche of support from more than 100 Hollywood figures including the likes of Woody Allen, Mike Nichols, Martin Scorsese and David Lynch. The veteran actress Whoopi Goldberg defended Polanski on ABC's morning talk show, "*The View*," saying he had pled guilty only to having unlawful sex with a minor, not rape. Goldberg said she was certain Polanski was sorry for his mistake. (The crime with which Polanski was charged was originally known as "statutory rape" in California but eventually changed to "unlawful sex with a minor."

Polanski's supporters cited his remarkable filmmaking credits which included such hits as "*Chinatown,*" "*Rosemary's Baby*" and "*Tess.*" Nearly 25 years after he fled the United States, Polanski won an Academy Award in absentia for his film, "The Pianist." He found a new home in Paris with its more tolerant life style. He married a young actress, Emanuelle Seigner, and they had two children. He made 10 movies overseas up to the time he was arrested on the extradition warrant in Switzerland.

Joining the filmmakers in the chorus of protest was Polish Foreign Minister Radoslaw Siroshi who expressed "consternation and shock" at Polanski's arrest Also voicing dismay was former Polish leader and union activist Lach Walesa who spearheaded the revolt against the Soviet style Communism in his country. France's Minister of Culture, Frederic Mitterand, said he was "dumbfounded" by the developments.

While Hollywood's big names joined together in denouncing Polanski's arrest, there was little sympathy in the rest of America. Polls showed the vast majority of those surveyed strongly believed that Polanski should face the bar of justice. The Los Angeles *Times* noted that the Polanski case "...points to a sharp divide between Hollywood and Middle America."

The "Hollywood family" has a long history of indulging unlawful sexual activities in its ranks and the term "celebrity justice" has an ugly connotation for critics of the justice system in California. Some examples: Errol Flynn bedded down with a 16-year -old girl who was with him when he died of a heart attack. Flynn had earlier been acquitted by a jury on two counts of statutory rape involving teenage girls. Charles Chaplin had his way with Lita Grey who was just 15 when he married her. Chaplin was perhaps Hollywood's most notorious "womanizer" who usually preferred the company of teenage girls. After billionaire Howard Hughes became a movie producer one of his favorites was a 16-year-old budding star, actress Ida Lupino. Rock Hudson's penchant for young boys was swept under the rug by the studio moguls who married him off when they foresaw big movies bucks in the handsome actor's future romancing the likes of Doris Day.

I may be one of the few reporters left who was around 31 years before when Polanski was arrested, then indicted by the Los Angeles County Grand Jury on six felony counts. And I am convinced that while Captain Alfred Dreyfus was finally freed when the truth became know, there are shades of gray and black in the Polanski case by which we may never know the whole truth. An example of a blatant mistruth came when a Polanski advocate, attorney Jeffrey Lowe, gave the case a Dreyfus-like overtone when he wrote in an L.A. legal newspaper that the judge in the director's case, Lawrence J. Rittenband was an anti-Semite and a member of a country club that barred Jews. In truth, Judge Rittenband was Jewish and friends said he was extremely proud of his heritage. Furthermore, he was a member of the predominantly Jewish Hillcrest County Club.

Much of the furor over Polanski's detention resulted from an Emmy winning HBO documentary broadcast in 2008, "Roman Polanski: *Wanted and Desired.*" The program was written and produced by one of my former journalism students at USC, Marina Zenovich. It aired accusations by the original prosecutor, Roger Gunson, and defense attorney Douglas Dalton, that Judge Rittenband was guilty of judicial misconduct by reneging on a deal to let Polanski go free after "diagnostic testing" at a state prison to determine if Polanski was a mentally disordered sex offender. Judge Rittenband was not around to defend himself, having died in 2004 at the age of 88.

Compounding the misconduct charge was another allegation in the documentary by a second deputy district attorney, David Wells, who claimed he gave Judge Rittenband the idea of using the diagnostic testing as a form of punishment. Such a conversation with a prosecutor would violate judicial ethics. But Wells said *"I'd like to think of it as an inept statement, but the reality is that I lied."* Associates said Wells had long been upset because he was not assigned the original prosecution of Polanski. Wells said he very much regretted the problems he had caused the court and the District Attorney's office.

But another reporter advised me that Wells had also told him the same story about his involvement in judicial misconduct. Based on what Prosecutor Gunson, Wells and defense lawyer Dalton said in the documentary, Polanski's attorneys presented it as evidence of judicial misconduct. The presiding judge of the L.A. Superior Court criminal Division, Peter Espinoza, said he found substantial evidence of misconduct by Judge Rittenband but could do nothing because Polanski was a fugitive.

After Polanski was arrested in Zurich, a spokesperson in the District Attorney's office told me that many of the original documents in the 32-year-old court case had disappeared and they were attempting to reconstitute the file. Fortunately back in the 1970s I copied the transcripts of the various proceedings in the Santa Monica courthouse, and maintained a fairly precise record of the events. As an example, one of the things I have not seen mentioned in the numerous accounts of the case is the fact that Judge Rittenband delayed Polanski's sentencing for 90 days so he could make a movie in Europe. Another item virtually ignored by the press was Rittenband's statement in court that he did not want Polanski placed in the general prison population because he might be harmed by other inmates.

The date of the Polanski affair was March 10, 1977. It took place at the home of actor Jack Nicholson shrouded by high shrubbery off Mulholland Drive on L.A.'s Westside. Nicholson was not home that day. The grand jury was quickly convened and indicted Polanski on six felony charges.

Testifying before the grand jury without a lawyer, the 13-year-old girl said she was terrified of Polanski and wanted to cry; that she begged him to stop, but he didn't. She said when it was all over Polanski told her, *"Don't tell your mother about this. It is our secret."* Then he drove her home.

It didn't remain a secret for long. The girl, Samantha Jane Gailey, was overheard by older sister Kim telling her boyfriend over the phone what Polanski had done to her.

Kim told her mother, Susan Gailey, who promptly called police. At the time Samantha was in the ninth grade at the Hughes Middle School in the San Fernando Valley suburb of Woodland Hills, which is said to have fostered a new breed of young women described as fun-loving "Valley Girls." Classmates said the beautiful Samantha, who lived in a father- less home, wanted to be a model or an actress.

A probation report prepared for the court indicated she was not an "innocent" by any means. Quoting from the report Judge Rittenband said:

*Although just short of her 14th birthday at the time of the offense, the prosecutrix (Samantha Gailey) was a well developed young woman who looked older than her years and regrettably was not unschooled in sexual matters. She had a 17-year-old boyfriend, with whom she had sexual intercourse at least twice prior to the offense involved. The probation report further reveals that the prosecutrix was not unfamiliar with the drug Quaalude, she having experimented with it as early as her 10th or 11th year. I believe the statement of the defendant was that he was told by her that she had stolen the Quaaludes that she had used in the past from her mother. Now this was the same drug which was furnished to her by the defendant. However, although the prosecutrix was not an inexperienced, and unsophisticated young girl, this of course was not a license to the defendant, a man of the worlds in his 40s, to engage in act of unlawful sexual intercourse with her."The part played by the mother in permitting her daughter to go to the Nicholson home, unchaperoned, is to be strongly condemned although there is some evidence that the mother asked to go along on the venture."*

Samantha's mother, Susan Gailey, was known to friends in her hometown of York, Pennsylvania as an aspiring actress whose heart was set on a career on either the

New York stage or in Hollywood movies. In 1966 Susan married her third husband, Jack Gailey, an attorney and long time member of the Pennsylvania legislature. Samantha was just three years old. She never knew her real father, Susan's first husband. The girl was adopted by Gailey and became extremely close to him before Susan divorced him circa 1976. Susan then departed for California with Samantha and Kim, intent on making a name for herself in Hollywood. It didn't take long to launch her career. She got bit roles in TV shows such as "Police Woman," "L.A. Law" and "Starsky and Hutch," and found a modicum of artistic success doing a slew of car commercials on TV.

Details of the police investigation, grand jury testimony and personal interviews were the basis for the following sequence of events:

On Feb. 13, 1977 Polanski came knocking on the front door of the family home in suburban Woodland Hills, his sights set on Susan Gailey's 13-year-old daughter, Samantha. A mutual friend of Polanski and the Gailey family apparently arranged the director's introduction. Polanski said he was in between directing jobs and claimed he was on assignment for the French glamour magazine, "*Vogue Hommes*," to shoot pictures of beautiful young women. (A magazine official later denied Polanski was given any such assignment).

On meeting Samantha, Polanski was obviously impressed. He showed Mrs. Gailey and Samantha an array of "beauty shots" of young women from the magazine and said he would like to do a similar photographic treatment on Samantha. Both mother and daughter excitedly agreed to the photo shoot. One week later, on Feb. 20, 1977 Polanski returned to the Gailey home, with his 35-millimeter camera. Mrs. Gailey stood by as Polanski went to Samantha's closet and picked out her clothes for the shoot, a pair of blue jeans, a white shirt and a patchwork blouse. According to Samantha's grand jury testimony, she got into his car and they drove about a block to a hilly area which Polanski decided was adequate for the photo shoot. Samantha said they climbed up to the top of the hill and she stood next to a tree where he began filming her. After a few moments he asked her to remove her blouse and pose topless. She removed the blouse without complaint and he photographed her. It's estimated he took 60 to 70 pictures.

When she got home Samantha talked about the extensive photo shoot but never mentioned to her mother that she posed partially nude. Polanski later called and said the proofs didn't turn out too well. So Polanski informed Samantha there would have to be another photo shoot at a different location. Susan Gailey said she would like to tag along, but Polanski insisted she stay away from the shoot because her presence might "inhibit" Samantha.

On March 10 Polanski first drove Samantha to the estate of actress Jacqueline Bisset in the Mulholand hills, an area populated with celebrities. Samantha said when they got there she saw "three guys and two girls." Polanski decided to move the shoot elsewhere, saying the lighting wasn't good. He told Samantha he was calling actor Jack Nicholson's home to see if he could film there. Polanski said a woman at the home told him to come right over – it was just five minutes away.

When they got to the actor's home Samantha said they were greeted by a woman with long black hair and two dogs. Later I was told by an LAPD investigator the woman was actress Anjelica Huston, daughter of the legendary director John Huston. Samantha said Polanski went to a refrigerator where he found a bottle of champagne and asked Miss Houston if he could open it. She said he could so he got some glasses and gave Samantha some bubbly. Miss Houston decided to leave and Polanski was left alone with Samantha. He coaxed her to the Jacuzzi where he told her to take off her clothes. Samantha told the grand jury she was frightened but complied because no one else was there. She said he took some pictures of her. Then he gave her part of a Quaalude tablet. Samantha said the combination of champagne and the pill made her feel woozy. She said she told Polanski she did not want to get in the Jacuzzi because she had asthma. Samantha told the grand jury she lied bout having asthma because she did not want to join Polanski who was nude in the steaming water. She said Polanski then jumped in the pool, swimming a lap before getting out. Finally he coaxed her into Nicholson's master bedroom where the various sexual acts took place. Samantha told the grand jury she was so dizzy from the combination of champagne and pills she could hardly remember much of what happened.

But what Samantha did remember was sufficient to indict Polanski on six felonies. She said Polanski first performed oral sex on her, followed by intercourse. Then he stopped and asked her if she was taking the "pill." Samantha said no, and then he asked "...*would you want me to go in through your back, and I went, 'no.'* " Samantha said he ignored her wishes and sodomized her. She said she cried because he hurt her. Then she said Anjelica Huston returned home and Polanski chatted with her through a crack in the bedroom door. A short time later Polanski drove Samantha home.

After Mrs. Gailey's phone call to the LAPD events began unfolding rapidly. LAPD Detectives Phil Vanatter (later a lead detective in the O.J. Simpson case) and John Rosenbrock, a rape investigator, accompanied by Deputy District Attorney David Wells, and four other officers descended on the Beverly Wilshire Hotel where Polanski was staying with a warrant for his arrest. They spotted Polanski in the lobby where he was waiting for some friends and handcuffed him. Then they searched Polanski's suite where they seized cameras, film and a bottle of Quaaludes. Vanatter said Polanski tried to pop a "lude" saying he was nervous but the cop took it away from him. The justice system moved at a rapid pace. Two weeks later Polanski was indicted by the Los Angeles County Grand Jury on the six felony counts. He was allowed to remain free after posting $2500 bail.

Why on earth, you might ask, would a man as internationally famous as Roman Polanski risk his career under such circumstances? There was a suggestion by Polanski himself that he might have lost his moral compass after his beautiful wife, actress Sharon Tate, was butchered by the Manson family. He also was said to be haunted by the death of his mother in a Nazi death camp.

There were several reports that Polanski had engaged in sexual escapades with other underage girls. A friend of Samantha Gailey told me she knew of another Polanski conquest, a second "Valley Girl" who was 16. Years later another report linked the director to an attack on a teenage actress in Europe. This last incident was publicly confirmed on May 14, 2010 in the midst of the tenacious legal battle over Polanski's extradition from Switzerland to the United States. British actress Charlotte Lewis came forward and said Polanski raped her in his Paris apartment "...in the worst possible way when I was just 16."

She said she was in France appearing in the movie "Pirates" directed by Polanski when he assaulted her. It was learned that Miss Lewis told her story a year previously to prosecutors in the L.A. District Attorney's office.

That alleged incident in Paris occurred nine years after the District Attorney at that time, John Van de Kamp, acting on the request of Susan Gailey and her ex-husband, Jack Gailey, dropped five of the felonies in the indictment in return for Polanski's plea of guilty to a charge of "unlawful sexual intercourse with a minor." Appearing in a Santa Monica court on August 8, 1977, Polanski pled guilty to the unlawful sex charge in count three of the indictment despite being warned by Judge Laurence Rittenband that he was giving up the right to confront his accusers and could face prison time. Asked by prosecutor Roger Gunson exactly what he had done, Polanski answered, "*I had sexual intercourse with a person, not my wife, under the age of 18.*" Asked by Gunson if he knew the penalty for the crime, Polanski answered, "*It's one to 15 to 20 years in state prison.*" He also acknowledged that he knew Samantha was just 13 when he had sex with her.

Gailey family attorney Lawrence Silver pleaded with the court not to send Polanski to prison. He told the court, "*My view, based upon advice from experts, and the view of the girl's parents, is that such a trial may cause serious damage to her. Long before I had met any other attorney in this case, my clients informed me that their goal in pressing the charges did not include seeking the incarceration of the defendant. He should remain under the supervision of the court in a program to insure complete rehabilitation. The plea of guilty by the defendant is contrition sufficient for my clients to believe their goal may be achievable.*"

Polanski counsel Douglas Dalton argued against hard time for his client, saying, "*This offense (unlawful sexual intercourse) doesn't have the connotation of rape. It's not even a criminal offense in about 13 of our states and in many places of the world.*"

A probation report prepared for the court said Polanski had been examined by two psychiatrists who determined that he was not a "mentally disordered sex offender." The report recommended that Polanski be placed on probation – with no jail time. Dr. Alan Davis, a psychiatrist who interviewed Polanski for the report, wrote: *"The incarceration of Polanski would impose an unusual degree of stress and hardship because of a highly sensitive personality. He was one of those great creative minds who came to Hollywood from Europe. While enriching the community with their presence, they have brought with them the manners and mores of their native lands, which in rare instances have been at variance with those of their adopted land."*

Prosecutor Roger Gunson denounced the psychiatrists for concluding that Polanski's sexual activities with the teenager "occurred naturally and mutually." Gunson noted that Polonski claimed to be a teetotaler but was drinking alcohol on the day in question and furnished it to a minor child along with a powerful Quaalude. Said Gunson, *"It does not appear these are the normal job or work projects involved in photographing a 13-year-old girl."*

Judge Rittenband praised both the prosecution and defense lawyers for their arguments and said the sentencing in the case was a "most troublesome and difficult task." He then announced his decision. Roman Raymond Polanski would be sent to the diagnostic facility at the state prison in Chino, California for a period of 90 days for an "in depth diagnostic evaluation to reach a fair and just decision as to the sentence to be finally or eventually imposed." The judge said confinement in the facility would allow Polanski to be kept away from the general prison population where he might be harmed. (Nowhere in the official record is there any indication that the judge agreed to let Polanski go free in exchange for time served at the prison diagnostic facility).

Then Douglas Dalton appealed to the court to delay the diagnostic test for 90 days so Polanski could complete work on the movie *"Hurricane"* which was being filmed in Europe. Dalton said the film was budgeted for millions of dollars and involved the services of hundreds of people who would be thrown out of work if the film were halted.

Judge Rittenband not only agreed to the 90 day delay, but said he might be willing to give Polanski another extension if more time was needed on the movie. After he returned Polanski would go directly to Chino for the evaluation. Some weeks later the judge was angered when shown a wire service photo of Polanski partying at an Octoberfest celebration in Munich, Germany. The picture showed Polanski holding a beer stein and smoking a cigar in the company of two attractive young women. Judge Rittenband said the picture caused him "great consternation." But finally he was satisfied by Polanski's lawyers that the director was really hard at work on the movie.

On returning to the U.S. at the end his 90 day stay, Polanski entered the state prison facility at Chino where he was examined by more psychiatrists who ruled he was not a mentally disordered sex offender or a threat to society. He was released after just 45 days. After reading the psychiatric report, Judge Rittenband called it a "whitewash." On January 30, 1978, the judge met in chambers with defense counsel Dalton and prosecutor Gunson to discuss the report. The judge said there was no mention in the report of any discussions either by counselors or psychiatrists relating "...*to the serious and more aggravated charges of rape by drugs and alcohol, sodomy and oral copulation of a 13-year-old girl.*" The judge said he would ignore the recommendation that Polanski be placed on straight probation with no additional jail time. He said he intended to send the director back to Chino to serve out the 90 day sentence given him originally.

The judge said on completion of the time at Chino Polanski should be deported by the U.S. Immigration and Naturalization Service because keeping the director out of the country would be in the best interests of the people of California. The judge acknowledged he did not have the power to deport Polanski but said it was only a recommendation.

The matter was continued until February 1, 1978. Released from prison the previous day, Polanski fled the country. The judge then issued a bench warrant for his arrest.

Rittenband appeared to be caught off guard when Dalton filed a motion a few days later stating that the judge was biased against Polanski and could not grant him a fair sentence. He asked that Rittenband be disqualified. The judge said, *"I am not now and have never been biased against Mr. Polanski and I know that Mr. Polanski would receive a fair and just sentence from me."* The Los Angeles County Counsel ruled there were insufficient grounds to disqualify the judge. But Rittenband stepped down anyway, noting that attorney Dalton had publicly stated that "Mr. Polanski might return for sentencing if another judge is assigned to the case." But, of course that never happened.

In his 1984 autobiography, *"Roman by Polanski,"* he described the events that led him to flee. He wrote: *"On September 16 Judge Rittenband told Dalton that the diagnostic study in Chino would constitute my punishment. Now, after I'd done my time, he announced that the report, which recommended probation, was the* worst he'd ever seen, 'a complete whitewash' and he was determined to send me back inside. 'I'm getting too much criticism,' he confided to Dalton. 'I'll give him an indeterminate sentence.' He also expressed surprise that I'd spent only 42 out of a possible 90 days in prison. This was almost absurdly disingenuous, since he knew as well as anyone that the average time for a diagnostic study was 47 days."

Polanski's 42 days at Chino were spent in an isolation area with other inmates who might be harmed if they were placed in the general prison population. He said bad as it was being in prison, he enjoyed himself after a few days because he was out of the glare of the "public eye." Polanski said he was treated fairly at all times by guards and the prison authorities but it was less than pleasant living among snitches, killers and habitual criminals. One of those in protective custody with him was a former "hit man" for the Mexican Mafia turned informant who had killed 16 people.

Polanski made it clear to his attorneys he did not want to go back to Chino or face the possibility that the judge would give him a longer sentence. He said he reviewed the situation with his lawyers but they could not offer any assurance that Rittenband would relent and "...let me go free after a full 90 days."

On January 31, 1978 Douglas Dalton picked up Polanski following his release from Chino and drove back to L.A. where they ended up in Dalton's office. "What had I to gain by staying?" Polanski asked. "The answer appeared to be nothing." Polanski said he borrowed a car and drove to the office of fellow director Dino De Laurentis where he explained his plight. He said Dino loaned him a thousand dollars. They hugged each other, and he departed. Polanski said at first he planned to go to Mexico. He wrote:

*"Then I thought the better of it. I made a U-turn and drove to L.A. International Airport. I got there with 15 minutes to spare before the next British Airways flight to London, and, with my American Express card, bought the last seat on the plane. My exhilaration was almost manic. I didn't sleep a wink all the way."*

Once in London, he called Dalton immediately and told him what he had done. "He didn't say much," Polanski wrote. "And I knew why. I was putting him in a spot." A short time later, Polanski said Dalton flew to Paris and tried to convince him to return to L.A. for sentencing. But Polanski was adamant. He would not return to the United States unless Dalton could assure him he would not be going back to prison.

The Polanski case was pretty much dormant until Dec. 30, 1989 when Samantha Gailey filed suit for damages against the director using the name of "Jane Doe." Her attorney was Lawrence Silver who a dozen years before had asked Judge Rittenband to allow Polanski to plead guilty to just one of the six felony counts so Samantha would not be forced to testify at a public trial. Now, she was a beautiful young woman of 25 and her identity would soon become a matter of public record.

The court quickly became awash in legal documents containing thousands of pages of legal motions and challenges. Polanski was asked to return to L.A. to give a deposition to Gailey's lawyers but he refused to set foot on U.S. soil. His attorneys demanded that Samantha be the first to give a deposition, but her legal team said no, Polanski had to be the first to testify. Finally Polanski was deposed in Paris for four days in May of 1993.

Polanski invoked the U.S. Constitution's Fifth Amendment against self incrimination when questioned about the original allegations of sodomy, oral copulation, and giving booze and pills to a minor. He would only admit to unlawful sex with a minor. In the course of the deposition attorneys for both sides began discussing a possible settlement. Following a conference later in the year in Los Angeles, both sides began coming to terms.

It was decided that Polanski would give Samantha $500,000 in a lump sum plus interest until the money was paid. The court issued a stipulated judgment authorizing the payment but collecting it proved difficult. By 1996 the money was still owed Samantha. Attorney Silver swung into action with another flurry of legal documents that set the stage for garnishing all of Polanski's earnings from several major studios including Warner Brothers, Sony Pictures and Mandalay Entertainment. Silver hit the jackpot with Mandalay Entertainment, opening a small window on the salaries paid top directors in Hollywood. The corporation revealed that it had advanced Polanski $750,000 to direct a picture called "The Double" and that he would be entitled to $2.5 million more payable in installments if the picture were completed under budget.

Silver had put the squeeze on the studios and the men running them were dead set against being dragged into the Polanski affair. So Polanski had no choice but to pay up if he wanted to keep doing business in the company town. That was the frosting on the cake for attorney Lawrence Silver. At this point the legal war abruptly ended. Polanski now owed Samantha Gailey $601,583 with accrued interest. There is no court record of the money being paid, there didn't have to be. Samantha, now married and known as Samantha Geimer, acknowledged she had received the settlement. As of this writing Mrs. Geimer lives with her husband and three children in Hawaii, far removed from the glare of Hollywood and the tabloids.

In 1997, I was working as a news consultant for television station KTLA in Hollywood when one of my law enforcement sources advised me that something was in the works involving the Roman Polanski case, and that the fugitive director might return to Los Angeles in a matter of days. I called Polanski's original prosecutor, Roger Gunson, in the D.A.'s office and he abruptly told me, "...*there is nothing I can discuss with you about the case. I have nothing to say.*" Little did I realize at the time that Deputy D.A. Gunson would soon shock his colleagues by implying that the deceased Judge Rittenband had reneged on an agreement to release Polanski for the 42 days served at Chino Prison's Diagnostic Center. My instincts told me to keep digging.

I called the Santa Monica courthouse to see if there was anything new in the Polanski file. But a clerk told me the file was gone. So I asked two of my researchers, Vic Cook and Linda Hackett, to go to the county archives in downtown Los Angeles and see if they could locate the file. But the name of Roman Polanski was nowhere to be found in the criminal index, which was rather perplexing. Then Hackett discovered the name of "*Raymond Roman*" on the index along with a case number. Cook handed the case number to a clerk and a few minutes later he gave them the criminal file on Roman Raymond Polanski. At this point it seemed to me that some sort of subterfuge was taking place. It was a troubling development and I could only speculate it was part of some sort of cover-up.

Buried out of order near the bottom of the file dated December 5, 1996 was a memorandum from Superior Judge Larry Paul Fiedler stating that he had conferred in chambers with attorney Douglas Dalton and Prosecutor Roger Gunson and the trial of Roman Polanski was set for "January 31, 1997 at 10:30 a.m. in his department. Obviously that was an error because Polanski had pleaded guilty 20 years previously. Perhaps he would be tried for jumping bail and fleeing the jurisdiction of the court. But a follow up memo deleted the language regarding the trial, and stated that a further conference in chambers was set for January 31, 1997. There was no public record of what happened on that date.

I was told by two sources in law enforcement that all the court proceedings were held secretly in Judge Fiedler's chambers. There was no court reporter present, but the sources said a deal had been worked out to have Polanski return to Los Angeles and surrender before Judge Fiedler on a fugitive warrant. The judge would then grant Polanski his freedom in exchange for the 42 days served in the Prison Diagnostic Center. On September 27, 1997 I broke the story about the secret court talks on KTLA, and it provoked an immediate uproar. The *Associated Press* picked up the story and sent it worldwide.

Three days later another memorandum from Department 122 was entered in the Polanski file at the courthouse. It simply stated: "Court (Judge Fiedler) and Counsel (Dalton and Gunson) confer in chambers. The conference is not reported. Bench warrant remains outstanding."

I was later told my story effectively squelched the Polanski "deal." For one thing, he wanted zero publicity should he return, and now that was impossible because of my story.

In doing the story I had no ulterior motives although some persons suggested I acted as a "tool of law enforcement." In my view, the judiciary cannot operate secretly in a democratic society and engage in "deal making" that leaves no paper trail such as a transcript or summary of the proceedings. It's hard to believe that it was a clerical accident when Polanski's name was eliminated from the court's criminal index and he was simply referred to as "*Raymond Roman*." If we hadn't found the file, no one would have ever known about the secret court proceedings.

Meantime, after the settlement was paid out Samantha Geimer unexpectedly came to Polanski's defense when appearing on the TV show "*Inside Edition*" in 1997 when legal moves were under way to force the director's return to L.A. While admitting she was in tears at the time of the sexual encounter, Samantha said Polanski "...wasn't forceful or mean. It wasn't rape." In an article that appeared in the L.A. *Times* on February 23, 2003 in advance of the Academy Awards in which the director had been nominated for an Oscar, Geimer urged that Polanski be allowed to return to the United States without facing jail time. She wrote: "*My attitude surprises many people. That's because they didn't go through it all; they didn't know everything that I know. People don't understand that the judge went back on his word. They don't know how unfairly we were all treated by the press. Talk about feeling violated! The media made that year a living hell, and I've been trying to put it behind me ever since.*"

The D.A.'s office was unmoved by Samantha's plea on behalf of the director. L.A.'s new district attorney, Steve Cooley, kept his focus on Polanski. Soon the DA's office was monitoring Polanski's travels in Europe, hoping to arrest him on an extradition warrant. There were several missed opportunities. The drumbeat for Polanski's freedom generated by the HBO documentary seemed to intensify the D.A.'s efforts to bring Polanski before the bar of justice. Switzerland had a firm extradition treaty with the United States, and when the director showed up for the Zurich Film Festival in September of 2009 he was promptly taken into custody by Swiss police. Eventually he was placed under house arrest at a Swiss villa he owned. Polanski's lawyers filed one court motion after another to halt his extradition to the U.S, including a request that he be sentenced in absentia, which was denied. Ten months after receiving the extradition request from the U.S. Government, it was formally denied by the Swiss Ministry of Justice which sided with the contention of Polanski's lawyers that the 42 days he served at the Chino Prison Diagnostic Center constituted the intent of his sentence in 1977 for the crime of having sex with a minor. It meant that Polanski was a free man, at least in Switzerland as well as France where he was a citizen and which had no extradition treaty for child rape. But he could be subject to arrest once more in any other country that has an extradition treaty with the U.S., and Los Angeles County District Attorney Steve Cooley vowed to go after Polanski should he step outside his protected boundaries.

Critics called the Swiss decision another case of "celebrity justice." The Los Angeles *Times* editorialized that the Swiss "...may share the moral myopia that has made Polanski an object of affection throughout Europe."

To repeat myself, there is no evidence anywhere in the public record that the late Judge Lawrence Rittenband agreed to sentence Polanski to the 42 days he spent at a prison diagnostic center to determine if were a mentally disordered sex offender. The facts are obvious. Roman Polanski pled guilty to having sex with a 13-year-old girl and fled the country before he could be sentenced. And his lawyers went to any length they could to prevent his presence before the bar of justice in California. Call it what you will, but in my view "celebrity justice" simply prevailed again.

# 30

## THE SUBWAY TO NOWHERE

During my brief retirement in the year 2000 I taught a graduate course in investigative reporting at the University of Southern California, and the students' collective assignment was to investigate the cost of L.A.'s brand new 17-mile-long subway. One of my pet peeves over the years was the way government officials dismantled L.A.'s great public transportation system known as the "Red Cars." The privately owned Pacific Electric system, launched at the beginning of the 20th century, covered 600 miles of track and could take you just about anywhere you wanted to go in the greater Los Angeles area. In my high school years I remember riding red cars that hit top speeds of close to 70 miles an hour. But after World War II Detroit car manufacturers and the oil industry lobbied long and hard for a freeway system to replace the red cars and they got their wish. The red cars vanished and Los Angeles Freeways would gradually become the world's worst traffic nightmare. It was great news for the automakers, and a bonanza for big oil. In oil company parlance, L.A. became "pad number one," the biggest consumer of oil and gas of any metropolitan area in the world.

My thesis at the UCLA Graduate School of Journalism in 1957 was on the birth of the Los Angeles Freeway system. My conclusion: the entire system was obsolete from day one. L.A.'s growth was so quick and so enormous that in just a few years the freeways would be overwhelmed with traffic. They were simply too small and too poorly planned to take L.A. motorists into the future.

By 1954 heavy traffic was quite common but the L.A. County Board of Supervisors turned a collective deaf ear to a plan by private enterprise to relieve the pressure on the freeways by building a monorail system at a cost of roughly $4 million. Not needed, the Supervisors said. In 1960, the builder of the Disneyland Monorail, made an offer to the Supervisors that seemed too good to refuse. Sixten Holmquist, the president of Sweden's Alweg Monorail Company, offered to build a county-wide monorail system on his own dime. There would be no expense to the taxpayers. The five county supervisors, who were known as the "five kings" in the days before women were elected to the board, gave a flat turn down to Holmquist, saying his plan wasn't "artistic enough" to meet L.A.'s high standards. Could it be that Mr. Holmquist failed to offer some remuneration to those on the county governing board in order to sell his proposal? Perhaps he might have done better with some sizable campaign contributions.

In 1975 at the ABC station, Dick Carlson and I received the Grand Award of the Los Angeles Press Club for an expose on the failure of the Southern California Rapid Transit District to replace the red cars with an urban transit system that would help relieve freeway congestion. The Transit District spent millions of dollars on studies, but had failed to implement anything that even resembled rapid transit. The best thing they could come up was a bus corridor along the San Bernardino Freeway.

As the traffic worsened the public began demanding action and government planners decided what L.A. needed was high speed underground subway system that would span 200 miles and greatly reduce freeway congestion. To finance the subway the voters would have to approve a half cent increase in the sales tax. So in 1980 the voters said okay, build the subway and we will ride it. But the subway planners fumbled and stumbled with their design plans and finally conceded they didn't have enough money to proceed. So in 1990 they asked the voters for another half cent increase in the sales tax, and once again the electorate said okay, we'll throw millions more dollars your way.

Now the Transit District had a new name, the Metropolitan Transit Authority and its directors announced they were prepared to start construction on one of the world's most modern subway systems. The name change didn't help a bit. The project was a disaster from day one. Cave-ins, fires, methane gas leaks and cost over-runs hampered construction from the start. The first leg of the system was completed by 1993; the last leg in 1999. But the route from downtown L.A. to North Hollywood stretched only 17 miles, a far cry from the 200 miles promised the voters. By now the meatheads at MTA had run out of money. The main contractor, the Tutor Saliba Company, was suing the MTA for a variety of claims, and the transit agency was suing right back. Legal bills ran into the hundreds of thousands of dollars with the taxpayers picking up the tab as usual.

My assignment to the USC grad students was not an easy one. I asked them to determine just how much debt the MTA acquired on the subway project. The agency kept its financial records in a warehouse and the students were allowed to inspect them somewhat grudgingly. MTA officials had no choice because every financial transaction was supposed to be a matter of public record. It was such an arduous and time consuming project that I detected the students were beginning to hate me. But the project was guided by a strong team leader, a young woman who had excelled in one of my earlier journalism classes and the grad students succeeded in getting a crystal clear picture of the subway's cost. The subway was supposed to cost a billion dollars a mile. But the cost overrun was roughly $6 billion. The sales tax revenue provided million dollars for the project, but it was far less than needed and the idea of a 200 mile subway seemed to be a bad pipe dream. The MTA had no choice but to sell junk bonds on Wall Street to keep out of bankruptcy. The voters must have very short memories because in November of 2008 they gave the transit agency another half cent increase in the sales tax to build a "Subway to the Sea" along with a several other transit projects.

The new "Subway to the Sea" was supposed to lighten the traffic load in West Los Angeles where some of the heaviest traffic in the nation had been reported. Don't bet on the project being completed any day soon. And don't bet that half cent sales tax increase is going to pay for the project.

Incidentally, the 17 mile "Subway to Nowhere" pretty much operated on the honor system for the first 16 years of its existence. Commuters were supposed to buy tickets from machines, but there were no ticket takers, no turnstiles and no security barriers to trap cheaters. It was the only big city transit agency in the country to operate on the honor system. Studies indicated the transit agency was losing $5 million a year in rider fees.

Once in awhile the cops checked to see who hadn't bought a ticket, and violators could be fined as much as $250. But most of the time the cops had more important things to do. Finally in 2009 the Metropolitan Transit Authority began trying to catch up with the times and installed turnstiles at several locations on a "trial" basis.

Just how bad is L.A. traffic? A 2007 study showed the average freeway commuter spent 77 hours a year stalled in traffic. In the West Los Angeles area, the 405 Freeway became the symbol off all that is bad about L.A. traffic. It was in almost constant gridlock from morning to night from the San Fernando Valley to the beach cities. It's estimated nearly 500,000 people commute every day to jobs on L.A.'s Westside, and the crush of cars simply overpowers the 405.

Meanwhile, several civic groups started campaigns to bring monorail to L.A.'s west side on grounds it would be a lot cheaper than building a subway. But the MTA brass was adamant in its opposition. The chairman of the MTA told me trains and subways are the only way to solve L.A.'s traffic mess. So who is going foot the bill? The voters have been fooled before. And by the way, those monorails in Miami and Tokyo are artistic enough as far I'm concerned and certainly get the job done.

One of my USC students joined me and reporter Christina Penza at my newest place of employment, television station KCOP, in putting together a detailed report on the subway's financial problems. The story won an Associated Press award for investigative reporting. It was a real credit to the young men and women in my class and their dogged pursuit of the story.

# 31

## COP KILLER TURNED FAMILY MAN

One of the most fulfilling moments of my journalistic career came nearly half a century after I became personally involved in an unsolved murder case during my first year at Los Angeles City News Service.

The date was July 22, 1957, one day before my 27th birthday. At that time I was living at my parents' home in the L.A. suburb of Manhattan Beach, reduced to near poverty by my salary at City News Service. I left for work about 9 in the morning in my battered 1948 Plymouth and was driving east on Rosecrans Avenue when I came to a boulevard stop sign. Suddenly a young man with surfer like blond hair bolted out from behind a large house shrub and began pounding on the passenger side window while yanking the handle on my car door. He screamed that he wanted a ride. I wasn't in the mood to pick up a raging stranger and drove off in a hurry. Looking at my rear view I saw the young man run back behind a small white frame house. I turned on my car radio and about 10 minutes later radio station *KMPC* broke into its music programming with a detailed news report about a gunman who killed two El Segundo police officers after they stopped him for running a signal shortly before 2 a.m. near the Standard Oil Refinery at Rosecrans Avenue and Sepulveda Boulevard, not far from Los Angeles International Airport. I was fairly certain the gunman was the same man who yanked on my car door. I recalled that he was wearing a white tee shirt and jeans and seemed very distraught, almost crazed.

The area where I had the encounter was about five blocks from the point where the officers were executed. Rosecrans Avenue straddled the beach cities. On the north side was the giant refinery which is situated in El Segundo and protected by a huge barbed wire fence. On the south side was the city of Manhattan Beach where the street is lined with California cottages built after World War II. When I got to work 20 minutes later I immediately called the El Segundo Police Department and said I had spotted a possible suspect. The cop who answered the phone said he was too busy to talk to me and hung up. I called back several times, always identifying myself as a reporter, but no one would take my information. Later I was told the Police Chief had told his officers not to discuss the case with reporters.

So I called the L.A. County Sheriff's Homicide Unit where I had made some excellent contacts while working the police beat and told Detective Ned Loretovich and his partner what I had observed. The sheriff's dicks, known as the "Bulldogs," took copious notes. Eventually the Sheriff took over the case from the small town police department which had pretty much bungled the investigation and had lost an opportunity to search for the killer in the area where he had hidden, and as I later learned, left his gun in the backyard of the home where I spotted him.

The sequence of events the night of the cop killings began in a lover's lane on an unpaved road in the city of Hawthorne where a young gunman robbed four teenagers, two boys aged 16 and 17 and two girls aged 15. He raped one of the young women, then tied them all up and fled in the car of one of the boys, a 1949 Ford. About 90 minutes later patrol officers Milton Curtis and Richard Phillips saw the Ford run a red light at Sepulveda and Rosecrans and pulled the driver over near the oil refinery. The young man got out of the car and fired six gunshots, fatally wounding both cops. But before officer Phillips died he got off three shots, wounding his killer in the back. Then Phillips staggered to his patrol car radio and his last words were, "call an ambulance." The gunman abandoned the 1949 Ford he stole from the teenagers a few blocks from the murder scene and fled. The teenagers he robbed and raped provided a fairly good description of the killer. So did a neighborhood woman who said a young man matching the description of the killer came to her door complaining of an injury to his back and asking for a glass of water.

Officer Curtis, 25, left behind a wife and two children. Officer Phillips, 28, a Korean War veteran, was survived by his widow and three children. It was the first time in the history of the department that officers had been killed in the line of duty. The city of El Segundo, a small town that resembled something right out of America's heartland, went into mourning with American flags draped at half staff from almost every home and store.

In 1959, two years after the murders, one of the homeowners on Rosecrans Avenue found a watch and a chrome plated revolver with a missing cylinder beneath shrubbery in his backyard. The man tossed the items on a garage shelf. A year later he was rototilling the backyard when he heard the sound of scraping metal which turned out to be the gun's cylinder. He immediately turned the revolver over to police and a ballistics test identified it as the murder weapon. (The home was at the exact spot where the young man had tried to force his way into my car.) Police searched the back yard and found another watch. It, like the watch recovered earlier, belonged to two of the teen-age robbery victims. The 22-caliber revolver had been purchased a week before the murders at a Sears store in Shreveport, Louisiana. The buyer gave the name of G.D. Wilson and a phony address in Miami. Florida. Nothing much came out of that information. But all of it was kept in meticulous detail in the "murder book" maintained by the sheriff's Bulldogs who had taken over the investigation from the El Segundo police.

Fast forward to February 2003, 45 years after the cop killings. I was working on the assignment desk at KCOP TV, Channel 13, moving reporters and cameramen and women around the city covering the day's events. One day I got a call from Sheriff's Detective Kevin Lowe who said he and his partner, Dan McElderry, wanted to meet with me to discuss the 1957 cop killings. They found my name in the original notes in the murder book, no thanks to the El Segundo Department. He said he and his partner were going to ask me to identify a possible suspect. They were relatively young guys, and I doubted either was born at the time of the murders.

They brought with them what's generally called a "six pack" in police parlance, a photo lineup with six mug shots. But this particular pack had eight pictures. As I said, it had been 45 years since the incident on Rosecrans Avenue, but I told the detectives I'd give it my best shot. The grandfatherly man I picked out of the visual lineup came slowly into focus. He was completely bald unlike the young man with flowing blond hair who tore at my car door in 1957. But there was no forgetting the face. It was that of George Fiten Mason, a retired 68-year-old businessman who lived in a three-bedroom brick home with his wife of 40 years in an upscale neighborhood in Columbia, South Carolina.

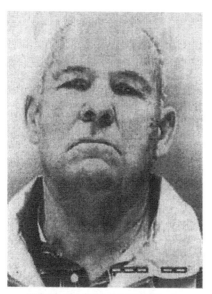

**GERALD MASON
BOOKING PHOTO 2003**

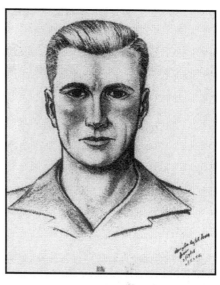

**GERALD MASON
COMPOSITE SKETCH 1957**

Before Mason retired he owned and operated a service station. He and his wife raised two daughters and he gave the appearance of being a solid family man. Neighbors described Mason as a pillar of the community, a "Good Samaritan" who often came to the aid of widows who needed a "man's help" around their homes. But obviously "Mr. Fix It" as he was known wasn't always a "Good Samaritan."

In 1956, a year before the El Segundo murders, Mason was fingerprinted when he was arrested for burglary in South Carolina and then convicted. Those prints were kept on file for 46 years and eventually fed into a national data base. At the time of the cop killings there was no automation in the fingerprint process. Analysts had to "eyeball" each print on file and compare it with those found at the scene of the crime. Murderers who moved from to state were difficult to apprehend through fingerprint evidence. In the early 1980s automation gradually started becoming a fact of police life with the creation of national and state fingerprint data bases. Richard Ramirez, the so called "Night Stalker" who may have killed as many as 30 people, was identified through the California fingerprint data base shortly after it went on line. State Attorney General John Van de Kamp invited me to Sacramento to see the data base in operation and I found it truly spectacular, one of the most significant innovations in modern crime fighting other than the discovery of DNA.

The 1949 Ford abandoned by the cops' killer on Sepulveda Boulevard was carefully dusted for prints by Deputy Howard Speaks. He found a partial print on the steering wheel and another partial print on the chrome in the inside door.

In 2003 El Segundo Police received a call from a dying man who said he could identify the cop killer. The information turned out to be false but Detectives Lowe and McElderry decided it might be worth taking a fresh look at the 45-year-old case. On learning there were two half prints left behind by the cop killer, they turned them over to forensic identification specialist Don Kier. He made a full digital print out of the two partial prints. The digital print was then run through the FBI's data base, known as the Universal Latent Work Station which was first activated in 2002. The system is able to provide a match with the most familiar print or prints in the data base, high technology that didn't exist in 1957. The composite print on the system provided a direct link to Mason and his 1956 arrest. The digital print and the two half prints were then viewed by three fingerprint experts who unanimously agreed they matched the prints taken in 1956, and detectives had gotten the right man. "I thought the day would never come," said retired deputy Howard Speaks, now 88, who had dusted the 1949 Ford for prints. The experts said Speaks did his job to perfection. A team of sheriff's detectives, including Lowe and McElderry, went to Columbia, South

Carolina where they put Mason under surveillance. On the day of his arrest they first watched him play a round off golf with friends at a local course. When they went to Mason's home, they announced they were there to arrest him for the murders of the two El Segundo police officers. Mason replied, "Oh, you're here for that. It was such a long time ago."  Mason's wife was in tears and said she knew nothing of his hidden past.

Mason's brother, Don, insisted it was a case of mistaken identity. "For over 40 years Jerry has been a loving husband, father and grandfather, and a friend of this community," Don Mason said. "Jerry is not capable of this type of behavior. We know he's innocent." One neighbor after another praised Mason as a good man, and refused to believe the charges. His golfing and bowling buddies said he never once displayed a violent streak.

The deputies said a search of Mason's home revealed he had applied for Belgian citizenship recently, an indication he might have planned to leave the country. They also found a 22-caliber revolver quite similar to the one used in the El Segundo murders. And they found a tell-tale scar on his back that most likely resulted from the gunshot fired at him by officer Phillips before he died.

At first Mason threatened to fight extradition to California. But confronted with the overwhelming evidence against him, he admitted his guilt under a plea agreement. He was at the point of tears when he appeared in Los Angeles Superior Court, and listened as the children of the slain officers described their grief. Keith Curtis, son of officer Milton Curtis, said his sister had died the year before without ever knowing who killed their father. "Gerald Mason," he said. "Your family may be shocked but my family has been devastated." Carolyn Phillips, the daughter of officer Richard Phillips, looked directly at Mason and said, "There is no way to describe the emptiness and anguish we have felt all our lives without Dad. We cannot and will not forgive you." Mason bowed his head and apologized to the families of the slain officers. Then he pleaded guilty to two counts of first degree murder in the deaths of officers Milton Curtis and Richard Phillips nearly half a century before on a darkened street near the Standard Oil refinery in El Segundo. A judge sentenced him to life in prison with the possibility he could be released on parole one day.

Under the plea agreement Mason received a major concession from the court. He was allowed to serve his time in a prison in South Carolina so he could be close to his family. Was justice served? You be the judge.

-O-

KCOP, the independent station where the Mason story was broadcast, was once one of L.A.s' leading news outlets, but in recent years it had fallen on hard times. For the most part the staff was young and enthusiastic, but sometimes we were simply overwhelmed by the much larger manpower in the news departments of the network owned stations. In 2003 my life would change dramatically. No longer would I be assigning camera crews and reporters to cover the daily news grind.

News Corporation Chairman Rupert Murdoch, owner of the Fox TV network, purchased KCOP, thereby forming a "duopoly" with KTTV, the Fox station in L.A. We soon moved out of the creaky old barn-like building we occupied on the edge of Hollywood into a gleaming three story structure on L.A.'s west side which had several levels of underground parking. News boss Jose Rios assigned me to his investigative unit with the admonition to start shaking things up. I gave it my best shot.

# 32

## CHASING DOWN CON MEN

Many years ago in journalism school a professor told us one of our main missions in life was to champion the cause of the underdog. These words are repeated over and over again in newsrooms but I've often wondered how many reporters take them seriously. Over the years I frequently obtained good stories from viewers asking for help with their problems, most of the time fighting a bloated bureaucracy that was deaf to their pleas. Time and time again they'd tell me it was virtually impossible to get anyone in authority to listen to them.

A case in point was the 70-year-old woman referred to me by a busy news assignment editor who found time to listen to her story. What she told me was quite compelling and newsworthy. Donna Radley said she had purchased what she thought was a health insurance plan to supplement her Medicare coverage. It wasn't too expensive. In fact it was dirt cheap at $49 a month. Just one problem, she couldn't find a doctor or medical facility willing to accept it. By coincidence, just after I talked to her I got a call from Philadelphia from one of my longtime sources, Christine Henrick, a medical researcher with an incredible knowledge about the failings of the health insurance industry. Chris told me she had spotted a number of ads for cut rate health insurance all over Philadelphia. She said the ads could be found in weekly shoppers, market bulletin boards, and on telephone poles. Prices ranged from $29 to $49 a month. The ads promised hospitalization and just about every other known medical benefit. The principal seller, according to Chris, was the United Family Health Group doing business out of Los Angeles. The company name bore a close resemblance to that of the nation's biggest health insurance company, United Healthcare. It soon became clear to me that a con was going on and that a lot of innocent people were being scammed, particularly the poorest of the poor who could not afford hefty health insurance payments.

I paid a visit to Donna Radley, the woman who said her United Family Health Group policy was worthless. Her lawyer, Constance Zarkowski, was present and helped fill in the blanks for me. Mrs. Radley said a man who sold her the policy over the phone insisted it was a supplement to Medicare.

But when she received the company's handbook it stated the health plan was not a Medicare supplement. Mrs. Radley said she was also told by the salesman that she could only obtain the policy by having it deducted monthly from her checking account so she gave him the name of her bank checking account number. A short time later she asked the company to cancel her policy. But the company declined to do so and kept deducting premium payments from her account month after month. Finally she hired a lawyer, and the payments were halted.

Checking public records I determined that United Family Health Group was owned by the Kohl Corporation, a hardy band of phone sales persons, so-called telemarketers, who ran into big trouble with the feds for charging people substantial fees to provide information about "bargain priced" foreclosed government homes and "seized and repossessed cars." The Federal Trade Commission's summary of the Kohl Group's activities strongly suggested that a fraud was being perpetrated on the consuming public; that once a person paid Kohl a fee which was described as "refundable," the customer never got his or her money back. The case was settled when the Kohl Group promised the FTC it would mend its misleading ways and agreed to pay a fine of $1,138,428 plus post a $100,000 performance bond.

Next stop for the Kohl Group was the health insurance industry, and why not? Some 40 million Americans lacked health insurance. So here was the opening for a new con, health insurance so cheap you couldn't afford not to buy it. Here's what The United Family Health Group offered prospective customers in its brochure:

*Hospitalization*
*Doctor Services*
*Dental*
*Eye Care*
*Hearing Aids*
*Chiropractic Care*
*Alternative Care*
*Long Term Care*

There was even a toll free number to a United Family Health Group Service Center. How could you pass that up for pieces ranging from $29 to $49 a month?

My first inquiry went to the service center and I asked if the health plan was a Medicare supplement as Mrs. Radley had been told. "No, it is not," a voice on the other end of the line told me. "You have it all wrong. We are simply a health care savings program."

So obviously something was "rotten in Denmark" as Shakespeare once wrote and I was determined to get to the bottom of it. Quite by coincidence I received a letter from a former company employee who said he resigned after determining United Health Group was a so-called "boiler room" operation with the sole purpose of ripping off gullible consumers in desperate need of health insurance. He said the sales staff was instructed to always get bank checking information so that automatic deductions could begin immediately after a policy was purchased. As for the health insurance offered by the group, the letter writer said it was an out and out fraud.

Next step was to get someone from the Kohl Group to tell the company's side of the story. We got a turndown from the company's corporate officers who referred us to their attorney, David Gurnick who immediately went on the offensive with me. Gurnick insisted United Health Group was a legitimate operation and the Fox network would be sued if we reported anything negatively that hurt its business. Under the law, damages from so-called business libel can be quite hefty. He also assured me I would hear from a company spokesperson in short order who would answer all my questions. In fairness to Gurnick, he gave me a list of health providers who, he said, accepted the Health Group's coverage.

There were 12 medical facilities in the L.A. area on the attorney's list and I checked out every one of them. Each medical facility did business with UnitedHealthcare but not one accepted insurance coverage from United Family Health Group. What's more, most facilities had never heard of the company although some remembered rejecting its health cards.

So I decided to take reporter Phil Shuman and a cameraman on the road to track down this mysterious company. The first stop was the address on the company's pamphlets, a building near the Pacific Ocean in Marina del Rey. Lo and behold the building was empty and there was no forwarding address. Then I learned the company had acquired a new name, Launchpad Communications, and had moved to a glitzy building in a section of Wilshire Boulevard known as L.A.'s "Miracle Mile."

So along with Phil Shuman and cameraman Nick Hankocy, we decided to make an unannounced visit to Launchpad Communications with camera rolling all the while. How could I be so rude as to breech the privacy of a business without its permission, trespass if you want to call it that? I wasn't ready to stand on journalistic formalities at this point. A newly created state agency supposedly charged with clamping down on health insurance fraud expressed indifference to our investigation, never once returning a phone call. The Spanish language station in Los Angeles owned by NBC had been running ads for United Health Group nightly. I learned the station's sales department persisted in running the ads despite complaints from more than 300 viewers, mostly poor Mexican immigrants, that the insurance was worthless. The station's own news department, at the time, was investigating the United Health Group. But TV sales types love to trample all over news people when advertising dollars are at stake.

So we walked in uninvited on Launchpad's swank offices with phone banks everywhere, and it seemed as if everyone working there ran for cover. No one was manning the phones, and suddenly the big boss, known only as "Mr. Hill," emerged from his huge office and told Shuman: "Our attorney has already talked to your attorney regarding this," and Shuman shot back, "Well he hasn't talked with us." Yes, Gurnick had called our counsel at Fox News, David Keneipp, and told him he was going to sue Fox for our errant ways. Keneipp told him to go ahead and sue.

Thank God for a company lawyer who wasn't intimidated by counsel for some shady operators.

If we were dealing with a health insurance company, there was nothing to show for it at Launchpad Communications. The simple truth is we had invaded the space of a telemarketing company that would sell anything for a price including totally worthless health insurance policies. Why did they hide the name of the health insurance company from public view in their new office? An ex-employee told me they didn't want the thousands of people they'd cheated to find out where they were located and start knocking down the doors.

After repeated denials, Mr. Hill demanded we vacate his office so we did. As luck would have it we got on an elevator with three young women who worked for Launchpad. They readily admitted they were telemarketers and pitched the low cost health insurance, unaware it was a fraud. All their comments were filmed inside the elevator with their permission.

On Dec. 20, 2004 Fox 11 News in Los Angeles presented the results of our investigation in a seven minute report. Not long after, lawyer Gurnick served Fox with a nine page retraction demand. He never got it. Then Launchpad Communications exited the insurance business after state officials finally decided to clamp down on health insurance fraud. And it all came about because a little old lady who realized she'd been conned decided the bad guys were not going to get away with it.

# 33

# TRICKS OF A FRAUDSTER'S TRADE

There's no con man anyone could quite compare to Bernie Madoff, the New York fraudster who ripped off investors in his Wall Street investment company for a goodly $60 billion before he finally admitted to the swindle in 2009. It may sound like hyperbole, but if anyone ever came close to being a Madoff clone it James Anthony Rojas. A hulking ex-convict with a criminal but very analytical brain. Rojas kept many steps ahead of law enforcement until we caught up with him. In all truthfulness it was one of the hardest stories I've ever worked because it took so long to unravel a well-constructed scheme that made Rojas one of the largest land owners in Los Angeles County. In the end it was another case of someone who was easily able to manipulate the bureaucracy, the banking industry and the gullible public in the days leading up to the "Great Recession."

The story began with another phone call, this one was from a woman named Anna Barralles who told me the grant deed to the home she shared with her husband and five children had been forged by a man named James Anthony Rojas.

Mrs. Barralles, a well-spoken employee of the Los Angeles School District, said she was trying to save her home from bank foreclosure when she suddenly learned it was no longer in her name. The bank had assigned the foreclosure process to a so-called "reconveyance agency" in El Cajon, California. I checked with the agency and a representative told me the foreclosure process had been halted because Rojas had "fractionalized" the grant deed. What he had done was put the grant deed in the name of three companies he owned, all of which were listed as being involved in federal bankruptcy court pro-ceedings. The reconveyance agent said the filings meant the foreclosure was brought to an immediate halt until the bankruptcy cases were resolved. As for possible fraud on Rojas' part in signing the grand deed over to himself as a gift, I was told that could not be an issue because he had not been charged with a crime. Talk about "Catch 22!"

Mrs. Barralles told me shortly after Rojas took control of her home he obtained a second loan on it for $75,000, a pattern we would find and over again on homes he seized throughout Southern California. In another case he took out a loan for $525,000 on a home he acquired through a forged grant deed. Loan officers weren't much for ask-ing questions in those days just before the great mortgage meltdown, a major culprit in the "Great Recession" of 2009 caused by all the easy money floating around.

Rojas also picked up a load of money by leasing homes he didn't really own to people looking for a place to live on Craigslist. One radio disc jockey told us he put down several thousand dollars as an advance payment on a lease and Rojas even helped him move into the place and make repairs. But soon the DJ and his family were evicted by the bank which held the mortgage. "I really thought he was a nice guy at first," the DJ said. "He really took me."

I discovered that James Rojas was an ex-convict and that he had spent three years in federal prison for fraudulent real estate loan activity. Reporter John Schwada and I found him doing business in an office across the street from the San Fernando Police Station. We went to the lobby and asked a receptionist if we could to speak to Rojas. He was one of those guys who could smell a TV camera a mile away and the very scent drove him into our waiting arms. Cameraman Mike Sioss started rolling immediately. Rojas said he was a legitimate businessman; that he was trying to help people save their homes from foreclosure. Often times, Rojas said, he gave his clients money to tide them over through a crisis. Rojas said there were a lot of "bad guys" out there using his name and stealing property from homeowners. He said he knew who they were and would tell all to the authorities. Several times when our questions became too pointed to suit Rojas, he bolted from the camera and walked away. But each time he returned in a matter of seconds and continued to extol himself for the services he was performing to save the homes of people in distress.

Things really started to unravel for Rojas after we broadcast our first investigative report on his shady activities on the Fox station in L.A. Dozens of people called us to say Rojas had forged their grant deeds. A woman in San Fernando said Rojas took out a loan for $175,000 on her home, and she was forced to make payments on it by the bank if she wanted to stay there. Another woman with an elegant home in the foothills said she was at a loss to explain how Rojas took title to her very expensive home. Her husband was about to go to work one morning when they found an eviction notice on the front door. Rojas had taken out a half million dollar loan and the bank wanted its money or the home now.

I went to the U.S. District Bankruptcy Court in Woodland Hills, California and learned that Rojas had filed nine bankruptcy petitions on behalf of companies he claimed to own with such English sounding names as "Victoria Holdings" and "Windzor Properties," names quite similar to actual companies. Eventually the court caught up with Rojas but it took many months to unravel his bankruptcy manipulations which went unpunished by the feds.

We then went to the Los Angeles County Registrar-Recorders office and were stunned at what we found on the computers. As many as 300 properties appeared to be listed in Rojas' name which certainly made him one of the bigger landowners in Los Angeles County. All of the grant deeds had been properly notarized and stamped with the recorder's seal. Take the case of Tommie and Johnnie Mae Joyce of Inglewood, California. A notarized grant deed said their home was a recent "gift" to Rojas. Trouble was Tommie Joyce had been dead since 1989 and his wife since 2004. The property was in probate court when Rojas somehow forged the Joyce's names to a grant deed and got away with registering it as a "gift" to himself. There was a million-dollar condominium in Long Beach that Rojas acquired through similar subterfuge and he immediately took out a $60,000 loan on it and used the money to post bail for a shady associate.

I couldn't believe how seemingly indifferent public officials seemed to be about the massive fraud. Registrar-Recorder Connie McCormick told me her agency was powerless to stop the fraud because it handles thousands of filings every day and is nothing more than a public "filing cabinet." Nick Hankocy, our cameraman, was so outraged he shouted in disbelief, "Nothing but a filing cabinet?" It meant that a phony grant deed could shoot right through the system, as James Rojas proved, and no one would be able to detect the fraud. Quite frankly it made me wonder if our public servants were out of their collective minds, or were just simply too lazy to get the job done?

I was told Rojas sometimes walked into the Recorder's office with as many as 20 to 30 grant deeds and no one ever checked their authenticity. All of the notaries whose names were found on the grand deeds reported to police that their notary seals had been stolen.

The LAPD's real estate fraud unit expressed indifference to our findings. It took the tiny San Fernando Police Department to get the ball rolling by filing the first charges against Rojas. Suddenly criminal filings began coming in from jurisdictions all over Southern California and a task force put together by the L.A. District Attorney came up with 126 felony cases.

Lawyers began calling me from as a far away as San Francisco to find out how the fraud worked. There were so many filings and so much evidence to assemble that the District Attorney decided to try Rojas on just 14 felonies. Prosecutor David Fleck laid out a strong case and Rojas was convicted by a jury on all counts. He was sentenced to seven years and eight months in state prison. So what happened to the thousands and thousands of dollars Rojas collected in bank loans and rents on homes he didn't own? An informant told me that Rojas buried much of his money in paper bags at several locations in the L.A. area. As far as I could determine, no law enforcement agency made any real effort to "follow the money" as the saying goes. On the positive side the homes of many people were saved by our investigation. Sadly, Anna Baralles, the woman who tipped us the massive fraud, finally lost her home and there was nothing we could do to help her.

# 34

## THE LAPD GOES "HIGH TECH"

DNA might be best described as a blueprint of the human body and its genetic makeup that can map and identify every cell, even track ancestry, truly one of the great scientific discoveries of the 1900s. The use of DNA in criminal cases was slow to take hold, but finally won virtually universal acceptance as a major crime solving tool at the start of the 21st century.

Leading the way in bringing DNA to the forefront in L.A. were my good friends, Leroy Orozco and Paul Tippin, a couple of retired cops who had been partners in the Robbery-Homicide detail where they were known as "The Plug" and "The "Stump" in reference to their sturdy but short statures. After retiring from the LAPD, Orozco teamed up with me, first at KNBC-TV and later at KCBS-TV, where we worked in the investigative units at both stations. He had solved a number of big criminal cases and I found his news "instincts" to be better than many of my newsroom contemporaries.

Always somewhere in the recesses of Leroy's very active mind was a case dating back to March 17, 1983,

St. Patrick's Day. Elaine Graham, a married 29-year-old nurse, had gone back to college in the hope of becoming a writer. On that day she first dropped her infant daughter, Elyse, off at the home of a babysitter, then left for an English class at California State University, Northridge, in the heart of the San Fernando Valley.

That was the last time she was seen alive. Apparently she was kidnapped somewhere on or near the campus. Posters of the missing Elaine and her car were tacked up at numerous locations and shown on TV news broadcasts. A week later her dusty yellow 1971 Volkswagen was found many miles away in the parking lot at the Fashion Square Shopping Center in Santa Ana by a woman who worked in the Bullock's Department Store. But there was no trace of Elaine. Her husband, Dr. Stephen Graham, disturbed at what he perceived to be a lack of progress by the cops, hired a controversial private eye from Chicago, Anthony Pellicano, to find Elaine. (This was the same Pellicano who 25 years later would be sentenced to 15 years in federal prison for running an illegal wire tapping operation in which he was paid large sums of money to snoop on the rich and famous including a score of Hollywood celebrities and entertainment figures. He was also given a three-year sentence for terrorizing L.A. Times reporter Anita Bush.)

The publicity-seeking Pellicano went on TV and said his investigation indicated that Elaine Graham had probably run off with another man and he was going to find them. Orozco was blunt and to the point with Dr. Graham. He said there wasn't an iota of evidence that Elaine had a lover and in all probability she was dead. He told the doctor Pellicano was "ripping him off" and urged him to fire the private eye. Dr. Graham took Orozco's advice and dumped Pellicano.

Eight months later, Pellicano's story went down in flames when several hikers found Elaine's skeletal remains in Brown's Canyon in the hills above the San Fernando Valley community of Chatsworth. Acquaintances said there was a deep groove in one of her rib bones and it was obvious that she had been stabbed to death with a large dagger.

Elaine Graham had everything to live for. Her husband, Stephen, was on the medical staff of the prestigious Cedars-Sinai Medical Center in Los Angeles. She was a nurse, he an intern when they met, fell in love and were married. They moved into a home in the fashionable community of Sherman Oaks and two years later daughter Elyse arrived.

Many times before Elaine went to bed she would write a letter to her baby daughter, usually about something that happened that day. On March 16, 1983, the night before she vanished, Elaine told her husband about her dream that she and Elyse were detectives searching for a criminal. Dr. Graham urged her to write about it in a letter to Elyse. This is an excerpt from that letter:

*"Dear Elyse,*

*"Last night I dreamed of you-it was a funny dream & when I told your Dad about it he suggested that I write it down... You and I were detectives-we were following some crooks-we got out of our car to follow them or stake-out & they began dropping trash cans on our car from several stories above. Soon I was captured but not you. Suddenly my captor opened a bucket and offered a lollipop. Before I could blink you were at my side..."*

**Elaine Graham with daughter Elyse in 1983**

Perhaps Elaine Graham had some sort of premonition about her fate. Many years later it was her grown daughter Elyse, who, through the instrument of DNA, would bring her mother's killer to justice. Strangely enough one of the critical events helping to identify the killer began in what's recognized as a very gossipy forum, a beauty shop. A week or so after Elaine's dusty yellow Volkswagen was found in the shopping center parking lot, the detectives got an anonymous phone call from a woman in Santa Ana. She told them the previous day she was in a hair styling salon when she overheard a beautician talking to another customer about the Elaine Graham case, which was front page news all over Southern California. She quoted a Miss Kathy Marr as telling the beautician her brother unexpectedly showed up at her apartment the evening of March 17 and when she put all the facts together thought he might be a suspect in Elaine Graham's murder. Orozco and Tippin reacted quickly and interviewed Kathy Marr. She told them after her brother, Edwin Jay Marr, arrived on her doorstep the evening of March 17 she took him to a St. Patrick's Day party where he appeared sullen and withdrawn. She told the cops she asked Edwin to leave the next morning. Kathy Marr said she found  it strange that Graham disappeared from the Northridge campus while her brother was at the home of their mother across the street from the university, then showed up at her place about 60 miles away in Santa Ana  that evening. The sister said once Graham's car was found in the Fashion Square parking lot just two blocks from her home she began to wonder if he were the actual kidnapper, and perhaps the killer.

Orozco and Tippin swiftly picked up the 25-year-old Marr's trail. The detectives learned Marr showed up at his mother's Northridge home across the street from the university on March 16. Earlier in the day Marr had been kicked out of the U.S. Army at Fort Irwin in Barstow, California for being a chronic drug abuser. He had gone through a drug rehab program in the Army, but apparently it didn't take. When he flunked a drug test at the Army post he was booted out. His mother, Frances Marr, said she told him he had dishonored the memory of his father, a career Army man, who had been killed in a plane crash during the Vietnam fighting exactly 21 years to the day Edwin was drummed out of the Army. She told him to get out of her home the next morning, St. Patrick's Day, the day Elaine Graham vanished.

There was no love lost either with sister Kathy Marr who said she wasn't about to let Edwin stay any longer than one night in her apartment. She told the cops as a teen-ager he experimented with an assortment of drugs including PCP, LSD and marijuana; that he had a very violent streak and slapped her around repeatedly.  Kathy said he had a strange obsession with guns and often bragged about the burglaries he committed in the neighborhood. The sister said after Marr left her apartment he moved in with some friends a mile or so away. Another person who knew Marr well said he had a "macho" image of himself and a deep hatred of women because he thought "they played games with his mind."

Edwin Jay Marr was born in Georgia. He was just four years old when his father was killed in Vietnam. His mother remarried, and as Edwin grew up he frequently battled with his stepfather when he got into trouble. Acquaintances said as a youth Marr sometimes hiked in Brown's Canyon, the site where Elaine Graham's body was found. Despite an assortment of juvenile problems, Marr was graduated from Cleveland High School in the San Fernando Valley in 1975. He attended Pierce College in Woodland Hills, then transferred to Santa Ana Community College where he majored in police science. Relatives said he was intent on becoming a cop, and worked part time as a security guard at Children's Hospital of Orange County. He applied to the Santa Ana Police Department and was accepted. But the job offer was withdrawn after it was discovered he had once been arrested on a felony drug charge.

Orozco and Tippin figured they had enough circumstantial evidence to arrest Marr, though Graham's body had not yet been found at this point in time. But prosecutors in the D.A.'s office disagreed, saying they simply didn't have enough to go on. Meantime, 24 days after Elaine Graham vanished, Marr was arrested for armed robbery in the city of Westminster in neighboring Orange County. It was 2:30 in the afternoon on April 11, 1983 when Marr walked into a dry cleaners on Westminster Avenue, pointed a 45-caliber revolver at owner Theresa Lynn Hooper. "Let me have all your money or I'll blow your head off," he told her. Hooper handed over $140 from the cash register to the gunman. The dark-skinned Marr fled and covered his head with an Afro wig, trying to disguise himself as a black man in a clumsy attempt to elude capture. He was spotted by patrol officer Russ Silva a few blocks away on a residential street. The wig didn't fool the cop who ordered Marr to freeze, seized his 45-caliber revolver and took him into custody.

When they got to the station Marr told officer Silva he had hidden his back pack behind a bush near the spot where he was arrested and asked the officer to retrieve it for him. When the cop recovered the back pack he opened it and found a large double edged dagger, a discovery that would eventually become the critical turning point in solving the murder of Elaine Graham. Silva booked both the knife and the other contents of Marr's back pack into evidence and there it remained under lock and key while Marr was held for trial. Marr was convicted of armed robbery and sentenced to three years in state prison. On September 1, 1983 Detectives Orozco and Tippin questioned Marr at the state prison in Jamestown in Northern California's Gold Country. Marr repeatedly denied involvement in Elaine Graham's disappearance. Asked about a report by one witness that Marr was loitering on the Northridge campus on March 17, he admitted being there but said he gone to the library to see if he could check out some books on modern dance. He told the cops he needed the books because he was hopeful of landing a job at the Fred Astaire Dance School. Orozco said Marr repeatedly lied during questioning, saying he had been at his mother's home for several weeks when, in fact, he had been there only one night. He also insisted he took a series of bus rides to get to get to his sister's home in Santa Ana, while the evidence strongly indicated he drove there in Elaine Graham's car. Despite the preponderance of circumstantial evidence, prosecutors in the District Attorney's office once again maintained there simply wasn't enough to prosecute Marr for Elaine Graham's murder.

On Dec. 3, 1983 following the discovery of Elaine's skeletal remains in November of 1983, an autopsy was held in the Coroner's office which showed that she had died from a wound inflicted by a large knife or dagger.

Orozco and Tippin were aware that the Westminster cop had confiscated a large dagger from Marr's back pack after the robbery. They were told the knife was still in the evidence locker and a few days later they picked it up and booked it into evidence at the LAPD Crime Lab. Technicians examined the knife and found traces of blood under the handle. But at that time DNA was an unknown commodity and there was no way to prove the blood on the knife was that of murder victim Elaine Graham.

After Elaine's remains were found, the two detectives went back to the prison at Jamestown once more to question Marr. But he cursed at them and walked away without submitting to a second interview.

Once released from prison, Marr moved to Cathedral City which neighbors Palm Springs, California. He became a licensed cosmetologist, and had frequent run-ins with the law. There were several reports that he stalked women in the area. Marr's picture was posted in the newsroom at KMIR, the NBC affiliate TV station in Palm Springs, after he stalked reporter Susan Hendricks day after day. Miss Hendricks reportedly lived in fear of her life and finally fled Palm Springs. In 1994 Marr's stalking ways caught up with him when he was sentenced to 90 days in jail for harassing a Miss Annette Samuelson whom he had been following in Palm Springs. In 1999 he was accused of being a partner in a Palm Springs area narcotics ring but pleaded guilty to a reduced charge of marijuana possession and was sentenced to 120 days in jail.

In 2001 the LAPD formed a so-called "Cold Case Unit" to investigate the thousands of unsolved murders in the department's files. By then Leroy Orozco was no longer working with me in TV news, and had gone back into law enforcement as welfare fraud investigator for the Orange County District Attorney. Paul Tippin, meantime, retired from the LAPD, and went to work in the Orange County D.A.s' unsolved murder unit. They frequently discussed the Elaine Graham case and decided it might be something the detectives in LAPD's new Cold Case Unit could sink their teeth into. After all there was a pretty good suspect, one Edward Jay Marr. Orozco and Tippin told Detective Rick Jackson that Marr's double edged dagger was in the LAPD evidence locker and newly developed DNA techniques might yield some viable evidence linking him to the Graham murder.

The Cold Case Detectives got to work immediately and asked the LAPD's Scientific Investigative Division for a new analysis of the dagger. A forensic criminalist had determined through ordinary serology the blood type on the dagger was the same as that on record for Elaine Graham. But there were no existing samples of Elaine Graham's blood. DNA was not even on police radar when her body was recovered and besides all that was left of her body were her skeletal remains. But the criminalists were able to turn to DNA for help. They were provided with a blood sample from daughter Elyse. And the tests concluded that the blood's markers on the knife had a direct genetic link to Elyse, and that was sufficient to prove a genetic link to her slain mother. On Monday, February 10, 2003 detectives arrested Edwin Jay Marr outside his home in Cathedral City for the murder of Elaine Graham. His bail was set at $1-million.

Marr was scheduled to stand trial on March 14, 2005, 22 years after the Graham murder. But just as jury selection was about to begin he pleaded guilty to a charge of second degree murder, and admitted he used the dagger to kill her. The following month he was sentenced to a term of 16 years to life in state prison following tearful testimony in the court from daughter Elyse Graham, now a young woman, who said she was relieved at Marr's guilty plea but could never forgive him for denying her the right to know and cherish her mother. Dr. Stephen Graham, who had remarried, said he intended to be present at every one of Marr's parole hearings to make certain he was never again allowed to return to society. "I will be there representing Elaine," Dr. Graham said. At the conclusion of the trial Special Prosecutor John Lewin had high praise for retired detectives Orozco and Tippin and their "dogged determination" in staying with the case despite their retirement and helping bring Marr to justice. Lewin said in all probability Marr was angry at his mother because she kicked him out of the house, and kidnapped and killed Elaine Graham because she was the first woman he encountered after leaving home that day.

Marr, incidentally, was the first person arrested for an old murder by the LAPD Cold Case Unit since its formation. Since then Cold Case detectives have solved dozens of old murders with an assist from DNA. One even involved a female officer with a spotless record who was accused of killing the wife of the cop's former lover.

Detective Stephanie Lazarus was a highly decorated officer who was assigned to the LAPD's elite Art Theft Unit. She was linked to the murder of Sherri Rasmussen 23 years before in a gated community by a speck of saliva found on the slain woman's body. The saliva had been saved by the crime lab over all those years and DNA testing eventually linked it to Lazarus. Investigators said Lazarus and the slain woman's husband, John Ruetten, were lovers when they both attended UCLA and they speculated she hoped to win him back by killing his wife, Sherri Rasmussen. Sherri, the director of critical care nursing at a Glendale hospital, was beaten with a blunt instrument and shot four times, a crime so brutal the cops thought the killer must have been a man. Cold Case detectives familiarized themselves with the case and had the saliva sample tested for DNA by the crime lab. The test show the saliva came from a woman. Based on past information the detectives began following Lazarus on her errands. One day she discarded a paper cup, and the cold case cops picked it up and took it the crime lab. A DNA test concluded the saliva found at the murder scene was a match to that found on the body of the murdered nurse. Then they arrested Lazarus, who, as of this writing is awaiting trial.

Other technological innovations besides DNA literally took police science out of the "horse and buggy" era. The identification of fingerprints at crime scenes took countless hours because detectives had to "eyeball" the prints to determine a match. At best it was an imperfect science.

The first killer identified through new fingerprint technology in California was a man known as "The Night Stalker." He called himself Richard Ramirez although his true name was Richard Leyva. A chronic drug abuser since his teens in Texas, Ramirez dressed like a street bum and left upside down pentagrams representing the rule of Satan at the scene of his crimes. He was an avid fan of the AC/DC singing group and his favorite song was their version of "Night Prowler."

On August 30, 1985 the LAPD released a photo of Ramirez after his fingerprints were found on an abandoned car following a brutal crime in Orange County. Four days earlier, on August 26, Ramirez broke into the home of a woman and her boyfriend. He shot the man in the head and raped and sodomized the woman after making her swear allegiance to Satan. A teenager wrote down the license number of the car when he saw Ramirez driving suspiciously through the neighborhood. Police found the abandoned car and dusted it for prints. A newly computerized fingerprint identification system, among the first in the nation, had just gone on line in the office of State Attorney General John Van de Kamp in Sacramento. The prints found on the car were rushed to the state capital and in a matter of minutes there was a match as the computer spit out the name of career criminal Richard Ramirez. He was directly linked to the murders of 13 people in Southern California and three in San Francisco. A picture of Ramirez was found from an earlier arrest and quickly circulated all over Southern California, appearing on all the city's TV stations. A dozen hours later Ramirez, apparently unaware he had been named a wanted killer, was recognized by a group of angry citizens in predominately Hispanic East Los Angeles and nearly beaten to death before he was rescued by police.

It was a Saturday morning and I had the day off at KNBC-TV where I was managing editor. The previous night I had assigned our morning camera crew to cover a story in Newport Beach many miles away. I was buying a piece of halibut at a San Pedro fish market when my pager went off. I called Assignment Editor Kris Knutsen who told me there seemed to be a lot of activity at an apparent crime scene in East L.A. and would I object if she diverted the camera crew to that area. "By all means," I told her. Our photographer, Dino Castro, was the first newsman on the scene and got exclusive video of Ramirez cowering in the back seat of the police car, trying to hide from the angry mob outside. News director Tom Capra then called me and asked whom he should contact to find out if Richard Ramirez was the one actually arrested. I told him my old friend, Leroy Orozco in the Robbery-Homicide Division, had the case and to call him immediately. Somehow Capra figured out that Orozco might be at the Hollenbeck Station which was close to the arrest scene. He was right. Orozco came to the phone and confirmed that Richard

Ramirez, "The Night Stalker," had at long last been captured. For the rest of the day KNBC-TV carried live coverage about the arrest of Ramirez. We were the only station in town that had video of the guy.

Ramirez' victims included little boys and girls, young men and women and elderly people. He raped and sodomized, forced women to orally copulate him, and tortured many of them. He drew pentagrams on some of their faces and left other Satanic signs at crime scenes. At his trial there were 165 witnesses and 658 exhibits. The jury took no mercy on devil worshiper Ramirez. He was convicted of 13 murders, 12 sexual assaults and 14 burglaries, and sentenced to die in San Quentin's gas chamber. At this writing, 25 years later, he remains a senior resident on "Death Row," lawyers filing appeal after appeal on his behalf. One of his longtime companions at San Quentin prison is another equally notorious monster, albeit a brilliant one, who became known as "The Dating Game Killer." His horrible crimes covered 40 years of my reporting career but there's still doubt that justice will be served in his case.

# 35

## FROM THE "DATING GAME"
## TO DEATH ROW

In 1978 when the producers of television's long running "Dating Game" took a look at 34-year-old Rodney James Alcala, they undoubtedly considered him the perfect candidate to charm one of the beautiful young ladies who appeared on the show in search of the perfect date. Alcala seemed to have everything, boyish good looks, college degree, gainfully employed by the Los Angeles Times where he worked in the composing room as a typesetter. What else could you ask for? For one thing there was Alcala's two-year stint in the California prison system for kidnapping, raping and nearly killing an eight- year-old girl. But no one bothered to tell the producer that Alcala was on parole when he made his TV debut, classified as a mentally disordered sex offender. And of course no one knew at the time that Alcala was a very active serial killer. The show's producer apparently didn't have a clue to his background. And, if my assumptions are correct, the only things male guests were screened for were charm and good looks.

On a Dating Game show broadcast on Sept. 13, 1978 Alcala was one of three male candidates competing for the charms of Cheryl Bradshaw, a buxom redhead and aspiring actress. Cheryl was almost starry eyed when she sized up the handsome Alcala and chose him for her "perfect date." Alcala smiled broadly and told her from the winner's circle, "We're going to have a great time together Cheryl." No one seems to know if they had a "great time." Years later a fellow contestant on the show said he doubted Cheryl went on a date with Alcala because he seemed "creepy." But he wasn't certain.

*Serial Killer Rodney Alcala on TV's "Dating Game" 1978*

*Cheryl Bradshaw picks Alcala as her "perfect date".*

I found a tape of "The Dating Game" show featuring Alcala in the office of the Orange County Clerk, just one of nearly a thousand pieces of evidence against a man now described by authorities as a horrific serial killer.

If DNA testing is to be believed, and there is not much reason to doubt it, Alcala committed at least three rape murders in California in the year leading up to his appearance on the Dating Game and one after it. Fingerprint evidence linked him to still another rape murder in L.A. during that time frame. There was also evidence that he murdered two other women in New York much earlier.

None of this was known at the time Rodney Alcala wound up on San Quentin's death row for the June 20, 1979 kidnap slaying of 12-year-old Robin Samsoe of Huntington Beach, California. Robin was riding her bicycle on her way to a ballet class when she disappeared. Her dismembered body was found a week later many miles away in the Angeles National Forest. Alcala claimed he, too, was miles away, looking for work at Knott's Berry Farm in Buena Park. However, a witness placed Alcala and his camera in the precise area where Robin vanished. Alcala had recently quit his job in the L.A. Times composing room after he was accused of still another sex crime.

Robin Samsoe's earrings, along with many other pieces of jewelry and pictures of several hundred women and children were found in a storage locker Alcala maintained in Seattle, Washington. Such revelations led Orange County prosecutor Mark Murphy to speculate that Alcala may have been involved in as many as 50 murders across the United States. Over the years I observed that serial killers often retained keepsakes from their victims, jewelry, small items of clothing, and other tangible remembrances of their crimes. There have been several cases in which serial killers posed as photographers and lured pretty young women to their death by having them poise for modeling jobs, and kept their pictures as "trophies." Alcala had extensive background as a photographer and those pictures in his locker must have had some significance according to Murphy, just as the earrings belonging to Robin Samsoe.

**Some of the 200 pictures found in 1979 in serial killer Rodney Alcala's storage locker in Seattle, Washington.**

The DNA testing of Alcala and nearly 700 other inmates on California's death row was approved by the courts and enacted despite a lengthy challenge by the American Civil Liberties Union. Alcala and his well-to-do family, including a brother who was a high ranking Army officer, provided funds to help the ACLU oppose the DNA testing. Alcala's DNA was taken on death row and the stunning results released in 2005 linked him to three unsolved murders in the Los Angeles area. It was quite by accident that I learned of Alcala's involvement in the murders. Reporter Phil Shuman and I were doing a special report on DNA testing with a county prosecutor who mentioned she had just learned that a man on death row had been linked to four old L.A. area murders through DNA and new fingerprint technology. I asked if she knew the man's name, and she said it was "Alcala." Did that give me a jolt! It was the same Rodney Alcala I had been tracking for nearly four decades.

As best I can tell, Alcala's life of crime in California started on September 25, 1968 when he kidnapped an 8-year-old girl in a Hollywood neighborhood, then raped and beat her into unconsciousness. An eyewitness, a motorist who saw the kidnapping, followed Alcala to his home, then called the LAPD from a pay phone. Alcala appeared shirtless in front of a window when the cops arrived and he told them to wait a minute. When he didn't return the officers knocked down the door and were startled to find the girl unconscious in a pool of blood. She had been raped and beaten. Alcala escaped. He fled to New York where he assumed a new identity, that of "John Berger," and went back to college. Fortunately the traumatized child survived despite the horrible ordeal that left her scarred for life. The cops called it a "miracle." My instincts told me that I should keep on top of the story and I began learning all I could about Rodney Alcala, so much so that many years later L.A. County District Attorney Steve Cooley publicly praised my "dogged pursuit" in piecing together the details of Alcala's life of crime while announcing Alcala would be tried for the four previously unsolved murders.

After the attack on the 8-year-old girl I learned quite a bit about the missing Rodney Alcala. He was a handsome Native American, a full blooded Indian, who had spent his early years on a reservation. He dabbled in photography, had a near genius IQ and was an honors graduate of UCLA with a major in fine arts. (I must point out that as of this writing not a single college graduate has been executed for a capital crime in California). On the dark side Alcala had been booted out of the Army for viciously beating a woman in New York and using dangerous drugs, including LSD. That was about the extent of his known criminal record at the time.

Three years went by before Detective Steve Hodel of the Hollywood Division persuaded the FBI to place Rodney James Alcala on its "Ten Most Wanted" list. (This was the same Steve Hodel who later wrote a book linking his father to the "Black Dahlia" murder.) The ploy paid off almost immediately. Two students at a girls school in George's Mill, New Hampshire saw Alcala's picture on a wanted poster at the local post office and called the FBI, saying Alcala was one of their teachers.

Detectives learned that after Alcala fled L.A. he enrolled as John Berger at New York University, where he took a number of film making courses and enhanced his skills as a photographer. According to the New York Post, one of Alcala's photography teachers was none other than the famous director Roman Polanski. Sometime in 1970 Alcala was hired to work as a counselor and photography instructor at the New Hampshire girl's school. Some years later New York police identified Alcala as the suspect in the murder of Cornelia Crilley on June 12, 1971 during his tenure at the girls' school. The 23-year-old TWA flight attendant was raped and strangled in her apartment on East 80th Street. I also found a confidential police report stating that a young woman at the girl's school disappeared while Alcala was teaching there.

Detective Hodel got a warrant for Alcala's arrest, took him in tow at the girl's school and flew him back to Los Angeles where justice was swift. Alcala was found guilty of kidnapping and raping the 8-year-old; declared a mentally disordered sex offender, and sentenced to a term of one year to life in the California Prison system.

In the 1970s sex crimes were not taken too seriously by the prosecutors and the courts. On May 19, 1972 Alcala was admitted to the Atascadero State Mental Hospital. Hard to believe but he was paroled less than two years later on August 3, 1974. Two months after his release it was back to prison again for kidnapping and raping a 13-year-old girl in Huntington Beach, California and also forcing her to smoke marijuana. In June of 1977 Alcala was paroled again and more innocents were placed in harm's way. At that time convicted felons were sentenced to California prisons under the state's indeterminate sentencing law which made them eligible for parole at just about any time after the first year in custody.

One month after his release Alcala asked his female parole officer for permission to travel to New York and she agreed to let him make the trip despite his record as a sexual predator. Ostensibly he wanted to visit a girlfriend in Connecticut and see his brother, an Army officer, in Washington D.C. After that he said he would attend a photographer's convention in Chicago. However, witnesses placed a man strongly resembling Alcala in Manhattan at the same time a young college grad named Ellen Hover disappeared between July 13 and 15, 1977 after telling friends she was going to spend the weekend with a friend in the Hamptons. Ellen, a piano virtuoso, grew up in Beverly Hills but moved to New York where she lived alone. She was the daughter of Herman Hover, owner of the famous Ciro's night club on the Sunset Strip where the "rat pack" led by Frank Sinatra and Dean Martin were regulars, and also frequent guests at the Hover home. Ellen told friends Frank and Dean were like "grandfathers" to her.

Hover's mother hired a private investigator, retired NYPD investigator Nat Laurendi, who persuaded her to place an ad in the New York Times seeking help from anyone who might have seen Ellen and the suspect who accompanied her. The ad contained a composite sketch of a man described as a white male or Hispanic with a long pony tail who worked as a professional photographer.

Almost immediately a young woman came forward who had attended the girl's school in New Hampshire where Alcala taught before he was arrested for the rape of the 8-year-old Los Angeles girl and identified him as the man in the composite sketch. Then NYPD detectives determined Alcala matched the description of the man who dated the missing Ellen Hoover.

Eleven months later Hover's decomposed body was found in a shallow grave on the grounds of the state park originally known as the Rockefeller Estate in Westchester County. Another young woman came forward and said she had posed for a photographer named Rodney Alcala at a spot about 100 feet from where Ellen Hover's body was recovered on Dec. 14, 1977. At the request of New York City police, L.A. homicide detectives and FBI agents interviewed Alcala about the murder of Ellen Hover. Alcala admitted he was in Manhattan and saw Hover but insisted that was before she disappeared. He was asked to take a lie detector test but declined. The New

York cops decided they did not have enough evidence to prosecute so Alcala was turned loose.

To place this in perspective, newly developed fingerprint technology showed that only two days after Alcala was questioned in L.A. about the Hoover slaying, he brazenly murdered a beautiful blonde nurse in her Malibu apartment. Her name was Georgia Wixted and she was 27 years old. It was alleged that on December 16, 1977 Alcala smashed open a window to get inside her apartment, raped, bludgeoned and strangled the young woman. A bloodied hammer was found next to her body.

The new technology determined that a palm print left on the woman's bed frame belonged to Alcala. Police theorize Acala may have spotted the nurse dining with a friend after she got off work at the hospital and followed her home. In a touch of irony, after her slaying Miss Wixted's younger sister, Ann, was married to LAPD officer Al Michelena who eventually would become commander of the Robbery- Homicide detail and was present for many of Alcala's court proceedings.

The first murder linked to Alcala through California's newly computerized DNA system took place the month prior to the Wixted murder. The nude body of 18-year-old Jill Barcomb was found in Franklin canyon near Beverly Hills on Nov. 15, 1977. She had been raped, bludgeoned with a rock and strangled with the legs of her blue pants. There were three bite marks on her right breast. Just three weeks earlier Miss Barcomb had moved to Los Angeles from Oneida, New York where she was one of 11 children. The LAPD's "Hillside Strangler Task Force," which was investigating a dozen murders by a serial killer or killers, decided the slaying of Jill Barcomb might be one of their cases.

I learned that early in 1978 they decided to focus on Rodney Alcala as a possible suspect in all the Hillside Strangler murders and questioned him at length, but finally cleared him. At the time there was no such thing as DNA testing to nail down a killer. (Kenneth Bianchi and his cousin, Angelo Buono, were eventually convicted of the Hillside Strangler murders and sentenced to life in prison.)

Although Alcala had a degree from UCLA and lots of credits from NYU, he was busy during this period taking a photography course at Pasadena City College, a class in electrolysis at Citrus College and still other general education courses at East Los Angeles College. Veteran cold case detective Cliff Shepard told me he suspected Alcala was simply taking the courses to troll for new female victims.

The next victim before Alcala's Dating Game appearance was that of legal secretary Charlotte L. Lamb, of Long Beach, California who was apparently murdered on her 32nd birthday, July 24, 1978. She had met Alcala at a disco. Her raped and strangled body was found inside a large washing machine at an El Segundo apartment house. Once again Alcala's sample in the state DNA bank fingered him as the killer. Lamb's earrings were also recovered from Alcala's storage locker in Seattle.

On Feb. 13, 1979 Alcala picked up a 15-year-old girl in Sierra Madre, California and took her to a deserted area in Riverside County where he raped, sodomized and choked her into unconsciousness. When the girl came to she pretended to be friendly toward Alcala who drove her back into town where she escaped from his car and called police. Alcala was arrested and released on bail. He then resigned from the Los Angeles Times after his latest criminal activity was revealed. But there was no stopping his murderous rampage.

On June 13, 1979 Jean Marie Parenteau, 21, was found raped and murdered in her Burbank apartment. The night before she and a friend ran into Alcala at the Handlebar Saloon and Disco in Pasadena. Her friend, Kathleen Franco, said they both brushed off Alcala. Days later the cops identified Alcala as their prime suspect, but the charges were dropped after a critical witness refused to testify. The charges were reinstated a quarter century later after Alcala's DNA was tied to Parenteau's murder.

It was just seven days later, on June 20, 1979 that 12-year-old Robin Samsoe of Huntington Beach disappeared while riding her bicycle to a ballet class. A girl-friend of Robin's identified Alcala as the photographer who stopped them, earlier in the day to take their pictures. A forestry worker said she spotted a man resembling Alcala with a blonde girl on a hiking trail not far from where Robin's body was found. Next police got a search warrant for Alcala's storage locker in Seattle where they found Robin's earrings. Alcala would claim he had earrings identical to those worn by the 12-year-old girl but the cops didn't buy it.

On July 24, 1979 Orange County detectives served a search warrant on Alcala's home in Monterey Park, and arrested him for the murder of Robin Samsoe. The story was front page news in Orange County where Alcala was indicted for the murder and a judge issued a "gag" order preventing any discussion of the case outside the courtroom.

At that time, of course, nothing was known about the four murders linked to Alcala 25 years later through DNA and fingerprint evidence. I decided to check out public records about Alcala in Los Angeles County. Orange County records were off limits to me because of the gag order. I was stunned by what I found out. Crime files in the L.A. County Clerk's office detailed Acala's arrest at the girls' school in New Hampshire and suggested he may have been involved in the disappearance of one of the students.

Another report mentioned that he was a possible suspect in two murders in New York City. There was also information that he was seriously considered a suspect in the slaying of Jill Barcomb long before his DNA positively linked him to her death, and for a time he was thought to be one of the notorious "Hillside Stranglers." I produced a lengthy story about Alcala's criminal career which appeared on KNBC-TV in Los Angeles. I was told the trial judge was furious about my story but couldn't hold me in contempt because I had not violated the terms of his gag order. All my information came from Los Angeles public records file, nothing from Orange County.

Justice came quickly to Alcala, or so we thought. On April 30, 1980 a jury found him guilty of murder and kidnapping with special circumstances and recommended that he be executed in the gas chamber. But then began a series of legal maneuvers that would make Alcala one of death row's longest living residents and trigger a revolt against the justice system by California voters.

Alcala's lawyers appealed his sentence on grounds that evidence of his prior crimes should not have been admitted at the murder trial. In August of 1984 the California Supreme Court overturned his conviction for that reason.

Two years later another Orange County jury convicted Alcala once again and he was sentenced to die. This time the California Supreme Court upheld the conviction, but California Chief Justice Rose Bird dissented from the decision. The court's decision to overturn Alcala's first guilty verdict produced a firestorm of criticism. Alcala soon became the poster boy for a movement to reinstate the death penalty in California. Then in 1987 in a campaign that highlighted the fact that Chief Justice Bird had voted against the death penalty 61 times, the voters overwhelmingly removed her from office. I had mixed feelings about Justice Bird's fate. A few years earlier she asked me to serve on a panel which successfully adopted rules enabling TV cameras and newspaper photographers to cover courtroom trials in California. It was a major breakthrough for the news media and a dozen years later the murder trial of former football star O.J. Simpson became the most watched courtroom proceeding in the nation's history.

One law and order move triggered another in California. The death penalty was reinstated. California got rid if its indeterminate sentencing program which meant a prisoner sentenced to a term of one to 25 years could be released at any time after the first year. It was replaced by a determinate sentencing law which said in effect if a prisoner were given five years he or she must serve all five years. Another addition was the "Three Strikes Law" which stated anyone convicted of three felonies would serve a life sentence without the possibility of parole. And for the first time hearsay evidence was allowed at pre-trial hearings for criminal defendants along with the introduction of past criminal records.

Despite the new hard line law and order stance of the state, Alcala and his lawyers were once again busy stalling his date with the gas chamber. They succeeded when on June 27, 2003, a three-judge panel of the U.S. Ninth District Court of Appeals threw out his second conviction. There were a number of factors in the court's decision, but the main one appeared to be that his counsel was "ineffective."

The following year the State Crime Lab released the results of its DNA test on Alcala linking him through blood and semen to the murders of the three L.A. area women.

So Alcala was removed from Death Row and returned to the Orange County Jail along with 16 boxes of legal material he had accumulated in San Quentin where he also found time to write a book proclaiming his innocence, "You the Jury." I covered his return to court for his third arraignment for the Robin Samsoe murder and it was a far different Rodney Alcala from the suave pony tailed charmer of years gone by. His long hair was gray and there was a stoop in his walk as Alcala, the senior resident of California's Death Row, shuffled into court carrying a brief case. Had it not been for his orange jail house jump suit, he could easily have been mistaken for a defense attorney. He was quite articulate as he made several motions, including one to review the numerous pieces of evidence in his case. Five years dragged by before, Alcala, his hair grown down to his shoulders, was allowed by Orange County trial judge Francisco Briseno to represent himself on five counts of murder "despite serious misgivings" by the jurist.

It goes without saying that the legal morass created by defense lawyers, the courts and Alcala himself, is a sad commentary on our judicial system. And the ordeal has been brutal on the victims' families. Robin Samsoe's mother, Marianne Connelly, attended every one of Alcala's court appearances in Orange County dating back to 1979. Tears streaming from her eyes at her home in Norco, California, she told me and reporter Chris Blatchford, *"I've watched Robin die hundreds of times in my nightmares. I've watched what he did to my little girl. Every time I want to help but I can't. Thinking that we have to relive another trial and come face to face with this monster again is terrifying."*

Alcala's efforts at defending himself were of little conse-
quence. His contention that he wore earrings identical to
those of the murdered Robin Samsoe when he appeared
on "The Dating Game" went for naught. The jurors looked
at a 20-second clip of Alcala on the show, but the earrings were hardly detectable. His long, rambling defense
against the validity of DNA testing likewise left the jurors
cold.

Prosecutor Mark Murphy told the jury Alcala should be
put to death, saying he "was an evil monster who raped
and tortured his victims because he enjoyed it." On Feb.
25, 2010, after deliberating less than two days, a jury found
Rodney Alcala guilty as charged of all five murders, and
two weeks later the same jury gave him five new death
sentences. One of those testifying against him at the trial's
penalty phase was Alcala's first known victim, a woman
who was just eight years old in 1968 when he raped and
bludgeoned her, then left her to die in a pool of blood
only to be saved by police.

**Rodney Alcala is given the death penalty for the
third time in 2010.**

A veteran detective told me that based on past precedent it was unlikely Alcala will be executed despite the old adage that he who represents himself in court "has a fool for a client." "The odds are," he said, "that Alcala wasn't a fool; that he knew what was doing and the appeals process will keep him alive for many more years. In all probability, he'll die of old age at San Quentin Prison." The justice system being what it is, I had to agree.

### POSTSCRIPT NEW YORK, N.Y

On January 19, 2011 the Manhattan Grand Jury indicted Rodney Alcala for murdering two young women in the 1970s. Almost a year later he pleaded guilty to killing TWA flight attendant Cornelia Michelle Crilley in 1971 and piano virtuoso Jane Hover in 1977. Both women were 23 years old. Both were raped and both were strangled. Alcala's horrific crimes in California were outlined to the Grand Jury by Los Angeles Police Cold Case Detective Cliff Shepard.

Alcala was sentenced to 25 years to life in New York which, does not have the death penalty, then returned to California's San Quentin Prison to await execution on Death Row.

In the summer of 2011 cold case cops in San Francisco identified Alcala as the killer of a young actress-model. In 1977 the body of aspiring actress Pamela Lambson, 19, was found on a dusty trail on Mount Tamalpaia, not far from Alcala's future home on San Quentin's death row. Pamela had told friends she was going to Fisherman's Wharf to have portrait pictures taken by a professional photographer. One of Miss Lambson's portraits was among 200 seized by police from Alcala's storage locker in Seattle. It left detectives wondering just how many other murders might be linked to the well traveled Alcala.

# 36

## UNFINISHED BUSINESS
## IN THE COLD CASE FILE

The Los Angeles Police Department and the Los Angeles County Sheriff have an estimated 15,000 unsolved cases between them since they began keeping record late in the 19th Century. In recent years a good many of the cases have been gang murders, often drug related. At one point in the 1980s the county coroner had so many cases there was no where to store the bodies properly prior to autopsy. Once we found at least 20 bodies stacked on gurneys outside the old Coroner's office in the Hall of Justice.

A lot of "cold cases" caught my attention over the years, but four murders in particular consumed many hours of my time without resolution. Here are the details of those four cases:

### IN SEARCH OF ROBIN GRAHAM

A body has never been found in one of the coldest cases in the LAPD's cold case file. Young Robin Graham disappeared one night, apparently in the clutches of a killer who drove a distinctive turquoise and white Corvette.

Over a span of 35 years I spent countless hours working on Robin's disappearance on November 15, 1970 on the Hollywood Freeway.

Robin Graham was just 19 when she disappeared, apparently kidnapped. She had gotten off work late in the afternoon on November 14 at the Pier One Imports store in Hollywood and went on a date with her boyfriend, Michael Hadden. She returned to the store parking lot shortly before 2 a.m. Sunday morning, got in her car and headed home to the Silver Lake area a few miles away. She was in the southbound lanes of the freeway when her Dodge sedan (a converted black and white Highway Patrol car her father had purchased from the state) ran out of gas near a call box where a stranded motorist could phone for help. This, of course, was in the days before cell phones. City records showed that at 2:04 a.m. Robin used the call box and asked the operator to contact her parents to tell them to come and get her. The parents were not home but the city operator got through to Robin's 16-year-old sister, Bonnie Jean, and left a message. Robin's parents, Marvin and Beverly Graham, got home minutes later and rushed off to help Robin.

When the parents got to the freeway's Santa Monica Boulevard off-ramp about 10 minutes later the Dodge was still there. But Robin was gone. There was no sign of foul play, no indication of a struggle. Marvin Graham asked, "How could Robin have run out of gas. I gave her two credit cards for such an emergency." The father drove the Dodge home where, in a burst of nervous energy the next day, he washed it, very probably removing the suspected kidnaper's fingerprints from the hood. However, police found one fresh fingerprint atop the engine but were never able to identify the person who left it there.

The investigation into Robin's disappearance was botched on several fronts. The Los Angeles *Times* castigated the LAPD editorially for delaying the investigation for 24 hours because "...*that's what's always done in missing person cases.*" The *Times* argued that wasn't a valid excuse. It editorialized: "*This was no ordinary missing person's case.*"

Then, there was the role of the Highway Patrol officers patrolling the freeway that night. It became clear from the start that the CHP officers did not get the license number of the Corvette parked alongside Robin's stalled car although they passed the scene numerous times. What is even more amazing is the account the lead CHP officer provided my investigative unit 20 years later while I was preparing to update the Robin Graham story.

The night of Nov. 14, 1970 officer Jerry Stone said he and his partner were patrolling a 10-mile stretch of the Hollywood Freeway which began in the West San Fernando

Valley. They were on a southbound pass approaching the Santa Monica Boulevard exit when they saw a 1968 Dodge stalled on the shoulder, sticking out onto the freeway's slow lane. Stone said he saw Robin at the call box and she told him she had contacted her family. Stone said because of traffic he couldn't back up to move the Dodge on to the freeway shoulder, so they drove to the next exit and returned. Then both officers pushed Robin's car out of harm's way.

The officers resumed patrolling the freeway, looking for speeders and drunken drivers. Stone said he saw a Corvette, maybe 10 years old, coming on to the freeway. Then it exited about a mile down the road. Stone and his partner made another pass and saw the same Corvette parked behind the disabled Dodge. On the next pass the Corvette was gone and Robin was sitting in her car. Still another pass and Stone said the Corvette was back and the man was pouring gas into Robin's tank. The officers made another pass and saw the man looking under the hood of Robin's car. On the next pass the Corvette, its driver and Robin were gone but her car was still there. On another pass everyone was back. One more pass, Stone said, and everyone was gone, Robin, the young man, and his Corvette, and the Dodge which had been taken home by Robin's father.

Stone said he went on his break believing the man in the Corvette was the family member Robin called for help. No, Stone and his partner never jotted down the license number of the Corvette. One thing kept secret by LAPD investigators for years was an eyewitness report that a second car pulled up to the scene and talked briefly to the driver of the Corvette.

The LAPD said its officers with the help of other law enforcement agencies checked out more than 500

Corvettes and their owners but never came close to finding a suspect. The one thing that came out of Robin Graham's disappearance was a new California Highway Patrol regulation requiring officers to stay with any woman "in distress" on the freeway system until she was taken to safety.

We did several stories on the CBS station about Robin's disappearance. We noted that she was an outstanding student and was about to enter USC on an academic scholarship. But no one ever came forward to shed light on her disappearance.

In 1992, while producing "Murder One" for NBC, I resurrected the Robin Graham story once again and that was when we were able to obtain the statement from the lead CHP officer in the unit patrolling the freeway the night she disappeared. Hard to believe but that was 22 years after that fateful night on the Hollywood Freeway. But once again we struck out. Not a single witness came forward.

I got to know the Graham family fairly well over the years. They were warm, friendly people who were convinced Robin was dead but dearly wanted to know what happened to her. They had nine children and a slew of grandchildren. A granddaughter named Robin was the spitting image of her missing aunt. Marvin Graham was a retired employee of the Los Angeles Department of Water and Power. His health was not great the last time I saw him but he could recall every single fact about his daughter's disappearance. The Grahams always spoke of Robin in positive terms, and were particularly proud of her winning an academic scholarship to USC.

For 35 years the Robin Graham story had followed me from network to network.

In the summer of 2006 Jose Rios, Vice President of News at KTTV (Channel 11) asked me if I could produce a couple of news specials on famous missing person cases to run the same nights a new show, "Vanished," made its debut on the Fox network.

Then I said to myself, why not take another shot at the Robin Graham story. Beverly and Marvin Graham welcomed me with open arms. I was accompanied by reporter Chris Blatchford, a Peabody Award winning journalist who was quick to sense the terrible agony suffered by the Graham family over the past 36 years. Joining us was Detective Cliff Shepard of the LAPD Cold Case Unit who took swabs from the mouths of the parents which could be tested for DNA if Robin's body should ever be recovered and needed positive identification.

The story ran at 10 p.m. on a Saturday night on the Fox station and I must admit my expectations for turning up something that might solve the case were minimal. A good portion of our audience wasn't even born when Robin disappeared in 1970.

I was astonished when Blatchford received a letter dated August 23, 2006 from a man who signed his name "William Kad," and identified himself as the person in the second car that pulled up behind the turquoise and white Corvette on the freeway. Kad said the driver was talking to Robin alongside her stranded car. Remember, that was the one bit of information the cops initially held back, the existence of a second car at the apparent kidnapping scene.

Kad identified the driver of the Corvette as a friend he was following home on the freeway after a night of partying and trying "to score" with the ladies on L.A.'s trendy Westside. For legal purposes I'm changing the driver's name to "Anthony K." Kad said Anthony K. owned a turquoise and white Corvette identical to the one described by the highway patrol officers. The officers described the man seen with Robin Graham that night as about 21 years old. Kad said his friend would have been 21 at the time. Kad had remained silent for 35 years, but now he wanted to go on the record. In the letter Kad did not use his real name. But he gave us an address where he once lived with a relative and that helped us track him down in Riverside County, some   60 miles south of Los Angeles.

This was his declaration:

*"I pulled behind him (Anthony K.), and there was also a car in front of him. I only saw this in my headlights as he was opening the passenger side of his Corvette as most likely her auto broke down or he knew her and offered her a ride. I got out of my car for no longer than 30 seconds at most and saw a very fast glimpse of a very attractive, blonde young girl. I do remember that her hair was very straight. I asked if I could help him or the young lady. His answer was something to the effect of: 'Bill you are to forget what you see. You are never to talk about this.' Listening to your report on that missing girl, I remember what happened that night. The memory came flooding back to me like it was yesterday."*

Some years before our meeting with Kad, a member of the Los Angeles County District Attorney's staff said his investigators had long suspected that Robin Graham's disappearance and several other freeway murders of young women might well be linked to one man. There was the case of Rose Tashman, 19, whose car with a flat tire was discovered on a Hollywood freeway off ramp in May 1969, not far from where Robin was last seen alive. Flares had been neatly arranged around Rose's Mustang. Days later her body was found in a ravine off Mulholland Drive in the

Santa Monica Mountains. She had been raped and strangled. In June of 1975 Mona Jean Gallegos, 23, apparently
ran out of gas on a freeway in the city of Covina. When
her car was found all the doors were locked. Several
months later her skeletal remains were spotted in a wilder-
ness area of Riverside County.

We wanted to know more about "Anthony K." and
began checking public records at courthouses throughout Southern California where we found a massive
amount of information including details of numerous
appearances in civil and criminal courts over the years.
There were eight appearances in family law courts in Los
Angeles, Riverside and San Bernardino counties involving
wives, girlfriends and various businesses. All told Anthony
K. was involved in 57 different civil cases. There were child
support cases, lawsuits and numerous tax liens filed by the
state of California and the federal government.

Anthony K.'s criminal rap sheet was much shorter but it
opened a window on his past that indicated he might fit
the profile of the man who abducted and may have killed
Robin Graham. Minor charges included driving with a sus-
pended license; failure to purchase car insurance; diso-
beying a court order, violation of a protective order and
contempt of court. In 1998 a domestic dispute in which
a girlfriend was badly injured led to Anthony K. being
charged with three felonies by the L.A. District Attorney.

But the charges were dismissed because only one witness showed up to testify at his trial, the complaining victim. The house of another witness reportedly was shot up
two days before the trial began, and she failed to appear
in court. A deputy district attorney involved in Anthony K's
prosecution told me was very concerned about the safety
of the girlfriend who filed the criminal charges against
him. I asked if he were aware of Anthony K.'s life-long

fascination with Corvettes, and the prosecutor said yes, that had come up during his investigation.

By a stroke of luck I found the former girlfriend who filed the criminal charges against Anthony K. and she was willing to discuss her life with him provided we not disclose her name or whereabouts. She told a horrifying story of an obsessed and threatening personality who frequently raged that he would kill her and brutalized her endlessly until she escaped from him.

The very attractive woman, let's call her Rita, told me in a taped interview that she first met Anthony K. in the summer of 1996 during an outing with a friend at a public park and soon they began dating. She said, Anthony began a courtship unlike anything she had ever experienced. He sent her roses almost daily and had a limousine pick her up for their dates. They dined at fine restaurants and he appeared to be the perfect gentleman. Soon he moved in with her, and in no time she was pregnant. It was then her nightmare began.

Rita recalled driving through the desert with Anthony when he mentioned that she was going to give birth to a girl and told her, "*You know, if she grows up she's going to be just like you, a whore and a slut and I don't want her to be raised by you. I'd like to take you out to this desert somewhere and kill you and nobody would know where you are.*"

She said the worst was yet to come. Shortly after giving birth, Anthony became enraged at the baby's crying and told Rita she was giving the child too much attention and ignoring him. She said he ripped off her clothes and sodomized her over a bathtub, saying he was teaching her a lesson. Rita said she was bleeding profusely and tried to dial 911 but Anthony K. ripped the phone from a wall mount. At that point, Rita said, she started planning to escape with her child.

Rita said she was terrified by the contents of his closet. She said "he had three different sheriff's uniforms," one of which was inscribed with the insignia of the San Bernardino County Sheriff's Department. Rita said Anthony K. *"...told me he was a cop before he met me. All together he had about 16 different guns."*

There was no record of Anthony K. ever working for any law enforcement agency in Southern California. Rita said he also kept a box in his closet containing several hundred pictures, mainly of young women. She said the box also contained a photograph of a turquoise and white Corvette identical to the one identified by the CHP officers the night Robin vanished. Rita said she finally escaped from Anthony K and went into hiding at the home of a friend who lived about 30 miles away in the San Fernando Valley.

As far as I could determine, Anthony K. had been married five times and as of this writing would be 62 years old. I talked to two of Anthony's former wives and they indicated they were terrified of him. I briefed LAPD's Cold Case Unit on the results of our investigation, but ultimately the people in charge decided not to proceed with a formal investigation. William Bratton, the LAPD chief at the time, expressed indifference to looking at old criminal cases in which there was no DNA. But I'd like to think that Robin Graham's case deserves a second look based on what we learned in our investigation. The Graham family deserves nothing less.

### "THE LADY KILLER"

Ricardo Silvio Caputo was known as "The Lady Killer," a title bestowed on him by New York headline writers in the

1970s, and underscored in the best seller about his murder spree, "Love Me to Death" by Linda Wolfe. Caputo, a native of Argentina, was said to be schizophrenic and suffered from multiple personality disorders. He reportedly killed his victims after what were described as "nurturing relationships."

In 1971, a year after moving to the U.S., Caputo killed his 19-year-old fiancée, Natalie Brown in her Long Island home. He was sent to a state mental hospital for the criminally insane. He escaped in 1974 after killing his psychologist, Dr. Judith Becker. After that he was linked to two more murders, the 1975 slaying in San Francisco of girlfriend Barbara Ann Taylor, 28, and the killing of Laura Gomez, 26, in Mexico City in 1977.

**Argentine born Ricardo Caputo, the so-called "Lady Killer."**

In 1994 Caputo, accompanied by his brother Richard, surrendered to the NYPD and confessed to the murders. He had called his brother from Argentina saying he wanted to turn himself in because he was racked by guilt and plagued by hallucinations. The brother flew to Argentina and brought Ricardo back to New York to face trial. Caputo's lawyer said since his last murder, Caputo lived a quiet life in both North and South America, using many different identities and marrying twice, having two children by his first wife and four by his second in Argentina.

Caputo was sentenced to life imprisonment for the 1971 murder of Natalie Brown. Some suggested Caputo returned to New York because that state had no death penalty, and homicide investigators speculated he may have been involved in other murders across the country.

It was later learned that before going home to Argentina, Ricardo Caputo moved to Hollywood some time in 1980. Using the alias of Bob Martin, he found work as a kitchen helper at Scandia, one of Hollywood's most glamorous restaurants where Hollywood nobility such as Lana Turner and Rita Hayworth were nightly regulars. Devan Marie Green, a good looking 27-year-old blonde, worked as a chef in the Scandia kitchen, choosing not to follow in the footsteps of her mother, Sharon, a successful lawyer.

On the morning of April 7, 1981, Devan's body was found in a parking lot near the John Anson Ford Theater in Hollywood. Her body apparently had been dumped there by the killer. She had been beaten and raped. Her car was found 20 miles away next to the Hilton Hotel in Sherman Oaks. There was no evidence to indicate she was murdered in her car. The late John St. John, the LAPD's most famous homicide cop, questioned her boyfriend, a Latino, but cleared him after he provided an air tight alibi. St. John eventually established that kitchen helper "Bob Martin" was actually the long missing Caputo.

Co-workers said Devan Green and "Bob Martin" seemed friendly in the work place but there were no signs of romantic involvement. After St. John retired the case was turned over to Detective Brian Carr. Carr was preparing to go to Attica after Caputo was incarcerated to question him about Devan's slaying when the multiple killer dropped dead while playing basketball on a prison court in October of 1997.

Detective Carr was pretty much convinced that Ricardo Caputo was Devan Green's killer And perhaps with even more advancements in the use of DNA and fingerprint technology, science will prove the dead serial killer guilty of one more heinous crime, possibly more. There's no doubt in mind that Caputo killed Devan Green.

## DEATH OF A SOAP STAR

Candice Mia Daly was a beautiful actress best known for her role as the crazed "Veronica Landers" in the television soap opera "The Young and the Restless." She also starred in four other TV shows as well as a score of "B" movies and cult films such as "After Dark," "Liquid Dreams" and "Zombie Four." Her beauty also graced a number of national TV commercials, including a slickly produced spot for Mercedes. But on December 14, 2004 this glamorous star lapsed into a coma and died in a rundown shack in the L.A. foothill suburb of Glendale, where she and her aunt had been staying with a male friend. She was just 38 years old. I call her death a cold case, but the Glendale cops disagree.

*Candice Mia Daly*

On the surface the circumstances seemed pretty clear cut. The Los Angeles County Coroner said an autopsy showed that Candice Daly died of "multiple drug intoxication" although she had no prior record of drug abuse. The lack of interest on the part of the Glendale Police Department was evident from the start. The coroner's report noted that the lead investigator on the case did not attend the autopsy, as is normally done in such investigations. The Associated Press carried three paragraphs on Daly's death, saying it was related to drug abuse. A tabloid newspaper, "The Globe," wrote that Daly was fired from "The Young and the Restless" because of drug problems. A spokesperson for the soap denounced the report and called Daly "...a lovely, very professional woman who never gave us any problems"

One morning when I arrived at the Fox 11 investigative unit there was an e-mail waiting for me from night assignment editor Marla Fain, who suggested I call a Mr. Quentin Gutierrez. She said he had some very interesting information about the death of actress Candice Daly. I phoned Gutierrez and arranged a meeting with him the next day at the station. He turned out to be a very likeable guy, a Mexican-American kid who grew up in L.A.'s teeming Hispanic ghetto on the east side, attended Garfield High School, a local community College and went on to become the top car repossession man in town. He was also a state expert on the use of tear, and had qualified as a private investigator.

His story was straightforward. He and Candice Daly had been lovers. They fell in love several years before after running into each other at the House of Blues on the Sunset Strip. He said she was like a mother to his two teenage daughters. One day Candice disappeared with a car he had loaned her. Eventually he tracked her to a rundown house with boarded windows on the outskirts of Glendale with grass so high you could barely reach the front door.

Gutierrez said he was shaken by the glazed look in her eyes when she came to the door. Candice told him she was happy and did not want to leave. Gutierrez became alarmed and began talking to neighbors and others who frequented the area. One woman told him she believed

Candice may have been raped after someone partying at the house gave her the date rape drug GHB.

Gutierrez called the Glendale Police Department numerous times, saying he feared for Candice's life. Several times the cops went to the house but did nothing after Candice indicated she was all right. Gutierrez made it clear to the cops he was convinced someone was feeding Candice the date rape drug, but they ignored him. On Dec.13, 2004 Candice's half-sister, Colleen Madden, flew in from Las Vegas and begged Candice to leave with her. But Candice insisted she wanted to stay right where she was and Colleen Madden left the house in tears, saying she had a premonition that Candice was in grave danger. Her fears well founded. The next day Candice collapsed on the floor and sank into a coma. An ambulance rushed her to a Glendale hospital where she was pronounced dead.

Guiterrez asked the cops to have the coroner do a test for the date rate drug during the autopsy, but they failed to do so. The cops kissed it off as just another "druggie" death. In my conversations with Glendale homicide investigators they made it clear they thought Guiterrez was a nuisance and not to be believed. The Glendale Public Information Officer went ballistic when I questioned the adequacy of the police investigation. He screamed that I was an "idiot" and told me never to call back. I called the office of Police Chief Randy Adams at least four times and also sent him a fax in the hope of questioning him about the investigation, but he never once responded. Adams later came under state investigation when he became Police Chief of the corruption plagued city of Bell, California where he was given an annual salary of $457,000 a years by the city manager and allowed to claim a disability to escape paying most taxes on his pension. Adams and a number of other city officials resigned when their huge salaries and pension benefits came under scrutiny.

My interest in the work of Adams's cops in Glendale intensified when I found out that Gutierrez had spent $3,500 of his own money for a private autopsy on Candice's body. It was performed by Dr. David M. Posey, once a top ranking member of the Los Angeles County Coroner's staff. The post mortem proved conclusively that a heavy dose of Gamma-Hydroxybutyrate (GHB) was found in the vitreous fluid around Daly's eyes. Several other prescription drugs were found in her body including Phenobarbital.

In a sudden burst of energy prompted by our investigation the L.A. County Coroner did a second autopsy and determined that Dr. Posey was correct about the presence of GHB. A coroner's investigator even suggested that Candice may have been held by someone "against her will." But this compelling evidence made no difference to the arrogant Glendale cops who wouldn't budge or to the District Attorney's office which I had made well aware of the facts of the case. After half a century in the investigative end of newsgathering I could pretty well sense a cover-up, gross incompetence, or both.

The body of evidence strongly indicated to me and several other law enforcement sources, including the nation's top expert on the date rape drug GHB, that there was quite possibly foul play in the death of Candice Daly. But things are done differently in Glendale, California.

## AN ACTOR'S GRIEF

Blond haired Dennis Cole was described by a writer who covered the Hollywood scene as the "Robert Redford of Television." His good looks won him one major TV role after another after starting out as a studio stuntman. His first big break was a featured role on "Felony Squad" and soon there were demands for his services throughout the industry. He appeared in "Young and the Restless" on daytime TV and made regular appearances on such shows as "Bracken's World," "Police Story," "Fantasy Island" and "Charlie's Angels" where he met and fell in love with one of Hollywood's most beautiful women, Jaclyn Smith. They were married in 1978 and divorced five years later.

I was writing and producing "Murder One" at NBC in 1992 when I got a call from Dennis Cole asking for my help. He told me in December of 1991 his 30-year-old son, Joey, had been shot to death during a robbery outside a friend's home in the beach community of Venice and police were at a dead end in the case.

Dennis said Joey was his only child from his first marriage and they were very close. He said Joey was a phenomenal tennis player and also an excellent writer. Joey Cole, I learned, was a so-called "roadie" who chronicled the activities of Black Flag and the Henry Rollins Band, groups just slightly removed from the punk rock era.

**Television star Dennis Cole (right) and son Joey, who was murdered in a 1991 robbery.**

Rollins and Joey Cole became fast friends. The night of the murder they were going to have dinner at the rocker's home in Venice and went shopping at a local market. Rollins had just opened the front door of his home when two gunmen, described as "gangbangers" came up behind them and demanded they hand over all their money. Both men complied, but then Rollins said Joey Cole started running away. One of the robbers whirled around and shot him dead. Rollins said he ran through the house and escaped through a rear entrance.

Rollins said he was questioned for almost ten hours by detectives at the Venice Police station who implied he was involved in a drug deal that went sour and that led to Joey's death. The rocker insisted he never used or had any involvement with hard drugs like cocaine and tried marijuana only once and didn't like it.

We spent considerable time on the story and after some initial reluctance Rollins agreed to an on camera interview. But after our story aired no one came forward with information that might lead to an arrest.

Dennis Cole gradually quit acting and became deeply involved with several crime fighting organizations. He called me on a regular basis for many months to see if there was anything new in his son's case. Finally I lost track of him. Then in March of 2009 I got an e-mail from him. He said he had moved to Fort Lauderdale, Florida and was working as a real estate broker. I wished him well. Not too long after that, on November 15, 2009, Dennis Cole died of renal failure at a Fort Lauderdale hospital. He was 69 and went to his death not knowing who killed his son.

# 37

## THE CURIOUS DEATH OF MICHAEL JACKSON

Anyone watching television news or reading the news-papers in the summer of 2009 might have thought the death of singer Michael Jackson was the biggest story of the millennium. What other story could knock the worst recession since the Great Depression right off the front pages? When Marilyn Monroe died in August of 1962 "The CBS Evening News with Walter Cronkite" reported her passing as the last item on the broadcast, and my recollection is the story ran about 45 seconds. Frank Sinatra's death attracted a reasonable amount of coverage on broadcast news but it was infinitesimal in comparison to the coverage bestowed on Jackson, the so-called "King of Pop." The great Ella Fitzgerald was fondly remembered for a day, about the same for the legendary Nat King Cole. Both lived in L.A. The beautiful and talented actress Farrah Fawcett died on the same day as Jackson. But her passing after a courageous fight against cancer was almost unnoticed, trampled beneath the monstrous hoof beats of reporters and camera crews covering Jackson's death. Only a handful of camera crews showed up at the Roman Catholic cathedral in downtown L.A. to take note of Fawcett's funeral. One local TV news outlet didn't even mention it.

I'll be the first to admit that these are different times. The internet has provided a whole new world of rapid fire communications, seriously challenging the ability of the conventional media, newspapers and broadcast news to remain afloat. So maybe that explains why Jackson's memorial service rated live coverage on all the nation's TV networks. But many other questions remain. Why did his death become the fodder for constant speculation? Was Jackson murdered? Did he die from a prescription drug overdose? Was he injected with a fatal dose of the powerful anesthetic Diprivan, which was among the drugs recovered at his home after he died of apparent cardiac arrest? Could the doctors or others who provided him with such drugs be charged with murder or manslaughter? Did Debbie Rowe, his former wife who gave birth to Prince Michael Jr. and Paris Katherine, through artificial insemination, want the kids be returned to her? One web site boldly proclaimed that Rowe had accepted $4 million from Jackson's mother, Katherine Jackson, so she could retain custody of her grandchildren. Was the father of Rowe's children really Dr. Arnold Klein, the Beverly Hills dermatologist who employed Rowe as an assistant and did Klein, who treated the singer for 25 years, donate the semen instead of Jackson? And who was the mother of Jackson's younger son, Prince Michael II, also known as "Blanket"? The London Sun claimed the father was former child star Macaulay Culkin. And if Jackson's mother, Katherine, couldn't take care of his three kids, why did he ask in his will that they be handed over to singer Diana Ross? Obviously enough fodder to feed the gargantuan tabloid obsession with the story for months, maybe years, to come.

TV's pursuit of the story was relentless from Day One, June 25, 2009, when the tabloid news service TMZ was the first to report that the 50-year-old Jackson had died at his rented $25,000 a month home in the fashionable L.A. enclave of Holmby Hills. I had never before seen as many remote trucks and satellite units descend on the city at one time as there were the day of Jackson's memorial service at the downtown Staples Center. One hundred miles to the north another herd of satellite trucks was parked along the small road outside Jackson's three-thousand acre Neverland Ranch in Santa Barbara County amid speculation that he would be buried there. The news gurus weren't taking any chances on missing a single element of the story. And they paid as much as $1,500 to the owners of the Staples Center to park their satellite trucks on public property in front of the building for the L.A. memorial service. This at a time the TV networks were pleading poverty, virtually eliminating their overseas bureaus, and firing hundreds of employees. The LAPD provided the Jackson family with a motorcycle escort to the memorial service at the Staples Center, shutting down portions of the freeway to assure clear sailing for the entourage, as if they were some sort of royalty. L.A. City officials, faced with horrible budget problems, spent several million dollars on police overtime to insure everything came off without a hitch during the memorial service. A lot of taxpayers were not pleased. One year after Jackson's death the executors of his estate agreed to pay the city $1 million to help defray the cost of policing his memorial service, a fraction of the costs.

Emmy Magazine, the official publication of the Academy of Television Arts and Sciences, reported that the three-hour Michael Jackson memorial was broadcast live on 18 channels in the United States alone with a total audience estimated at 31 million. Jim Bell, executive producer of NBC's "Today" show, was quoted as saying he was not surprised by the astounding number of viewers. "Michael Jackson," he said, "is probably as big a star as we've ever had in this country." If I didn't know better I'd say Bell was kidding.

Day after day CNN, and its talk show host Larry King, in particular, beat the Jackson story to death. There was father Joe Jackson, defending his tough love for Michael as a boy and promoting his music business on the side. There was brother Jermaine Jackson and other assorted members of the clan, expressing disbelief at Michael's tragic death, and planning money making memorial shows. Sister LaToya Jackson was certain Michael was murdered and said she would soon tell all. She never did.

What no one seemed to want to discuss on TV were Michael Jackson's sexual proclivities. Congressman Peter King of New York boldly came out front and described the King of Pop as a "pervert and a pedophile" and asked why the nation had become so politically correct that no one wanted to talk about it. No one in Congress challenged his remarks. Columnist Steve Lopez of the L.A. Times broke with the ranks of Jackson's admirers in the Fourth Estate and wondered in print about Jackson's attraction to young boys whom he liked to take to bed with him.

Jackson first admitted to sleeping with boys in 2003 when questioned by Martin Bashir on a British television documentary about his life. He insisted the sleepovers had no sexual overtones. Ten years earlier Jackson agreed to a $22 million settlement with Jordan Chandler, a 12-year-old Santa Monica boy who had traveled with Jackson and spent considerable time bedded down with him. But after Jackson's death Chandler, by now a young man, said he lied about Jackson being a pedophile at the urging of his father, a dentist, who was dead by this time.

In 2005 Jackson stood trial in the city of Santa Maria in Santa Barbara County on charges of committing a lewd act with a young boy, administering the child an intoxicating agent, child abduction and false imprisonment. There was massive coverage of the proceedings. TV camera trucks and satellite units feeding live stories worldwide surrounded the small courthouse and remained there for the entire run of the month long trial. I covered portions of the trial and there was some incriminating testimony brought forth by the prosecution. However, a jury found Jackson not guilty on all charges. The boy's mother had serious credibility problems. A few years earlier security guards at a J.C. Penney store accused her of using her children to conduct a Fagin-like shoplifting operation. This left many with the impression that the charges against Jackson were a "shakedown."

In the case of Michael Jackson it's not easy to ignore the old Irish axiom of "never speak ill of the dead." The fact of the matter is Michael Jackson was never convicted of a crime. Like the late Elvis Presley, he was generous to a fault, giving millions to charity and the needy and never trying to glory in publicity. Jackson's will left 20 per cent of his estate to children's charities. But the case in point here is the credibility of modern news coverage. If the media merchants are going to bestow sainthood on this man shouldn't someone out there be playing devil's advocate? And above all that, was Jackson's death worthy of such mindless day to day coverage, or, might I ask, are we simply living in a mindless era?

It's a Monday night, 32 days after Jackson's death. I turn to CNN for the day's news and it's the Larry King show with a substitute host. There's a panel of four experts and all they're talking about are the latest developments in the Jackson case, which really amount to nothing but gibberish. Suddenly a graphic is super imposed on the screen and it changes the conversation. It reads: "Source says Jackson's doctor gave fatal injection." Later I learn the source is the Associated Press and the doctor in question is Jackson's personal physician, Dr. Conrad Murray, a Las Vegas cardiologist who was with Jackson when he died. Dr. Murray reportedly was paid $150,000 a month to minister to Jackson's medical needs. Seven months after Jackson's death Dr. Murray was charged with involuntary manslaughter based on allegations he recklessly dispensed dangerous drugs to Jackson time after time. A jury found Dr. Murray guilty and he was sentenced to four years in the Los Angeles County Jail. Jackson's family cheered openly in court at the verdict.

I must report that Larry King's total focus on the Michael Jackson story doubled the ratings on his talk show. And that's the bottom line in a business that is no longer considered a public service. I turn on CNN's sister channel, HLN, and there's Jane Velez Mitchell with still another panel of blabbing experts, including a former prosecutor, rehashing the Jackson case. There's one news break when Jane find enough time to pitch her upcoming self fulfillment book to the TV audience. It's the same Michael Jackson story on *Access Hollywood*, *Entertainment Tonight*, and of course, *TMZ*, the investigative mouthpiece for entertainment sleuthing and scum laden gossip that made the likes of Paris Hilton, Lindsay Lohan and Brittany Spears household words As one veteran reporter told me, "It seems we in the media have lost our way."

It may have come as a surprise to some people that Jackson spent an outlandish sum of money on his personal physician. But that's just the half of it. I reported he was catered to by a score of personal aides including his nutritional counsel, Cherilyn Lee, a registered nurse. Lee was the first to disclose Jackson's dependency on the anesthetic Diprivan, also known as Propofol, to stop his suffering from bouts of insomnia. The drug is widely used during surgery to induce unconsciousness. Miss Lee said she warned Jackson that the Diprivan could kill him, and refused his request to obtain the drug for him. Jackson's drug dependency was demonstrated by the fact that wherever he went he was followed his own personal ambulance, a large van complete with trained emergency medical technicians. The van was equipped with oxygen and any drugs Jackson might need or want during the course of his travels.

The new journalism breeds contempt for conventional news. Over and over again I saw local TV stations ignore coverage of California's budget crisis, the state's devastating water shortage, the health care debate in Washington, the wars in Iraq and Afghanistan and the bloody violence between the Army and drug dealers just south of our border in Mexico. The "impoverished" television networks found enough loose cash to spend millions on their after death coverage of Michael Jackson. Apart from all this, Rupert Murdoch, the Fox Network's majordomo, found many more millions to pay his hosts on "American Idol" after firing 120 newsroom employees at Fox 11 News in Los Angeles. Where's the justice in all this?

It seems to me this is all part and parcel of the reckless behavior that has infiltrated television and some newspapers, causing them to lose their way and their dignity in delivering the news to the American people. You must ask yourself, can the media be trusted to keep us informed about what's important, or are they going to let us wallow in the gossipy tabloid sinkhole where paying for a story and breaking privacy laws with cameras violates the basic principles of American journalism? And while they're at it, how about letting Michael Jackson rest in peace regardless of his failings in life!

# 38

## AN EYE ON TV NEWS

When I broke into television news in 1961 in depth reporting was quickly becoming the order of the day in the newsgathering world  that was brought to life by master innovator Sam Zelman, the man who created the nation's first hour-long news broadcast, "*The Big* News" at the CBS-owned station in Los Angeles, KNXT, now known as CBS2. "*The Big News*," which ran for more than 15 years, was a huge profit center for the network and considered a model for countless other news broadcasts both in the United States and overseas.

Zelman preached that TV reporters speak in conversational tones so the audience would fully comprehend their message.  At the same time they were expected to abide by journalistic standards requiring the inclusion of the "who, what, where, when and why" in every story. Zelman demanded stories with a beginning, a middle and an end. In my early years in TV news many of my investigative stories ran four to five minutes. My story announcing the arrests in the Charles Manson murder case ran almost 23 minutes. The narration was covered almost entirely by film. Conversely, a story about mob involvement in a

Beverly Hills housing development ran eight minutes, but had less than a minute of video. Many times Associated Press wire photos were used to visualize a story at which newsreel cameramen were absent.

The dynamics of early television news broadcasts were geared to an audience which got most of its news from daily newspapers. When the Big News debuted in late 1961 there were four newspapers serving metropolitan L.A. As of this writing, there is just one, the Los Angeles *Times*, and its circulation has steadily declined. Local TV news broadcasts, in the beginning, tended to take their cues from the newspapers, following up on print stories one after another. It was the same at the network levels with newsrooms at CBS, NBC and ABC leaning heavily on the coverage of the New York *Times* and the *Washington Post*.

The Big News, under Zelman's direction, took giant steps to reverse this pattern with original coverage that put us in direct competition with the newspapers. The idea of expanded news coverage spread across the country and local news broadcasts running 60 minutes became common place in a few years. But there was one major setback along the way. In 1967 an enterprising young male intern at WBBM, the CBS station in Chicago, offered to help film a "pot party" at Northwestern University and the news director bought his proposal. Problem was the "pot party" was a staged affair, paid for out of newsroom funds. The intern, an honors graduate of the Medill School of Journalism at Northwestern, actually set up the party. It was an invitation only affair in an apartment near the Northwestern campus attended  by six clean cut students, a teacher and two college dropouts, all of whom agreed to be filmed and interviewed about smoking marijuana. Their goal apparently was to show that smoking pot was "harmless."  WBBM spent a large sum of money advertising the two-part program entitled *"Pot Party at a*

University," and it obtained the desired result, huge ratings in a time spot where it usually got beat by the opposition. Northwestern University reacted immediately, charging in a press release that the program was a "staged affair" by WBBM news personnel to hype the ratings. The Federal Communications Commission launched an investigation and concluded that the program was indeed "staged" by the CBS station, that it actually paid for and manufactured the news. The FCC ruling came down hard on WBBM and its bosses at the CBS network. The FCC decided it would not take away the CBS broadcast license at WBBM for putting a "staged story" on the air. But it took the CBS brass to task for its "cavalier response" in denying there was any wrongdoing in the making of the marijuana program. The FCC said from that day forward news rooms should defer to station general managers on stories of such importance. It noted that the CBS organization had no rules to guide investigative reporting by its news staffers and ordered the network to put a policy in place at once.

The net result was that station managers, nearly all of whom rose up through the ranks of their sales departments, would be responsible for local news coverage. In effect this meant that because of one mistake, albeit a very big one, professional journalists would be taking orders from guys who started their careers selling commercials for used cars and panty hose. That was okay with the consultants because station managers were much more amenable to change than news types. And the GMs were the guys who paid for their advice. I saw the immediate impact at the CBS station. The News Director began clearing just about every investigative story I did with the general manager. I am convinced it was the GM who killed the story on the sex scandal in the administration of Governor Ronald Reagan.

The fallout from that FCC decision has been never ending, and I blame it for many of the failings that are obvious in TV news today. When news directors were in charge political advertising was seldom seen on TV news broadcasts. In Los Angeles, for instance, every station once had a policy banning political ads on news and public affairs shows. But in 1986 KNBC's new station manager John Rohrbeck, who had risen through the ranks of various sales departments, announced the station would begin carrying TV ads on all news programming and the other stations in town quickly followed suit. It's now difficult to differentiate between the paid political spots that saturate TV news and the actual news coverage. One political reporter told me he was greatly embarrassed when a political ad for a candidate appeared just before he started interviewing the same person on a live broadcast.

Soon after the FCC decision, TV news consultants led by Dr. Frank Magid, began worming their way into one newsroom after another where they found friendly receptions from the sales oriented general managers. When I worked at the ABC station in Los Angeles, the news director, Bill Fyffe, refused to let Magid inside the newsroom. Fyffe maintained the only safe place to meet with the consultant was in a neutral setting. Otherwise the newsroom staff would consider Magid's presence a sign of weakness on Fyffe's part. Magid said the TV news audience was getting older and another way had to be found to generate stories that would interest young men and women, the "TV Babies" who grew up watching *Captain Kangaroo* and all those animated shows that kept kids glued to their sets. We were told shorter news stories with lots of video edits were the order of the day. Politics was boring so keep those stories brief or don't run them at all. Crank up your consumer reporting and do more medical stories. Stay away from city hall and other government agencies. A cynical producer once told me we should do lots of stories about breast cancer because that gave us an opportunity to show video of women's breasts.

It was this sort of thinking that drowned out serious coverage of the political machinations at City Hall and led to massive helicopter coverage of car chases by the cops that began dominating local news following the famous O.J. Simpson "slow speed" police chase on L.A.'s freeway system in 1994. The former football star was being sought for the murders of his wife, Nicole, and her friend Ron Goldman when he was finally reigned in. The Simpson pursuit by the cops produced gigantic ratings. So why not interrupt a newscast or regular programming with something visually provocative such as a wild west like chase involving good and evil. Station after station across the country got involved in the car chase dynamics.

But then, one such pursuit turned ugly, ending in a personal execution before a stunned audience of several million. At the time I was out of work and the *Christian Science Monitor* solicited my opinion about the story for its editorial pages. It was about a deranged man waving a rifle in a pickup truck which brought traffic to a standstill on the Harbor Freeway not far from the Los Angeles Civic center A half dozen TV helicopters hovered overhead, and several zoomed in for a close up as the man set fire to himself, his dog and the pickup, then shot himself in the head. It was breaking news, it was live on all the TV stations, and it was ghastly. Thousands of complaining viewers lit up switchboards, particularly at my old NBC station, where the coverage of the horrible scene was extremely graphic. L.A. *Times* TV critic Howard Rosenberg called it "A total abrogation of journalistic responsibility."

My commentary in the Monitor was a virtual indictment of local television news operations, yet no one in the business challenged my conclusions. A number of reporters called to thank me for what I had written. Nevertheless, car chases soon resumed on a regular basis on local TV and pretty much continued to be a fact of television life for many years until the price of aviation fuel went out of sight, costing more than a thousand dollars an hour to keep a helicopter airborne. To the credit of NBC, veteran newsman Bob Long banned live coverage of all car chases from news broadcasts the day he became news boss at its Los Angeles station.

When I say that television is a "hot" medium I truly believe it has the capacity for good or evil; the capacity to inform or manipulate, to teach or propagandize; to engender love or hate. Back in the early 1960s when the "Black Power" movement was starting to take shape our newsroom at KNXT was vandalized by intruders who painted black power slogans everywhere. The incident prompted CBS to hire security guards for the first time and purchase security cameras. When I was at the ABC station a screaming man broke into the newsroom shouting obscenities and threatening people until he was subdued by several camera men. It was clear there were those who regarded us as the "enemy."

Perhaps the most startling incident occurred at NBC. Consumer reporter David Horowitz was on the air when a young man walked up to him in the studio and put a gun to his head. News director Tom Capra immediately told the director to go to black, and the news audience was really left in the dark. What the audience missed was seeing anchorman John Beard and security guards subduing the young man and taking away his realistic looking weapon which was just a toy gun, thank God.

It turned out the intruder was the son of Max Stollman, a druggist who, until a few weeks before, doled out pharmaceutical advice to viewers on the station's 4pm news broadcast. The young man said he was bitter about his father's termination and simply wanted to make a statement on television.

"Streakers," although relatively harmless, have frequently posed a problem, especially for reporters and camera crews doing live reports from the field. The audience may laugh but the people who run TV see no humor in a naked body shooting in front of a camera.

The fact of the matter is that it can be quite dangerous to be a television personality. News anchorwomen on television have to be extremely cautious about stalkers and over zealous fans. In October of 2008 Anne Pressley, an anchor woman for a television station in Little Rock, Arkansas, was beaten to death by an intruder in her apartment. A suspect was arrested and convicted of murder. Another anchorwoman in Mason City, Iowa, Jodi Heisentruit, disappeared off the face of the earth in 1999. In Palm Springs, California, TV reporter Annette Samuelson (Chapter 33) fled town after she was stalked just about everywhere she went by man who later pled guilty to a brutal kidnap-murder in Los Angeles.

I became personally involved in a case involving Kelly Lange, an anchor woman featured on both local and national television for NBC. Most people at the studio thought the guy sleeping every night in the company parking lot in his rusty 1956 Cadillac was relatively harmless. His name was Sonny Hudson. He was about 50 years old and tipped the scales at nearly 300 pounds. Eventually I learned that Kelly Lange was the imagined love of Sonny Hudson's life. He showered her with gifts, including his late mother's fur coat and jewelry. Kelly never responded to his entreaties and Sonny's gifts of passion remained boxed up in her office.

Months went by and then one day my assistant, Perdita Brown, told me, "Pete, you have to talk to this man on line one. Kelly's life may be in danger." I picked up the phone and the man on the other end told me in a calm voice that he ran a telemarketing company near the airport, one of those so called "boiler rooms" that sells just about anything over the phone, and he feared for Kelly Lange's life. He said Sonny Hudson was one of his telemarketers and told fellow workers that his long romance with Kelly Lange was over and that he was going to harm her physically. I asked him to elaborate. The man told me, "He's going home, and get a gun to kill her." I didn't hesitate for a second. On a hunch earlier I had found out where Hudson lived. I called a friend in the LAPD Robbery-Homicide Division and he and his partner raced to Sonny's home where they caught up with him just as he was walking out the front door. "Where are you going?" the cop asked Sonny." Without batting an eye, Sonny answered: "I'm going to Burbank to kill Kelly Lange because she doesn't love me any more." The detective immediately disarmed Sonny who was carrying two loaded weapons, a rifle and a police revolver. The handgun had once belonged to his father who many years before was kicked off the LAPD for "psychiatric reasons."

Sonny Hudson was convicted of threatening the life of Kelly Lange in a non-jury trial before Superior Judge J.D. Smith and sentenced to five years in prison. Once he got out he never bothered Kelly again. But he did start a letter writing campaign aimed primarily at the Roman Catholic Archdiocese claiming that I was guilty of framing him for a crime he never committed. It was obvious that mental competency was an issue in this case. But there's not much you can do about people like Sonny Hudson until they commit a crime.

As a young editor at City News Service I took my lumps for reporting the names of two firemen killed while fighting a raging blaze in an industrial building before their families were notified. A fire department duty officer had given me the names of the victims, but failed to mention that the families had not been told. I included the victims' names in my story that went to just about every radio and TV station in Los Angeles. And to my dismay both families learned of the deaths while watching TV.

The widow of actor Alan Ladd cried and described me as "heartless" for a story implying her husband had died from a possible overdose of prescription drugs, a finding that was later verified by the County Coroner. Comedian Groucho Marx wasn't laughing when he called me and threatened to kill reporter Harold Green for insinuating that the comedian was "senile" while describing his appearance in a Hollywood parade.

Then there are those who would manipulate the medium to their advantage. In 1975 I was introduced by KABC news director Bill Fyffe to Mike Brown, a squat, stocky man in his early 30s who described himself as the illegitimate son of billionaire Howard Hughes. To the best of my knowledge Hughes never had any children. Accompanying Brown was a good looking woman who stood at least six inches above him, and seemed mesmerized, possibly by the dollar signs she saw in his future.

I joined Fyffe and reporter Dick Carlson in meeting with Brown who seemed to have his act together at first. He knew a lot about Hughes, including a relatively obscure island in the Hawaii chain where Hughes sometimes sought peace and quiet. Brown was quite learned about Hughes financial empire and his storied history as a world class flyer and movie director. I must say I was impressed until Brown said, "There's one thing more I want to tell you. I'm always in touch with my father." I asked how so, and Brown said, "a year or so ago I was riding with Howard on the Hollywood Freeway. He pulled off the freeway and parked his car in front of Mount Sinai Hospital." Brown quoted Hughes as saying, *"I want you to be in contact with me all the time so you're going to have a simple operation in which the doctors will implant a very tiny radio transmitter in your brain. That way we can always be in contact. Well I had the operation and now Howard can talk to me any time he wants."* I exploded and told Brown and his lady friend to get off the premises immediately. Fyffe and Carlson seemed stunned and asked what prompted me to act so decisively without hearing Brown out. I said there was no story here. I explained that Brown was either a con man or a nut case. I maintained that any shrink would say Brown's story about the radio implant was delusional; that making such a claim is considered a psychosis in psychiatric circles.

It turned out Brown may have been crazy and a con man at the same time and didn't realize the shaky ground he was treading on with the implant story. One year later he was arrested in Las Vegas for swindling investors out of ten million dollars by selling them shares of the vast fortune he claimed he would inherit upon the death of his father, Howard Hughes. Mike Brown turned out to be a very bad bet in the gambling oasis. A jury found Brown guilty of the swindle and he got 10 years in prison.

Self-styled TV psychic Tamara Rand also found Las Vegas a good bet for her con game, one involving an attempt on the life of the President of the United States. On March 30, 1981 the nation was stunned when President Reagan, just 69 days in office, was shot and nearly killed while getting into a limousine following a speech at the Hilton Hotel in Washington D.C.

Twenty-six-year-old John Hinckley, unloaded six shots at the President. A bullet that ricocheted off the limousine lodged in Mr. Reagan's lung near his heart. His press secretary, James Brady was shot in the head. A Secret Service agent was shot in the stomach and a policeman took a bullet in the back. All survived although Brady was so badly hurt he could not return to his job. He soon became a leading advocate of gun control. A jury found Hinckley not guilty by reason of insanity after an investigation revealed he had once stalked President Jimmy Carter, and apparently shot Mr. Reagan to impress actress Jodie Foster. She became the object of Hinckley's obsessions after he watched the movie "*Taxi Driver*" 15 times. Foster played a 12-year-old prostitute in the film.

Both NBC and ABC saw a moment of opportunity after receiving a video tape in which the psychic known as Tamara Rand ostensibly predicted before Mr. Reagan's inauguration that he could be the victim of an assassination attempt. The network producers were told the prediction was made on a TV talk show with host Dick Maurice on KNTV, the NBC affiliate in Las Vegas. Responding to a question from Maurice, Rand spoke in cautious, fearful tones. "I feel he (Reagan) is in a crisis cycle," she intoned. "I hate to say it. In my mind, after he was elected, I saw a gun, shots all over the place. It might actually be an assassination."

Just about everyone fell for the tape, and Tamara Rand was all over the network including NBC's *Today Show*. If publicity was her goal, she got what she wanted. KNBC, the NBC station in Burbank, ran with the story much to my dismay and after a brief discussion with news director Irwin Safchik, a former New York *Times* editor, we decided that further checking was needed on Tamara Rand because the story seemed to have some holes in it. I started to suggest the name of a reporter, when Safchik interrupted and said, "Pete, take a camera crew and go to Vegas." So I did and I wasn't at all surprised by the results. Ed Quinn, the general manager of station KTNV, gave me carte blanche to check out every aspect of the story. Rand said her prediction was made in a show that aired January 6, 1981.

A review of the show broadcast on that date revealed no such prediction. It was quite obvious the tape supplied the networks was shot with just one camera and had limited camera angles. The usual *Dick Maurice Show* was shot with two cameras, technicians at the station told me. Then, another technician told me the day after the assassination attempt, a Saturday, Rand and Maurice showed at the station and asked to tape a segment. They finally rounded up a director and one cameraman. And then, with the tape rolling, Maurice asked her if Mr. Reagan's life would be in danger once he assumed the presidency. That was the same tape delivered to the networks. Station manager Quinn told me his investigation had revealed exactly what I had determined to be the case; that Tamara Rand and Dick Maurice in an attempt at attracting nationwide publicity had provided the media with a phony story. Returning home that night, I broke the story on KNBC's 11 o'clock news.

The NBC network news types were greatly embarrassed, but they never told the rest of the nation that the Tamara Rand prediction was a hoax despite having broadcast her phony tape on the "*Today*" show. The whole affair became available on You Tube and the most hilarious part is that of Dick Maurice trying to explain how the scam came about. It's one of those times when a con artist is hoisted on his own petard. Maurice fumbles, stumbles and almost falls before he concedes that fraud was possibly involved in the taping.

To repeat myself, television news is a "hot" form of communications, and it behooves everyone working in the industry to guard and protect its public trust from those who would manipulate it for their own personal goals.

# 39

# THE LESS THAN PERFECT TV FAMILY

June 5, 1968 was one of my darkest days in the news business. I've always prided myself on my ability to keep my emotions in check while covering a news story but I was reduced to tears of anger when I was told that Senator Robert Kennedy had been shot and critically wounded at the Ambassador Hotel in Los Angeles shortly after midnight. He had just finished his victory speech in the hotel ballroom before a cheering crowd after being declared the winner of the California Democratic presidential primary election over Senator Eugene McCarthy of Minnesota.

I was producing the election coverage that night at the CBS station, KNXT, and was preparing to go off the air when word of the shooting struck like a thunderbolt. The senator was exiting the hotel through the kitchen pantry service area shortly after midnight when 24-year-old Sirhan Bishara Sirhan wildly unloaded his 22 caliber revolver and started shooting, the bullets hitting Kennedy and five others, including two news persons. The five were not too badly hurt. Sirhan was seized immediately and disarmed by several persons, including former Los Angeles

Rams pro football star Roosevelt Grier, and Olympic track hero Rafer Johnson. Kennedy had been shot three times. He died from the bullet to his brain twenty six hours later in Good Samaritan Hospital.

Investigators served a search warrant on the Pasadena home where the gunman lived with his mother, Mary Sirhan and two brothers. Among the items seized was Sirhan's diary in which he wrote over and over, "RFK Must Die," in what would seem to be an obvious case of premeditation. One of our news writers at the CBS station, Robert Blair Kaiser, quit to write a book about the assassination entitled *"RFK Must Die."* In my view it was one of the most comprehensive studies of an assassin ever documented.

Sirhan, a Palestinian, was born in Jerusalem and came to the United States with his family when he was 12 years old. He attended local schools and held a number of odd jobs that included working as a stable boy at a local race track. Mary Sirhan said her son developed a hatred of Kennedy's because of his strong support for Israel.

Despite the preponderance of eyewitness evidence, for years there have been rumors and speculation that there was a second gunman at the murder scene and that Robert Kennedy was killed because of a well orchestrated conspiracy. One of the first to advance this theory was a Canadian journalist named Theodore Charach who joined forces with a former CBS copy boy who happened to be an eyewitness to history. The night of the election we assigned the copy boy, Donald Schulman, to the Ambassador Hotel to assist our camera teams and reporters. He was in the pantry when Sirhan fired his weapon.

Minutes later reporter Ruth Ashton Taylor questioned Schulman, and specifically asked him, "did you see anyone else firing at the senator?" Schulman answered, "No, there was only one gunman." His response was emphatic. A few weeks later Schulman quit his job at the station. The next thing we knew Charach called a news conference to introduce an eyewitness who said he witnessed a second gunman in the pantry firing at Robert Kennedy. The news conference was attended by a score of reporters and camera operators. And to our surprise, the eyewitness who supposedly saw the second gunman was none other than the same Donald Schulman interviewed by Reporter Taylor almost immediately after Kennedy was shot.

That night I ran Schulman's remarks about the second gunman first in our news broadcast; then followed it up with his original interview the night of the assassination in which he insisted there was only one gunman. Our story infuriated Charach who accused me of being a party to the cover-up, working hand-in-glove with the LAPD, FBI and CIA. His whole second gun theory had blown up in his face. Perhaps Charach was unaware of Schulman's original story, or else he figured that people working in TV news were just a bunch of dimwits. Despite our expose he kept insisting the second shooter was a security guard at the Ambassador named Thane Eugene Cesar, who was immediately cleared by the cops. We had knocked the guts out of his fabricated story and he knew it.

Despite the facts in evidence, Charach spent many months writing letters to congressman and senators taking me to task for blocking the true story of the RFK assassination. In 1970 Charach produced a documentary called "The Second Gun," which in the parlance of the trade was a box office "bomb."

Another theory making the rounds was that of a young British documentary producer who wasn't alive when Robert Kennedy was shot. The thrust of the 2007 documentary broadcast on British TV was that three CIA agents he claimed were present in the Ambassador that fateful night took part in the assassination. As proof he showed video of the crowded gathering where Kennedy spoke at the Ambassador Hotel the night of June 6, 1968 which he obtained from the archives of L.A. TV station KTTV where I was working. Mind you, this documentary was pieced together 39 years after the assassination. There was no way that I or anyone else could positively identify the men as actual CIA agents, and even if they were, how does that prove they were involved in the assassination?

I happened to learn that the British producer was working closely with Brad Johnson who was on the staff of the *Cable News Network* at its international desk in Atlanta, Georgia. Johnson insisted that the video used in the British documentary had been censored by a government agency since there were several long holes in the KTTV archival video. He was correct that something was left out of the video. What was missing were the commercials. When making air checks on tape nearly all television stations seldom recorded commercials, promotional material or public service announcements that appear on news broadcasts. Such deletions were standard procedure way back in 1968 when news programs were recorded on two-inch tape. That bit of information pretty much deflated his conspiracy theory. But you couldn't tell that to Johnson, who insisted it was all part of a major cover-up in RFK's death, and hounded television editors all over Los Angeles for what he believed to be the missing video. He never found it.

There were some aspects of Sirhan's trial that raised my curiosity level. For one thing, one of his lawyers was Russell Parsons who definitely had ties to organized crime. I had copies of several letters Parsons wrote to federal probation officers describing L.A. mob boss Mickey Cohen as a model citizen. When Parsons was in his mid 80s, he was disbarred for stealing from the estate of a wealthy woman who owned a very successful nursing home in Orange County. When she died, the estate went into probate, but Parsons managed to control it for 30 years, collecting huge profits until he was caught. He died a short time later and was never brought to trial.

Grant Cooper, Sirhan's lead attorney, was a personal friend and I knew him to be a man of great integrity. But I was really bothered by Parsons' mob ties. At the time I was writing a book about the assassination of President John Kennedy in which I indicated his death may have been the result of an underworld conspiracy. In fact the original title of the book was, "*Did the Mafia Kill JFK?*" But the publisher opted out of that title as being "too scary" and the book was renamed "*Legacy of Doubt,*" which was published in 1973.

Another thing I found bothersome about the trial was that the CIA planted an investigator on Sirhan's defense's team. I was duty bound by a source not to reveal the investigator's name. Perhaps the CIA got away with it because of national security but it was most certainly an illegal intrusion on the attorney-client privilege by a government agency.

Despite these odd bits of information I am convinced that Sirhan acted alone; that RFK's death was not a conspiracy involving the CIA, FBI or any other agency, foreign or domestic. I scoured hundreds of public records; checked out numerous interviews, and read everything I could find about Sirhan and his family to reach my conclusion that he acted alone that night in the Ambassador Hotel pantry.

Donald Schulman wasn't the only copy boy who tried my patience during my years at the CBS station. On one occasion we sent a copy boy in a company station wagon to the Burbank Airport to pick up news film of a late breaking story in Sacramento, the state capitol. Apparently our employee had done a little too much imbibing at lunch that day and he crashed the company wagon into a Boeing 707 on the Burbank air strip. The newsroom was stuck with an $8,000 bill to repair damage to the plane and I had to sign off on it, much to the displeasure of the company bean counters. I didn't fire the young man, who shall remain nameless, and eventually he became one of my best friends and a very successful entrepreneur in another line of work.

One who won't remain nameless is the copy boy turned convicted rapist who worked right under my nose at the CBS station. It was March of 1971 and I was producing the Saturday edition of the hour long Big News when I saw a husky Alan Janis twisting the arm of a copy girl behind her back, so hard that she was crying. I ordered Janis to let go of the girl and he asked if I were big enough to make him. I flattened him with one punch and when he came to his senses I told him to get out of the newsroom and never come back.

In those days we didn't have a human relations department to deal with and the managing editor's word was law. The following Monday I got a call from Lt. Dan Cooke, the legendary LAPD press spokesman who was frequently portrayed on the "Dragnet" television show. Cooke asked, "Pete, do you have an Alan Janis working there?" I replied,

"Not any more. I fired him on Saturday. Cooke responded, "That's good because we've just arrested him for raping as many as five young women." Cooke said rape investigators were able to track Janis down because he told each one of his victims, "My name is

Alan," apparently believing his victims thought highly of him. Janis spent less than two years in prison before he was paroled. Punishment for rape has changed drastically since 1971 and as of this writing nearly 40 years later Janis would probably be sentenced to life imprisonment.

I first learned that Janis had been granted an early parole while working at station KFMB- TV in San Diego in 1976. My longtime colleague in both Sacramento and L.A., former colleague Dave Browning, called me from a pay phone in Fresno, California. Browning, who had witnessed my newsroom confrontation with Janis at KNXT seven years earlier, said he had just spotted the convicted rapist's picture on a billboard as he was driving through the city en route to L.A. "There he was in all his glory," said Browning, featured as a sports anchorman at a local TV station." It was hard for me to believe that Janis was back on the street, much less working in TV news. Six months later in a bit of unmitigated gall Janis called me in San Diego. He said he wanted a job in a bigger market than Fresno and San Diego would do just fine. I hung up the phone in disgust.

My brief sojourn to Sacramento in 1965, the birthplace of muckraking hero Lincoln Steffens, wasn't exactly a watershed moment in my career, but as news director it gave me a lot of administrative experience. My assignment editor, the very same Dave Browning, went on to fame and fortune with the CBS network, eventually winding up as a producer for "Sixty Minutes." David was multitalented and could perform just about any job in the newsroom. But his main value to me was as an assignment editor. Anyone who has ever worked in TV news will tell you running the assignment desk is the toughest job in the newsroom. So when David quit for a job with CBS in Hollywood I quickly began looking for a replacement. Otherwise I would have had to do the job myself.

I made the mistake of hiring the first guy to walk through the door. His name was Keith Bonnet and he had a crooked nose that someone obviously had smashed in a brawl. He had a tough guy New York accent, not far removed from the Bowery. But what stood out on his behalf was an incredible letter of recommendation from an editor at the Los Angeles Times. It was typed on the newspaper's stationery, and I had no reason to doubt its authenticity.

Only years later did I learn that the Times employee who wrote the letter was a friend of Bonnet and he confessed to me he made the whole thing up to help him get a job. That's not considered fair play in our business. In reality Bonnet did not have a single credit as a newspaperman, and he had never even taken a journalism class. I doubt very much that he ever went to college except maybe to sweep the floors.

Three days after hiring him I was asleep at home when the phone rang at 2 in the morning and the sheriff of Yolo County was on the other end of the line. "Noyes," he said, "...send someone over to the jail to pick up these drunks who work for you." It turned out that Bonnet and reporter Myra Scott had been out on the town and after too much imbibing he wrapped the company car around a light pole. Both were pretty well banged up but recovered quickly. I should have fired Bonnet then, but I didn't. I couldn't believe how quickly he grasped the intricacies of assigning reporters and cameramen to cover stories, and as the saying goes, I was "covering my butt." One reason being an assignment editor isn't an easy job is that many TV news reporters have egos as big as Mt. Whitney, the tallest peak in California. And often they question just about everything they're asked to do. Will Rogers used to say "I never met a man I didn't like." My response, "Will Rogers never met a TV reporter." But Keith got a quick handle on the care and feeding of TV reporting types.

Months later I was also back in Hollywood, replaced at the Sacramento station by Tom Capra, son of the legendary movie director Frank Capra. Tom told me that Bonnet eventually worked himself up to the job of reporter and credited him with lots of "street smarts." I later heard he was hired by the CBS station in San Francisco and lost track of him after that. Fast forward 20 years to 1985 when I was working at the NBC station in Burbank, California. One day I got a long distance call from Bonnet who told me was in a Peruvian prison on trumped up drug charges. He said he was tortured and beaten brutally, day after day by the guards. He begged for my help and asked me to send him several hundred dollars so he could mount a legal defense. Again I should have known better. It never dawned on me for a second that I was dealing with one of the biggest drug smugglers in the western world. A lot of people in the newsroom knew Keith and we took up a collection that raised $600 for his "legal fees" and wired the money to him at the prison.

On Feb. 8, 1986 Bonnet sent me this telegram:

*"Escaped Peruvian prison 16 December1985. 5 weeks with Sandinistas. Crossed Equadorian border 4 February 1986. Cuban-coke-arms connection confirmed. Cuban trawlers "Rio Las Casas" and "Rio Damuji" supplying arms. Arriving 10 February 1986 Eastern Flight 505-Miami-LAX 1700.*

*Keith Bonnet"*

I began to wonder if we did the right thing in sending Bonnet the $600. My suspicions were confirmed three months later when a federal grand jury indicted Bonnet and seven others, including Bradford Witt, the former New Mexico Attorney General, on charges of delivering $3.5 million worth of cocaine to undercover police officers in Albuquerque. I never quite figured out how he got out of the Peruvian prison but it seemed obvious someone was paid off with the $600 in newsroom money.

The feds said Bonnet and the others operated a huge cocaine smuggling ring that stretched from Columbia, to Los Angeles and Albuquerque. Bonnet was described as a veteran newsman whose stints included working as a correspondent for CBS News in London and as a reporter for the San Francisco Chronicle. No one at the CBS network could recall Bonnett working in London, but of course, as I learned, he was fairly effective at juicing up his resume. He claimed in his defense, he went to Peru on an assignment to write a book about gun running. But investigators said what he was really doing was organizing a massive cocaine delivery to the U.S. mainland. Thank God no one mentioned our $600 contribution to his work in the field. In all my years in news, both print and broadcasting, I had never known a journalist who was involved in the sale of narcotics. Yes, there were journalists who used marijuana and during the late 1980s and 90s cocaine was a drug of choice for a few. But it was never tolerated by management. A second tier anchorman at the NBC Burbank station was identified as a coke addict and summarily fired. He later confessed to me that he was a heavy user and bought his cocaine from a technician on the Johnny Carson TV show which was broadcast at the station.

Bonnet did almost seven years in the federal lockup before he was released on parole. A few months later he robbed a bank of $6500, got caught and it was back to the pen for another four years. Last we heard he was living in Miami Beach, close to the water's edge, just one of those less than perfect people who found a temporary home in TV news.

The same might be said of Clarence Stanley Duke, one of the first black sportscasters in Los Angeles, who was involved in another emotionally jarring incident during my tenure as managing editor at the CBS station in Los Angeles. Duke was arrested by the LAPD for murdering a prominent white radio personality he found in bed with his estranged wife.

The night of Feb, 11, 1971 Duke, who preferred to be called Stan, finished his 11 p.m. sports anchor spot on the news broadcast and decided to pay a visit to his estranged wife, Faye Williams Duke, at her new apartment. Faye was the President of the Black Educators Association and a highly regarded junior high school teacher.

Duke said he peered through a window and saw his wife in bed with Averill Berman, a controversial left wing radio broadcaster with a fairly large following in Los Angeles. He said he went home, loaded his rifle, burst into the apartment and fired half a dozen shots into the closet where Berman was cowering, killing him instantly. After his arrest Duke told the cops, "It took me 17 years to get where I am and I blew it all tonight."

In 1968 there was tremendous pressure on television stations to hire minorities, and Stan Duke seemed like a perfect fit for the job of weekend sports anchorman. At the time he was a staff photographer for the local NBC station. He had been a track star at the University of Oregon and later transferred to Lewis and Clark College where he received a B.S. degree. He earned a Master of Arts degree in communications from UCLA and was just a few credits away from a getting a doctorate in the same field when he was arrested for killing Berman.

Duke pleaded not guilty and not guilty by reason of insanity to a charge of first degree murder. He was represented by a very able criminal attorney, Paul Caruso, who decided to avoid a jury trial and let the judge rule on Duke's fate. The judge threw out the insanity plea and found Duke guilty of second degree murder. Duke was sentenced to five years in state prison, which he described as a "Northern-style lynching."

He repeatedly insisted he had done nothing wrong because Averill Berman had invaded the sanctity of his marriage. Duke was paroled after serving just three years in prison, during which time he escaped but was quickly caught. Eventually he was granted a full pardon by Governor George Deukmejian.

Once back on the street Duke applied for work at numerous TV stations, but always got a turn down. It was too bad because his knowledge of sports was encyclopedic, but more than that, he was a solid broadcaster. He constantly pointed out to me that a white radio personality who called himself "Humble Harv," killed his wife about the same time, got out of prison after a couple of years and was back on the air waves almost immediately.

For a time Stan found employment as a sports information officer at the University of Caliornia, Santa Barbara. Then, in 1981 he married again. He and his wife, Ellen, had two sons, Brent and Brandon. Duke said he stayed home to raise the boys while his wife pursued a successful business career.

Duke died of heart failure in March of 2007. He had been an avowed atheist most of his life but at his funeral the minister disclosed that Stan had embraced Christianity before his death. We remained friends over the years and I had breakfast with him in Santa Barbara a few months before his death. He was still a very angry man who felt he had been cheated out of a broadcasting career because of a justifiable killing. So I was pleased to learn he had found a peace of sorts in his final days. The funeral was a crowded affair and I looked around for someone I knew. But I was the only news person from L.A. who showed up to say goodbye to Stan Duke. Television is a business filled with short memories.

# 40

## LEGACY OF DOUBT OR
## DID THE MAFIA KILL JFK?

In 1972 while I was putting the finishing touches on my book, *"Legacy of Doubt,"* about the assassination of President John Kennedy, I was invited to lunch by Jerry Cohen, one of the top reporters on the Los Angeles *Times*. Cohen told me right out that the newspaper wanted me as its new city editor. But there was one caveat. I had to stop work on my book, which was then called *"Did the Mafia Kill JFK?"* I had no idea how the *Times* knew so much about my JFK project. The thrust of the book was the linkage between President John Kennedy's assassination in Dallas and threats on his life by New Orleans Mafia boss Carlos Marcello who had been unceremoniously deported to Guatemala by the President's brother, the U.S. Attorney General Robert Kennedy.

Obviously what I was doing was against the party line at the *Times* which supported the Warren Commission's findings that Lee Harvey Oswald acted alone when he fired his rifle at the President from the Texas Book Depository on November 22, 1963. I gave the *Times* a flat turn down only to learn a few weeks later I was being fired as managing editor at the CBS station in Los Angeles. Fortunately the next day I was offered a producing job at double my CBS salary at the ABC station where News Director Bill Fyffe encouraged me to finish the book.

I have never regretted my decision to turn down the job at the *Times* although it had once been my boyhood dream. Nash Publishing of Los Angeles originally signed me to a book contract, printed a cover but then backed out when my editor became frightened of the content. Pinnacle Books of New York was quick to pick up the book. The title was changed to "*Legacy of Doubt.*" Then Pinnacle launched me on a cross country tour which started with a half-hour TV interview on KABC (Channel 7 in Los Angeles) in which I discussed my conclusions about the JFK assassination. There were numerous radio interviews culminated by an assassination seminar at Georgetown University where I was a featured speaker along with the likes of authors Norman Mailer and Peter Dale Scott, Senate Counsel Bernard Fensterwald Jr., Dr. Cyril Wecht, one of the nation's leading medical researchers and George O'Toole, a former CIA computer analyst. We pretty much agreed that in the eyes of the conventional press we were regarded as "lunatics" for challenging the views of the Warren Commission.

My theory, as I've mentioned, revolved around Mafia boss Carlos Marcello, known in New Orleans to his friends and enemies as "The Little Man." On April 4, 1961 the 5-foot 3-inch tall Marcello was deported to Guatemala for falsifying an immigration application on the order of Attorney General Robert Kennedy. Marcello was handcuffed by federal agents as he emerged from the U.S. Immigration office in New Orleans. He was placed on a plane bound for Guatemala, which he claimed was the land of his birth on immigration papers. He managed to sneak back into the country some months later.

I personally interviewed Las Vegas publicist Ed Becker who later swore under oath before Congress that he heard Marcello make the death threat on the President. Becker said the occasion was a meeting at Churchill Farms outside New Orleans to discuss to discuss an upcoming event in that city with Marcello and several associates. Becker said the angry Marcello vowed revenge against both the President and his brother for his deportation and said he would get a "nut" to do the job. Becker personally testified before the House Committee on Assassinations about Marcello's threat. The FBI advised the committee it considered Becker's testimony to be "credible."

I also developed information that David Ferrie, a former airline pilot and acquaintance of  assassin Lee Harvey Oswald, flew Marcello back into the country from Guatemala. (The information was contained in an FBI report which was shown to me by William (Matt) Byrne, the U.S. Attorney for the Central District of California.) At the time a federal grand jury in Los Angeles was looking into allegations that Marcello was trying to take control of the Queen Mary, the historic British passenger ship turned into a tourist attraction at the Port of Long Beach. In the days that followed Marcello's return Ferrie worked for the mobster as a private investigator. The day of the assassination Ferrie was at Marcello's side in a federal courtroom where a New Orleans jury found the mob boss not guilty of immigration law violations, thus allowing him to remain in the United States. The next day in Dallas several FBI agents mentioned Ferrie's name to an NBC news team as a possible suspect in the plot to kill the president.

The House investigating committee determined that Ferrie had once trained Oswald in his Civil Air Patrol Unit. Ferrie was a strange looking duck. He was totally hairless and did not have eyebrows, the result of a rare disease. He worked for United Airlines as a pilot until he was fired for "homosexual activities." He was also known to be amateur hypnotist. Ferrie died eleven days after he was charged with a role in murdering the President by Jim Garrison, the erratic District Attorney of New Orleans. Garrison failed to mention that Ferrie did "investigative" work for Marcello in addition to being his personal pilot. Garrison claimed that Ferrie committed suicide, but an autopsy stated the cause of death was an aneurysm.

The L.A. *Times* declined to review "Legacy" and the Chicago Tribune scoffed that I was "...using a new whip on a long dead horse." But the L.A. *Herald-Examiner* had high praise for the book as did a number of other papers across the nation. Two months after publication a Pinnacle editor told me that "Legacy" had made the New York *Times* best seller list. But then suddenly Pinnacle stopped printing the book. An editor confided to me that drivers in Jimmy Hoffa's Teamsters Union were ordered to stop delivering "Legacy" to book stores. I wasn't surprised. Hoffa was involved in the business of the Mafia for many years. I pretty much gave up on the book's future. To my astonishment several years later much of my material was lifted from Legacy by *National Enquirer* writer Sybil Leak and her colleague Bert Sugar for a book called "*The Assassination Chain*," which strangely enough was also published by Pinnacle.

I was victorious in a federal court plagiarism suit against Pinnacle and the two writers; and was awarded a cash settlement plus full rights to my book. Excerpts from "Legacy" appeared, with my permission in most cases, in numerous other books, was quoted by CBS newsman Dan Rather, and certain elements showed up in the movie "Executive Action."

My spirits were considerably dampened because no other publisher was interested in picking up "Legacy," and my investigation appeared to be a flop. But evidence kept building of sloppy work and even suppression of evidence by the FBI and strange dealings between the Mafia and the CIA over the years.

Congressional investigators were alarmed to learn that for a dozen years the FBI suppressed information that shortly before the JFK assassination Lee Harvey Oswald had gone to the Bureau's Dallas office and left a threatening note for special agent James P. Hosty, Jr. who had been investigating Oswald. Two hours after the assassination Hosty's superior told him to destroy the note and he flushed it down a toilet. It was things like this that in 1976 led to the formation of the Select Committee on Assassinations of the House of Representatives. I was pleased to note that the Los Angeles Herald Examiner wrote that "Legacy of Doubt" had laid the groundwork for the Congressional investigation.

Meantime, there was already an investigation in the U.S. Senate in the mid 1970s led by Senator Frank Church, an Idaho Democrat, which also delved into certain aspects of the JFK assassination as it looked into the so-called plot to kill Cuban dictator Fidel Castro involving the Central Intelligence agency and the Mafia.

Of particular interest to the Church Committee on Domestic Surveillance was the CIA's involvement with two notorious underworld figures picked for the Castro killing, Chicago Mafia boss Sam Giancana and L.A.'s Johnny Roselli, a dapper man about town who was known as the mob's ambassador to Hollywood. Roselli had a hand in several movie productions and was first name basis with many stars. In the early 1960s Giancana, Roselli and Florida mob boss Santo Trafficante Jr. were recruited into the CIA's spy program by Robert Maheu, a beady-eyed former FBI agent with a vast number of contacts in the intelligence community.

Testimony revealed the mobsters were assigned to elim-inate Castro, his brother Raul and another government official by having an aide drop poison pills in their drink-ing water. The plan apparently failed when the Castro aide was transferred. The very thought of using Mafia hoodlums to carry out the Castro assassination came as a shock to many Americans. But some members of Congress were livid at the Church Committee for exposing the CIA's innermost secrets. Years later one senator even blamed the committee for eventually causing the 9-11 disaster in New York City by weakening the agency's resolve in flush-ing out terrorists.

On July 19, 1975 Sam Giancana met with members of the Church Committee in Chicago which arranged for him to testify about the various assassination plots involv-ing the CIA and the Mafia. That evening he held a din-ner party for his daughter Francine De Palma and her husband and two other acquaintances, Charles English and Dominic Blasi. All had departed by 10 o'clock that night. Apparently someone known to Giancana entered the home a short time later. That person fired a bullet into the back of Giancana's skull with a 22-caliber silencer. Then the killer fired six more shots into his mouth and neck, the placement of the shots symbolic of Mafia justice for a squealer. Another Giancana daughter, Antoniette, was quoted as saying her father "...was killed by the same people responsible for killing the Kennedys."

Roselli, born Filippo Sacco in Esperia, Italy on July 4, 1905, had a criminal record and lived under the constant threat of deportation from the FBI. He twice testified before the Church Committee, In June of 1975 he was questioned about the plot to kill Castro.

In April of 1976 he was called back before the commit-tee. He was asked about a theory he had once advanced, that Castro might have engineered the Kennedy assassination out of revenge for the plot to kill the Cuban dictator. Roselli said he had no evidence to support the theory.

Roselli quietly disappeared from public view. After his last appearance before the committee, he moved into his sister's home in Plantation, Florida and stayed out of sight, for the most part. On June 16, 1976 he went to Fort Lauderdale where he dined with Santo Traficante Jr. Twelve days later he drove to a nearby marina in his sister's car. Once there he was met by two men who joined him aboard a yacht that would soon set sail. Ten days later fishermen came across a 55-gallon oil drum floating in the water. Inside was Roselli's body. His legs had been sawed off so his body would fit inside the drum.

The Select Committee on Assassinations obtained an FBI wiretap on Roselli's old friend, Traficante in which he was quoted as saying: *"Now only two people know who killed Kennedy and they aren't talking."* It was pretty ominous stuff, especially after the Washington Post's Jack Anderson disclosed he had been holding secret talks with Roselli for several years. He quoted Roselli as saying, "When (Lee Harvey) Oswald was picked up, the underworld conspirators feared he would crack and disclose information that might lead to them. This almost certainly would have brought a massive U.S. crackdown on the Mafia. So Jack Ruby was ordered to eliminate Oswald." Roselli told Anderson Ruby was not involved in the conspiracy to kill the president.

So who were the conspirators? Carlos Marcello appeared in executive session before the House Select Committee and insisted he had nothing to do with the JFK assassination. The Committee's chief counsel, Dr. G. Robert Blakey, said Marcello was specifically asked about the meeting described in my book at Churchill Farms outside

New Orleans in which an informant quoted the Mafia boss as saying he wanted revenge for his deportation to Guatemala by the President's bother, Attorney General Robert Kennedy. Marcello insisted he never said that but his face became flushed red with anger when he spoke about Robert Kennedy's efforts to deport him.

In a book co-authored with Richard Billings, *"The Plot to Kill the President,"* Dr. Blakey described *"Legacy of Doubt"* as "a meticulously researched book." Jim Braden, the mystery man who became a focal point of my investigation, claimed I had damaged his reputation in testimony before the Select Committee. He denied knowing members of the Mafia in contradiction to evidence obtained by the LAPD's Organized Crime and Intelligence Division as well as investigators for the U.S. Internal Revenue Service and the California Justice Department. Braden was identified in various reports as a suspected mob courier. Investigators noted that an eyewitness saw at least $50,000 in cash tumble out of Braden's golf locker at the La Costa Country Club in the San Diego area. At the time the club was owned by the notorious Mafia boss from Cleveland, Morris (Mo) Dalitz.

The Cabana Motel where Braden stayed during his Dallas sojourn was known as a mob hangout. Jack Ruby was said to have visited someone at the motel the night of the president's assassination. Braden reportedly had checked out of the motel at 2 p.m. that afternoon and flew to Houston on a commercial airliner.

Earlier, minutes after the assassination, Braden was arrested as he emerged from the Dal-Tech Building directly opposite the Texas Book Depository where presidential assassin Lee Harvey Oswald stationed himself on the sixth floor with his Mannicher-Carcano rifle. Braden was brought to police headquarters after a witness said he had been acting suspiciously in the Dal-Tech building. But Dallas police were unaware of his real identity and long criminal record including the fact that he had once been run out of town by Sheriff Bill Decker. He told the cops he entered the Dal-Tech building trying to find a pay phone to call his parents in Santa Barbara, California to tell them about the shooting of the president. He was quickly released from custody.

My report that Braden was in Los Angeles the night Senator Robert Kennedy was shot was described by Dr. Blakey as "...a troubling Los Angeles-Dallas parallel." That night Braden was registered at the Century Plaza Hotel on L.A.'s Westside, about 15 minutes from the Ambassador Hotel where Robert Kennedy was mortally wounded.

Under questioning by Committee members Braden admitted that he and his wife, Mildred Bollman, lived in New Orleans for the six months prior to the assassination. This came as a surprise to his parole officer who thought he had been living in California all that time. Two months before the assassination he was in California where obtained a new identity when he went to the Department of Motor Vehicles and changed the name on his driver's license from Eugene Hale Brading to Jim Braden.

As for Roselli, there were reports he was also at the Cabana Motel in Dallas that night, but that had not been proved or disproved to my satisfaction. A former CIA pilot named William "Tosh" Plumlee said in a written statement that he picked up Roselli in Tampa, Florida on November 21, then flew to New Orleans where several other men joined the flight. Plumlee said their destination was Dallas but bad weather forced them to first land in Garland, Texas. Eventually, Plumlee said he flew the party to the Redbird Airport in Dallas. Plumlee insisted Roselli was on a mission to prevent the assassination, and was not involved in a conspiracy although he apparently had knowledge of it.

Other sources told me, however, that Roselli was in Los Angeles the day of the assassination. Where the truth ends or begins I do not know. But it's reasonable to suspect Roselli was killed because he knew who plotted the assassination.

In its final report in 1979 the Select Committee on Assassinations of the House of Representatives left unanswered the question of was there a conspiracy behind the killings of President John Fitzgerald Kennedy in Dallas, Texas at 1:30 p.m. Nov. 22, 1963.

It took issue with the Warren Commission finding that Oswald acted alone and stated there was strong evidence to support a second gunman fired at the President in Dealey Plaza that fateful day, but his shot missed. The Committee said it was Oswald's shot that killed Mr. Kennedy.

This statement summed up the committee's conclusions:

*"The Committee believes, on the basis of evidence available to it, that the national syndicate of organized crime, as a group, was not involved in the assassination of President Kennedy, but that available evidence does not preclude the possibility that individual members may be involved."*

For many years now I've believed that the plot to kill President Kennedy was hatched by Carlos Marcello and the "nut" he selected to do the job was Lee Harvey Oswald who was recruited by David Ferrie. I have held to that opinion for nearly 40 years.

By 1999, Dr, Blakey appeared to be coming around to my point of view. Interviewed by ABC News, he was asked: "What connections do you point to between Oswald and Marcello?"

Dr. Blakey's response:

"I can show you that lee Harvey Oswald, when he grew up in New Orleans, lived with Dutz Murret (Oswald's uncle). Dutz Murret is a bookmaker for Carlos Marcello. Did Lee Harvey Oswald grow up in a criminal neighborhood? Yes. Did he have mob-connected friends? Yes. Was he known to them to be a crazy guy? Yes. He's out publicly distributing Fair Play for Cuba leaflets (in New Orleans). If you wanted to enlist him a conspiracy that would initially appear to be communist and not organized crime, he's the perfect candidate. Ex-Marine, marksman, possibly prepared to kill the President for political reasons"

That's about as definitive as anyone in authority has ever been about the plot to kill President John Kennedy. Nearly all the principals are dead. As I mentioned earlier, David Ferrie died or was murdered in 1966. Jim Garrison died in 1992 and Carlos Marcello in 1993. And of course the two mobsters recruited by the CIA to kill Fidel Castro, and suspected of having knowledge about the plot to kill JFK, Sam Giancana and Johnny Roselli, died violent deaths in 1975 and 1976 respectively while involved with a Senate investigating committee.

Not long ago I talked with Dr. Blakey, now a faculty member at the Notre Dame University School of Law. I asked if he thought the assassination might ever be solved. "Not in this lifetime," he answered, "maybe in the next life." And so the answer to the question, "Did the Mafia Kill JFK?" seems destined to remain a "Legacy of Doubt."

# 41

# IN RETROSPECT
# LESSONS LEARNED

I've always thought the most important story I covered over the years was the partial meltdown of the sodium reactor in 1959 (Chapter 17) at Atomic International's nuclear facility in the Santa Susana Mountains northwest of Los Angeles. Unfortunately our report on KNBC-TV in 1979 disclosing a 20-year cover up of the accident by the federal government and the plant operator was dwarfed by the media coverage of the partial meltdown at the Three Mile Island nuclear reactor in Pennsylvania. That was the same year we broke the L.A. story. The radiation released at the Atomics International facility (later known as Rocketdyne) far exceeded the amount at Three Mile Island. According to a UCLA study, virtually all of the hundred or so workers who took part in the cleanup there died of cancer caused by radiation poisoning. A half century after the sodium reactor blew up, twisting its steel rods like putty, the state of California ordered a cleanup of the contaminated area to meet or exceed the standards set by the U.S. Environmental Protection Agency. Builders have long wanted to put up expensive homes in that area, but that can not be done until the cleanup is completed. And no one seems to know how many years that will take.

One of the first "news commandments" I was taught is that a reporter must have two sources on every investigative story. I disagree. If the Coroner tells you his findings concluded someone important died from an overdose of drugs, do you wait for a second source, or do the story immediately? Does anyone in news mandate a second source for a revelation made to a reporter by the President of the United States? I'll readily admit I had only one source on the story about condemned Army Private Richard Hagelberger (Chapter 12). My source was an officer in the Army's legal arm, the office of the Judge Advocate General. The source told me that Private Hagelberger was about to be executed for two murders in Germany while the actual killer had been granted a commutation of his death sentence. Should I have waited for a second source? I think not. Had I waited Hagelberger might not be alive at this writing. However, I must concede that an editor has the authority to demand a second source on a story.

I was subjected to criticism from some of my colleagues at KNXT in 1969 because of my decision to broadcast details of the arrests of Charles Manson and his "family" (Chapter 9) for the Tate, La Bianca and Hinman murders. Several co-workers insisted I should delay the story because Police Chief Ed Davis planned to make a "major announcement" at a news conference that evening. I said 'No, we're going with the story on the 6 o'clock news." Davis did hold the news conference but never mentioned Charles Manson by name and had hardly anything to say in the way of detail other than the fact that the murders had been solved.

There were scary moments covering the news, especially when I was the subject of death threats. Confidence artist Jerry Dean Michael (Chapter 13) hired a con man to kill me, reporter Dick Carlson and D.A. Prosecutor Bob Youngdahl in 1974. Michael had dressed up as a woman, called himself G. Elizabeth Carmichael and promoted a phony three wheel car called the Dale which he claimed got 70 miles to the gallon. Investors were cheated out of many millions of dollars. When our expose at KABC-TV brought down his scheme he paid a gunman $6,000 to kill the three of us. Fortunately the hired gun decided that wasn't enough money for a triple kill, backed out of the plot and squealed to the District Attorney. In return a felony charge against the snitch was dismissed. I guess I should have been grateful.

In my early years as a reporter one of the overriding factors in ever investigative story I did was the threat of litigation. I studied libel law under one of the great thinkers on the subject, Professor George Wasson at UCLA. At the time, many states including California had criminal libel statutes on their legislative books and telling the truth did not always mean a reporter would get off Scott free on a defamation action.

In the late 1950s the editor of a right-wing newsletter and three former LAPD officers were successfully prosecuted for criminal libel in Los Angeles. They had been indicted by the L.A County Grand Jury for circulating a phony police affidavit that stated liberal California Republican senator Thomas Kuchel had been caught engaging in homosexual activity in 1949. Kuchel, married and the father of a daughter, was outraged by the allegations and pressed for an investigation. The defendants pleaded no contest to criminal libel, maintaining the slander of Kuchel was the result of a mistaken identity. None of them went to jail.

Today, if Tom Kuchel faced the same allegations, he would have little chance of winning a prosecution against his detractors. In 1964, an historic ruling by the U.S. Supreme Court in the case of Sullivan versus the New York Times established a new legal framework for prosecuting libel cases. The issue in the case was not a reporter's story but rather a full page advertisement in the New York Times paid for by several civil rights groups. L.B. Sullivan, a police commissioner in Montgomery, Alabama, sued the newspaper and the civil rights organizations on behalf of the Montgomery Police Department, the city and its elected officers. The lawsuit alleged the ad contained errors and false allegations about racial matters in the rigidly segregated city which had been targeted by the black civil rights leader, Dr. Martin Luther King.

In perhaps the most far reaching decision in U.S. history about character defamation, the high court unanimously ruled that politicians, and other so-called "public figures," could not seek redress against those they accused of libel, even when an error was made, unless they could prove the perpetrator of the libel acted with malice. The opinion was signed by Justice William Brennan who wrote: *"Debate on public issues should be uninhibited, robust and wide open."*

The overall effect of the court ruling was to weaken libel statutes in most states because the high court ruling affirmed the British common law principle that truth is a complete and unabridged defense against libel. The ruling virtually nullified the prosecution of criminal libel cases.

But reporters still had a major concern about everything they wrote because of the so-called "Law of Privacy," which for all intents and purposes did not even exist in the minds of most news editors in 1964 when the court considered *Sullivan versus the New York Times*. Actually, as far back as 1890 the courts ruled on the issue of privacy. But for the most part the "Law of Privacy" became a fact of legal life around the 1970s based on hodgepodge of court rulings and legislative actions.

During my career in TV news I never lost a libel suit on any story I did, and some were quite controversial. But it was a different story when it came to the "Law of Privacy" after I became involved in what's considered a "textbook case" on the subject in legal circles.

The year was 1979 and I was in charge of "Unit 4," a team of investigative reporters and producers of which much was expected from upper management. The team's debut on KNBC-TV was launched with a costly full page ad in the Los Angeles Times. Warren Olney, the son of California's famous corruption prosecutor Warren Olney III, was my lead reporter. Week after week we churned out hard-hitting stories, including an 18- minute report looking into allegations that the oil companies secretly manipulated their markets to create gasoline shortages so they could raise prices. By TV news standards the story was extremely long. But News Director Irwin Safchik was so impressed he threw out a score of commercials so there would be no interruption of our story.

It's always seemed to me that covering the news is a daily learning experience, and you can you can never learn too much. The early success of Unit 4 was tempered by a new learning experience about the law and the media.

A subject to which I had given a great deal of thought was the problems paramedics were having in saving lives in the city of Los Angeles. For one thing jurisdictional lines were often blurred since L.A. was such a large area and paramedics would often find themselves called to places outside the city limits. In life and death situations they could not very well deny help to any person in need even if he or she didn't live in their jurisdiction. Apart from that, there were a number of inefficiencies in the system.

Officials at the L.A. City Fire Department liked my idea of doing a series of special reports on the problems confronting their paramedics and gave the go-ahead for a number of "ride-alongs" with one of their units. The project got off to a rough start when the paramedic unit our crew was assigned to didn't get any calls for help the first few days. And then it happened. On the evening of October 30, 1979 Unit 4 producer Ruben Norte, cameraman John Parsons and sound engineer Stan Riley were alerted to a 911 call a few miles away and sped off to an apartment house in the 8200 block of Blackburn Avenue.

Inside the apartment a man identified as Dave Miller was unconscious on the floor of his bedroom after suffering an apparent heart attack. Our crew followed the paramedics into the apartment and began filming. Miller was on the bedroom floor face up. The image on film did not show the man's face. What the film showed was Miller's huge bare chest and paramedics working furiously to revive him. There were a few frames in the film of the man's wife, Brownie Miller, appearing very much in distress in the background. Producer Norte said at no time did Mrs. Miller ask him or the camera crew to leave so he presumed their presence as all right. The NBC cameraman kept rolling as the paramedics hoisted Miller on a gurney and placed him in an ambulance. They took him to Mt. Sinai Hospital where he was pronounced dead shortly after arrival. His face was never visible on our news film, but that didn't account for much on our judgment day.

It's fair to say Unit 4's five-part series on the problems confronting paramedics was an artistic and commercial success, producing a significant increase in the ratings. But that was simply the calm before the legal storm. Unknown to me, Tom Moody, the head of the KNBC Promotion Department, went to the library where our news film was stored and helped himself to the video of the paramedics trying to revive David Miller. Moody then inserted the video into a promo about a KNBC program on CPR (cardiopulmonary resuscitation). Brownie Miller never watched the news, but she loved soap operas and one day she suddenly saw herself and her dying husband in the CPR promo on an NBC soap.

It didn't take long for the lawyers to swing into action. Mrs. Miller and her daughter, Marlene, who saw the video while watching the news at her home in Laguna Beach, hired a lawyer and charged NBC, producer Norte and the city of Los Angeles with trespassing, invasion of privacy and emotional stress.

Tom Moody was no longer with the station, and I became the first fall guy from NBC to go on the legal firing line. I wouldn't say I was brutalized by the deposition taken from me in the office of a Beverly Hills lawyer but I was beaten down pretty badly. "Mr. Noyes," I was asked, "...after all the awards and honors you have received in the news business how could you allow something like this to happen?" How do you answer a question like that? I used the stock company answer, "We entered the home and when no one asked us to leave we covered the story under the protections afforded us by the First Amendment." That didn't go over too well. I was blistered by the attorney for being neglectful and not doing my job as a manager. I refused to acknowledge that we were trespassing.

The following year the case came to trial in Burbank Superior Court and to my relief NBC won the case when the judge ruled our news people had conducted themselves properly at the Miller home and found no grounds to support trespassing or an invasion of privacy. The judge held that we were exercising our First Amendment right as a component of the nation's free press in covering the story.

But that wasn't the end of the story. Six years after the incident at Brownie Miller's home, the California Court of Appeal set aside the verdict of the Burbank judge and ruled there was sufficient evidence to try the case before a jury. A written unanimous opinion by the court's four justices said: *"The NBC camera crew devoted little or no thought whatsoever to its obvious transgressions in an alarming absence of sensitivity and civility. They had no right to be there."*

The court's verdict returned on December 18, 1986 said the case should be put before a jury for trial on the issues of invasion of privacy, trespassing and the infliction of emotional distress. NBC's legal counsel decided as a matter of last resort to work out a settlement with Mrs. Brownie Miller. It was a confidential settlement but I was told the network paid her a sum in excess of $800,000 plus court costs, a fairly substantial amount for that time. A dozen years later the United States Supreme Court pretty much enunciated the privacy principles laid down in "Miller versus NBC" which is now considered a textbook case for journalists to bone up on. It was a learning lesson, a cautionary tale if you will, for all of us in the field of newsgathering.

After the Miller story, I hung around in news another 30 years. Gradually libel suits were few and far between but the tabloids exposed themselves to constant litigation for violating privacy laws. I never again became involved in any sort of litigation in news.

One of the problems I witnessed in my golden years was the total reliance many young journalists had on the internet. The net can be useful at times. But frequently the net contains misinformation, botched facts and unwarranted speculation. Over and over again I advised young news people to read a newspaper daily and watch the network news broadcasts. All too often I found them engrossed in blogs which more often than not were simply matters of opinion and not sources of information.

An example of that youthful dependency on the internet as a source of information came to mind in a story about a legendary broadcasting figure in Los Angeles. In 2010 the night assignment editor at KNBC News received a tip that 83-year-old Vin Scully, the voice of the Los Angeles Dodgers for more than half-a-century, was in the hospital. Now most hospital administrators maintain that privacy laws prevent them from giving out patient information. The assignment editor was well aware of that policy so he called the hospital and asked for Scully's room. A member of Scully's family answered the phone. The editor identified himself and his place of employment and asked the relative about Scully's condition. The relative replied that Scully was hospitalized after he fell out of bed but appeared to be in pretty good shape. The assignment editor then took the story to the producer of the news broadcast who thanked him and said he would try to find the story on the internet. No such luck. It was nowhere to be found on the net or even on the news wire services. It took a lot of arm twisting to convince the young producer that he had an "exclusive" but he finally ran the Scully story as the first item on the news broadcast that night. The story was picked by up by all the news media the next day. It was proof of the old journalism axiom, perhaps handed down by William Randolph Hearst: "The news is what people talk about." Another axiom: "Being first is better than being last." A very simple learning lesson.

I'm proud to say the assignment editor who came up with the story that night and fought to get it on the air was my son, Jack Noyes. And as we say in the news business, "that's 30."

# PHOTOGRAPHY CREDITS

1. Lana Turner, Watson Family Photo Archives
2. L. Ewing Scott, Watson Family Photo Archives
3. Barbara Graham. Watson Family Photo Archives
4. Eddie Wein, P&G Archives
5. President Gerald Ford with Pete Noyes, White House photo
6. Howard Hughes, Watson Family Photo Archives
7. Jerry Dean Michael, P&G Archives
8. Elizabeth Short, Bob Martin Photography
9. "Bugsy" Siegel, Watson Family Photo Archives
10. Eddie Cannizzaro, P&G Archives
11. Karen Kupcinet, ABC Television Productions
12. Jean Spangler and note, Peter Brooke Archives
13. Gerald Mason, Los Angeles County Sheriff's Dept.
14. Elaine Graham and daughter, P&G Archives
15. Cheryl Bradshaw and Rodney Alcala, Orange County Evidence File
16. Rodney Alcala on TV screen, Orange County Evidence File
17. Rodney Alcala in court, Fox News
18. Pictures in Alcala locker, Huntington Beach Police Department.

19. Robin Graham, courtesy Marvin Graham family
20. Ricardo Caputo, New York Police Department
21. Candice Mia Daly, courtesy Quentin Guiterriz
22. Dennis and Joey Cole, P&G Archives

# INDEX

# E

Made in the USA
Las Vegas, NV
03 February 2021